The Besterman World Bibliographies

The Besterman World Bibliographies

Music
and Drama

A BIBLIOGRAPHY OF
BIBLIOGRAPHIES

By Theodore Besterman

TOTOWA, N. J.

Rowman and Littlefield

1971

Published by
Rowman and Littlefield
A Division of
Littlefield, Adams & Co.
81 Adams Drive
Totowa, N. J. 07512

★

Copyright © 1939, 1947, 1965, 1971
by Theodore Besterman
Printed in the United States of America

★

Typography by George Hornby
and Theodore Besterman

ISBN 0-87471-046-4

Contents

Preface

I have explained in the Introduction to the successive editions of *A World bibliography of bibliographies* why I decided to arrange it alphabetically by specific subjects. Since that decision was taken, and after prolonged experience of the book in use, I have had no reason to regret it, nor among the many letters I have received from librarians has there been a single one complaining of the alphabetical form of the *World bibliography*.

The *World bibliography of bibliographies* covers all subjects and all languages, and is intended to serve reference and research purposes of the most specific and specialised kind. Yet contained in it are broad and detailed surveys which, if relevant entries throughout the volumes are added to them, can serve also the widest reference inquiries, and be useful to those who seek primary signposts to information in varied fields of inquiry.

Therefore I can only thank Rowman and Littlefield for having gathered together all the titles in some of the major fields found throughout the 6664 columns of the fourth edition (1965-1966) of *A World bibliography of bibliographies*.

Preface

These fields are:

1. Bibliography
2. Printing
3. Periodical Publications
4. Academic Writings
5. Art and Architecture
6. Music and Drama
7. Education
8. Agriculture
9. Medicine
10. Law
11. English and American Literature
12. Technology
13. Physical Sciences
14. Biological Sciences
15. Family History
16. Commerce, Manufactures, Labour
17. History
18. Geography

Of course these categories by no means exhaust the 117,000 separately collated volumes set out in the *World bibliography*, and the above titles will be added to if librarians wish for it.

Th. B.

Notes on the Arrangement

An Alternative to critical annotation

Consider what it is we look for in a normal bibliography of a special subject. Reflection will show, I think, that we look, above all, for completeness, just as we do in a bibliography of bibliographies. We desire completeness even more than accuracy (painfully uncongenial though it is for me to make such a statement); for in most cases a bibliography is intended to give us particulars of publications to which we wish to refer; thus we can always judge for ourselves (waiving gross errors) whether the bibliographer has correctly described these publications. On the other hand, anything that is omitted is lost until rediscovered.

The question is, therefore, whether it is possible to give some indication of the degree of completeness of a bibliography without indulging in the annotation which is impossible in a work of the present scope and scale. It seemed to me that this could be achieved, to a considerable extent, by recording the approximate number of entries set out in it. This method is, of course, a rough-and-ready one, but experience shows that it is remarkably effective: and I hope that its novelty will not tell against it.

The recording of the number of works set out in a bibliography has another advantage in the case of serial publications: it displays in statistical form the development of the subject from year to year—often in a highly significant manner.

This procedure, then, is that which I have adopted, the number of items in each bibliography being shown in square brackets at the end of the entry. This, I may add, is by no means an easy or mechanical task, as can be judged from the fact that this process, on the average, just about doubles the time taken in entering each bibliography.

Supplementary information in footnotes

I have said that this method of indicating the number of entries is intended to replace critical treatment; but it is not possible to exclude annotation altogether, for a certain minimum of added information is indispensable. Consequently many of my entries will be seen to have footnotes, in which the following types of information are recorded: a few words of explanation where the title is inaccurate, misleading, obscure, or insufficiently informative; a statement to that effect where a work is in progress, where intermediate volumes in a series have not been published, or where no more have been published; an attempt to clarify complicated series; a note that a book was privately printed or in a limited number of copies, where this does not exceed 500, or in some abnormal manner, as on one side of the leaf, on coloured paper, or in a reproduction of hand-writing, or with erratic pagination; when I have come across copies containing manuscript or other added matter, I have recorded the fact; substantial corrections and additions to bibliographies are sometimes published in periodicals, and I have noted a good many of these—but without aiming at anything even remotely approaching completeness, the attainment of which would be impossible. Various minor types of information are also occasionally to be found in the footnotes.

Owing to the great increase in the number of bibliographies reproduced directly from type-written copy, such publications are designated by an asterisk at the end of the entry; this device saves a good deal of space.

Place of publication

The place of publication is not shown when it is London in the case of an english book and

Notes

Paris in the case of a french one. In the case of a series or sequence of entries, however, the absence of a place of publication means that it is the same as the place last shown in the series. The same applies to the names of editors and compilers. The place of publication is given as it appears on the titlepage, but prepositions are omitted even if violence is done to grammatical construction.

The Order of entries

Under each heading the order of the entries is chronological by date of publication; in the case of works in successive volumes or editions the chronological order applies to the first volume or edition. In suitable long headings an additional chronological order by period covered has been created; see, for instance, France: History, or Drama: Great Britain.

Method of collating

An effort has been made, so far as space allows, to give detailed and accurate information of the kind more usually found in small bibliographies. For instance, I have paid special attention to the collation of bibliographies in several (or even numerous) parts or volumes. It is, in fact, difficult to understand why it is usually considered necessary to give collations of works in a single volume, where difficulties seldom occur (from the point of view of systematic bibliography), but not of a work in several volumes, where confusion much more frequently arises. An occasional gap in the collations of such publications will be noticed. This is because, naturally enough, I have not been able in every case to see perfect sets; and I have thought it better to leave a very small number of such blanks rather than to hold up the bibliography indefinitely.

Serial publications

Where successive issues of a serial publication are set out, the year or period shown is usually that covered by the relevant issue; in such cases no date of publication is given unless publication was abnormal or erratic in relation to the period covered.

Bibliographies in more than one edition

Where a bibliography has gone into more than one edition I have tried (though I have not always been able) to record at least the first and latest editions. Intermediate editions have also been recorded wherever it seemed useful to do so, that is, for bibliographies first published before 1800, and for those of special interest or importance; but in general intermediate editions, though examined, have not been recorded.

Notes

Transcription of titles

Titles have been set out in the shortest possible form consistent with intelligibility and an adequate indication of the scope of the bibliography; omissions have of course been indicated. The author's name, generally speaking, is given as it appears on the titlepage, amplified and interpreted within square brackets where necessary.

Anonymous bibliographies

Far too large a proportion of bibliographical work is published anonymously. This is due, in part, to the all too common practice of library committees and similar bodies of suppressing altogether or of hiding in prefaces the names of those who have compiled bibliographies and catalogues for them. I have spent a good deal of time in excavating such and other evidences of authorship, and the result may be seen in the large number of titles preceded by names enclosed within square brackets.

Th. B.

Music.

[bibliographies of individual composers are not repeated under this heading.]

Music

1. *Bibliographies*

LUIGI ALBERTO VILLANIS, Piccola guida alla bibliografia musicale. Torino 1906. pp.63. [100.]

MICHEL BRENET [*pseud.* MARIE BOBILLIER], Bibliographie des bibliographies musicales. Année musicale: 1913. pp.152. [1500.]

A CHECK LIST of thematic catalogues. Public library: New York 1954. pp.37. [350.]
— Addenda 1955–1956. [1957]. pp.3. [30.]*

2. *Periodicals*

ÉDOUARD G[EORGES] J[ACQUES] GREGOIR, Recherches historiques concernant les journaux de musique depuis les temps les plus reculés. Anvers 1872. pp.71. [300.]

WILHELM FREYSTÄTTER, Die musikalischen zeitschriften seit ihrer entstehung bis zur gegenwart. Chronologisches verzeichnis der periodischen schriften über musik. München 1884. pp.v.139. [400.]

LIST of periodicals to be included in cumulative index of music periodicals. Chicago public library omnibus project: [Chicago 1940]. ff.19. [175.]*

PAN AMERICAN magazines relating to architecture, art and music. Pan american union: Washington 1942. pp.[i].13.*

A. RIEDEL, Répertoire des périodiques musicaux belges. Commission belge de bibliographie: Bibliographia belgica (no.8): 1954. pp.48. [330.]

JEAN ADRIEN THOUMIN, Bibliographie rétrospective des périodiques français, de littérature musicale, 1870–1954. Institut national des techniques de la documentation: 1957. pp.xvii.179. [594.]*

[KARL HEINZ KÖHLER *and others*], Verzeichnis der in der musikabteilung der Deutschen staatsbibliothek nach 1945 laufend gehaltenen zeitschriften. Deutsche staatsbibliothek: Zeitschriften: Bestandverzeichnisse: Musik (no.4): Berlin 1958. pp.21. [200.]

ECKART ROHLFS, Die deutschsprachigen musikperiodica, 1945–1957 ... mit ... bibliographie der bisherigen literatur über musikzeitschriften. Forschungsbeiträge zur musikwissenschaft (vol.xi): Regensburg 1961. pp.xiv.108.xiv.115. [589.]

3. *History*

HERMANN RITTER, Repetitorium der musikgeschichte nach epochen übersichtlich dargelegt, nebst einem verzeichnisse der hauptsächlichsten wissenschaftlichen musikliteratur. Würzburg 1880. pp.279. [1000.]

WILHELM BRAMBACH, Die musiklitteratur des mittelalters bis zur blüthe der Reichenauer sänger-schule (500–1050 . Chr.). Karlsruhe 1883. pp.[ii]. 27. [20.]

ROBERT EITNER, Quellen- und hilfswerke beim studium der musikgeschichte. Leipzig 1891. pp. v.55. [500.]

VERZEICHNIS der im druck erschienenen musik-historischen arbeiten von Robert Eitner. Leipzig 1893. pp.8. [35.]

CATALOG der Schweizerischen musikbibliothek. . . . 1. Musikgeschichte und theoretische werke. Basel 1906. pp.[iii].39. [1000.]
no more published.

SELECTED list of works in the New York public library relating to the history of music. [New York 1908]. pp.36. [1000.]

AUSSTELLUNG: Schmuck und illustration von musikwerken in ihrer entwicklung vom mittel-alter bis in die neueste zeit. Kunstgewerbemuseum: Franfurt a. M. [1908]. pp.[vi].46. [279.]

CATALOGUS van de bibliotheek der Vereeniging

voor nederlandsche muziekgeschiedenis. Amsterdam 1919. pp.274. [2000.]

ERNEST NEWMAN, What to read on the evolu-
tion of music. Public libraries: Leeds 1928. pp.34.
[200.]

KATALOG. Musikkollegium: Ausstellung musik-
historischer dokumente bei anlass des dreihundert-
jährigen jubiläums. Zweite . . . auflage. [Winter-
thur 1930]. pp.27. [254.]

RICHARD SCHAAL, Das schrifttum zur musikalischen lokalgeschichts-forschung. Kassel 1947.
pp.62. [2000.]

ERNST C[HRISTOPHER] KROHN, The history of
music. An index to the literature available in a
selected group of musicological publications.
Washington university: Library studies (no.3):
St. Louis 1952. pp.[ii].xxi.463. [5000.]*

ÅKE DAVIDSSON, Catalogue critique et descriptif
des ouvrages théoriques sur la musique imprimés
au XVIᵉ et au XVIIᵉ siècles et conservés dans les
bibliothèques suédoises. Studia musicologica
upsaliensia (vol.ii): Upsala 1953. pp.83. [108.]

ERNST C. KROHN, The history of music. An
index to the literature available in a selected group

of musicological publications. St. Louis 1958. pp. [ii].xxi.463. [5000.]*

FRIEDRICH GENNRICH, Der musikalische nachlass der troubadours. Summa musicae medii aevi (vol.iv): Darmstadt 1960. pp.xix.177. [302.]

JOSEPH SMITS VAN WAESBERGHE, PETER FISCHER and CHRISTIAN MAAS, The theory of music, from the carolingian era up to 1400. Descriptive catalogue of manuscripts. Répertoire international des sources musicales: [1961]. pp.155. [250.]

4. Manuscripts

[see also section 12, below]

CATALOGO de' qvadri, partite, divertimenti, cassat. scherz. ed intrade . . . a diversi stromenti, che si trovano in manuscritto nella officina musica di Breitkopf in Lipsia. [Leipsic 1765]. pp.24. [400.]

SUPPLEMENTO I. [&c.] dei cataloghi delle sinfonie, partite, ouverture, soli, duetti, trii, quattri e concerti per il violino, flauto traverso, cembalo ed altri stromenti che si trovano in manuscritto nella officina musica di Breitkopf in Lipsia. [Leipsic].
    i. 1766. pp.56. [800.]
    ii. 1767. pp.48. [700.]
    iii. 1768. pp.36. [500.]
    iv. 1769. pp.32. [500.]

v. 1770. pp.32. [500.]

vi. 1771. pp.32. [500.]

vii. 1772. pp.40. [600.]

viii. 1773. pp.40. [600.]

ix. 1774. pp.40. [600.]

x. 1775. pp.28. [400.]

xi. 1776–1777. pp.36. [500.]

xii. 1778. pp.44. [600.]

xiii. 1779–1780. pp.32. [500.]

xiv. 1781. pp.58. [900.]

xv. 1783–1784. pp.82. [1250.]

xvi. 1785–1787. pp.46. [750.]

these are supplements to a series of catalogues entered under the appropriate headings.

[THOMAS OLIPHANT], Catalogue of the manuscript music in the British museum. 1842. pp.[v]. 107. [3000.]

— — [supplement, begins:] The following volumes . . . were bequeathed to the British museum by Domenico Dragonetti . . . in 1846. [*s. l.*]. pp.7. [200.]

— — [another edition]. Catalogue of manuscript music . . . by Augustus Hughes-Hughes. 1906–1909. pp.xxvi.615 + xxv.961 + xxiii.543. [17,500.]

A CATALOGUE of original letters and manu-

Music

scripts, in the autograph of distinguished musicians, composers, performers and vocalists, . . . collected by Thomas Mackingley. 1846. pp.[ii].20. [300.]

privately printed.

JUL[IUS] JOS[EPH] MAIER, Die musikalischen handschriften der K. hof- und staatsbibliothek in Muenchen. Catalogus codicum manu scriptorum Bibliothecae regiae monacensis (vol.viii): Muenchen 1879. pp.viii.379. [3000.]

[ERNESTO COLOMBANI], Catalogo della collezione d'autografi lasciata alla R. accademia filarmonica di Bologna dall'accademico . . . Masseangelo Masseangeli. . . . 1. Maestri di musica, cantanti e suonatori. Bologna 1881[–1896]. pp.xv.435. [2000.]

no more published.

ERNST PFADEL, Die musik-handschriften der Königl. ritter-akademie zu Liegnitz. Musikhandschriften aus öffentlichen bibliotheken (vol.i: Beilage zu den Monatsheften für musikgeschichte): Leipzig 1886. pp.74. [2000.]

[EGIDIO FRANCESCO SUCCI], Catalogo con brevi cenni biografici e succinte descrizioni degli autografi e documenti di celebri o distinti musicisti posseduti da Emilia Succi. Mostra internazionale di musica: Bologna 1888. pp.x.181. [886.]

TADDEO WIEL, I codici musicali contariniani del secolo XVII nella R. biblioteca di san Marco in Venezia. Venezia 1888. pp.xxx.121. [200.]

EMIL BOHN, Die musikalischen handschriften des XVI. und XVII. jahrhunderts in der Stadt-bibliothek. Breslau 1890. pp.xvii.423. [3000.]

[JOHANNES] EMIL [EDUARD BERNHARD] VOGEL, Die handschriften nebst den älteren druckwerken der musik-abtheilung. Die handschriften der Her-zoglichen bibliothek zu Wolfenbüttel (achte abtheilung): Wolfenbüttel 1890. pp.viii.280. [manuscripts: 315.]

[RICHARD BATKA], Aus der musik- und theater-welt. Beschreibendes verzeichnis der autographen-sammlung Fritz Donebauer. Prag 1894. pp.lxxx. 151. [1200.]

FRIEDRICH KUHN, Beschreibendes verzeichnis der alten musikalien-handschriften und -druckwerke des Königlichen gymnasiums zu Brieg. Monats-hefte für musikgeschichte (beilage): Leipzig [1896-]1897. pp.[iii].98. [600.]

[JOSEF MANTUANI], Tabvlae codicvm manv

scriptorvm praeter Graecos et Orientales in Bibliotheca palatina vindobonensi asservatorvm. . . . Volvmen ix[–x]. (Codicum mvsicorvm pars i[–ii]). Academia caesarea vindobonensis: Vindobonae 1897–1899. pp.x.421+vi.587. [5000.]

MANOSCRITTI e libri a stampa musicati esposti dalla Biblioteca nazionale di Torino. Esposizione nazionale: Torino 1898. pp.24. [68.]

A[UGUST] HALM, Katalog über die musikcodices des 16. und 17. jahrhunderts auf der Königlichen landes-bibliothek in Stuttgart. Monatshefte für musikgeschichte (beilage): Langensalza [printed] 1902. pp.58. [1000.]

[AMÉDÉE GASTOUÉ], Introduction à la paléographie musicale byzantine. Catalogue des manuscrits de musique byzantine de la Bibliothèque nationale de Paris et des bibliothèques publiques de France. [Société internationale de musique: Section de Paris: Publications: 1907]. pp.ix.103. [150.]

FRIEDRICH LUDWIG, Repertorium organorum recentioris et motetorum vetustissimi stili. . . . Band 1. Catalogue raisonné der quellen. Abteilung 1. Handschriften in quadrat-notation. Halle a. S. 1910. pp.[vii].344. [2500.]
no more published.

12

Music

OTTO GÜNTHER, Die musikalischen handschriften der Stadtbibliothek und der in ihrer verwaltung befindlichen kirchenbibliotheken von St. Katharinen und St. Johann in Danzig. Katalog der Danziger stadtbibliothek (vol.iv): Danzig 1911. pp.viii.188. [1400.]

CATALOGUE of the musical manuscripts deposited on loan in the British museum by the Royal philharmonic society of London. British museum: 1914. pp.16. [35.]

GEORG KINSKY, Musikhistorisches museum von Wilhelm Heyer in Cöln. Katalog. . . . Vierter band: musik-autographen. Cöln 1916. pp.[xxxi]. 872.32.[xxx]. [1750.]
325 copies printed.

[RUDOLF SCHWARTZ], Verzeichnis der autographen der musikbibliothek Peters. Leipzig 1917. pp.16. [50.]
a copy in the British museum contains manuscript notes.

HIGINI ANGLÈS, Catálog dels manuscrits musicals de la colleció Pedrell. Biblioteca de Catalunya: Departament de música: Publicacions (vol.ii): Barcelona 1920. pp.138. [846.]

HENRY GEORGE FARMER, The arabic musical

manuscripts in the Bodleian library. 1925. pp.18.
[17.]

WILHELM HITZIG, Katalog des archivs von Breitkopf & Härtel. Leipzig.
  i. Musik-autographe. 1925. pp.[vi].50. [348.]
  ii. Brief-autographe von persönlichkeiten die
      vor 1770 geboren sind. 1926. pp.[vi].50.
      [4000.]

[WILHELM ALTMANN], Preussische staatsbibliothek: manuscrits de musique. Exposition internationale de la musique, Genève 1927: Berlin 1927.
pp.46. [20.]
  [—] — Musik-handschriften. 1927. pp.48. [20.]

LIONEL DE LA LAURENCIE, Inventaire critique du
fonds Blancheton de la bibliothèque du Conservatoire de Paris. Société française de musicologie:
Publications (2nd ser., vols.i–ii): 1930–1931. pp.
3–107.19+3–112.35. [301.]
  covers the period 1700–1800.

WILLIAM BARCLAY SQUIRE, Catalogue of the
manuscripts in the library of the Royal college of
music. [1931]. ff.[ii].568.216. [4105.]
  4 copies reproduced from typewriting.

EDMUND H[ORACE] FELLOWES, The catalogue of
manuscripts in the library of St. Michael's college,

Music

Tenbury. Paris 1934. pp.[iv].319. [1386.]
220 copies printed.

JOSEPH SCHMIDT-GÖRG, Katalog der handschriften des Beethoven-hauses und Beethovenarchivs Bonn. Kataloge des Beethoven-hauses und Beethoven-archivs (vol.i): Bonn 1935. pp.76. [138.]

INVENTÁRIO dos inéditos e impressos musicais. Fasciculo 1. Universidade: Biblioteca: Publicações: Coimbra 1937. pp.xv.59.47. [300.]

LIST of the letters and manuscripts of musicians in the William Andrews Clark memorial library. Southern California historical records survey project: Los Angeles 1940. ff.[14]. [37.]*

HIGINI ANGLÉS and JOSÉ SUBIRÁ, Catálogo musical de la Biblioteca nacional de Madrid. . . . Manuscritos. Consejo superior de investigaciones científicas: Instituto español de musicología: Catálogos de la musica antigua conservada en España (vol.i): Barcelona 1946. pp.iii–xix.491. [300.]

INGEBORG LAGERCRANTZ, Lutherska kyrkovisor. 1. Finländska musikhandskrifter från 1500– och 1600–talen. Lutherska litteraturstiftelsens Svenska publikationer (no.2): Helsingfors 1948– .
pp.[iv].256+   .

ANSELM HUGHES, Medieval polyphony in the Bodleian library. Oxford 1951. pp.[iii].63. [51.] *a catalogue of manuscripts.*

EDWARD N. WATERS, Autograph musical scores and autograph letters in the [Gertrude Clarke] Whitall foundation collection. Library of Congress: Music division: Washington 1951. pp.18. [120.]

—— Revised. 1953. pp.ii.19. [130.]

OTTO EDWIN ALBRECHT, A census of autograph music manuscripts of european composers in american libraries. Philadelphia 1953. pp.xvii.331. [2017.]

ANSELM HUGHES, Catalogue of the musical manuscripts at Peterhouse. Cambridge 1953. pp. xvi.76. [400.]

GEORG KINSKY, Manuskripte, briefe, dokumente von Scarlatti bis Stravinsky. Katalog der musikautographensammlung Louis [Lajos] Koch. Stuttgart 1953. pp.xxii.361. [355.]

MEDIEVAL and renaissance music manuscripts. Toledo museum of art: [Toledo] 1953. pp.xv.40. [103.]

an exhibition catalogue.

[RENÉ JEAN HESBERT], Les manuscrits musicaux

de Jumièges. Monumenta musicae sacra (vol.ii): Mâcon 1954. pp.3–104. [125.]
the manuscripts are now in the Bibliothèque publique of Rouen.

EMANUEL WINTERNITZ, Musical autographs from Monteverdi to Hindemith. Princeton 1955. pp. [viii].154+vol. of plates. [125.]

BIANCA BECHERINI, Catalogo dei manoscritti musicali della biblioteca nazionale di Firenze. Kassel 1959. pp.xii.179. [2500.]

JOHN KIRKPATRICK, A temporary mimeographed catalogue of the music manuscripts and related material of Charles Edward Ives . . . given . . . to the library of the Yale school of music. [New Haven] 1960. ff.xxxv.279. [1500.]
114 copies reproduced from typewriting.

JOSEPHUS M. LLORENS, Capellae sixtinae codices musicis notis instructi sive manu scripti sive praelo excussi. Studi e testi (no.202): Città del Vaticano 1960. pp.xxiii.558. [660.]

KATALOG zu den sammlungen des Händelhauses in Halle. 1. teil. Handschriftensammlung. Halle an der Saale 1961. pp.332. [500.]

ÅKE DAVIDSSON, Musical treasures in the univer-

sity library. Uppsala 1962. pp.20. [29.]
an exhibition catalogue.

VINCENT [HARRIS] DUCKLES and MINNIE ELMER,
Thematic catalog of a manuscript collection of
eighteenth-century italian instrumental music in
the university of California, Berkeley, music
library. Berkeley &c. 1963. pp.[x].403. [1000.]*

FRIEDRICH WILHELM RIEDEL, Das musikarchiv im
minoritenkonvent zu Wien. (Katalog des älteren
bestands vor 1784). Internationale vereinigung der
musikbibliotheken: Catalogus musicus (no.i):
Kassel 1963. pp.xvii.139. [771.]*

ÅKE DAVIDSSON, Catalogue of the Gimo collection of italian manuscript music in the university
library of Uppsala. Acta bibliothecae R. universi-
tatis upsaliensis (vol.xiv): Uppsala 1963. pp.101.
[360.]

5. *General*

i. *Bibliographies*

VERZEICHNISS musikalischer bücher . . . welche
bey Johann Gottlob Immanuel Breitkopf . . . zu
bekommen sind. Leipzig 1760. pp.56. [500.]
— Zweyte ausgabe. 1761. pp.[ii].35–116. [750.]
— Dritte ausgabe. 1763. pp.[ii].59–88. [300.]
— Vierte ausgabe. 1770. pp.[ii].91–116. [300.]

— Fünfte ausgabe. 1777. pp.[ii].119–148. [400.]
— Sechste ausgabe. 1780. pp.[ii].151–172. [250.]

REVIEW of new musical publications. No.1
[–IX]. [1784]. pp.76. [100.]

[CARL FRIEDRICH WHISTLING], Handbuch der
musikalischen litteratur oder allgemeines systematisch geordnetes verzeichniss der bis zum ende
des jahres 1815 gedruckten musikalien, auch musikalischen schriften und abbildungen. Leipzig 1817.
pp.xii.593. [25,000.]

— — Erster [&c.] nachtrag.

 i. 1818. pp.viii.72. [2500.]
 ii. 1819. pp.vi.78. [3000.]
 iii. 1820. pp.vi.57. [2000.]
 iv. 1821. pp.vi.88. [3000.]
 v. 1822. pp.[iv].68. [2500.]
 vi. 1823. pp.vi.84. [3000.]
 vii. 1824. pp.vi.86. [3000.]
 viii. 1825. pp.[vi].66. [2500.]
 ix. 1826. pp.[vi].64. [2500.]
 x. 1827. pp.[iv].68. [2500.]

— — Zweite . . . auflage. 1828. pp.xii.1158.
[35,000.]

— — — Ergänzungsband.

 i. Bis zum ende des jahres 1828. Herausgegeben von C. F. Whistling. pp.[iii].iv.

Music

1159–1298. [3000.]

ii. 1829–1833. Angefertigt von Ad. Hofmeister. pp.viii.386. [10,000.]

iii. 1834–1838. pp.viii.407. [12,500.]

— — — Musikalisch - literarischer monatsbericht neuer musikalien, musikalischer schriften und abbildungen. Als fortsetzung des Handbuchs der musikalischen schriften. Dritte folge. Angefertigt von Ad. Hofmeister.

i. 1839. pp.160. [4000.]

ii. 1840. pp.176. [4000.]

— — Dritte . . . auflage. Bearbeitet . . . von Adolph Hofmeister. 1844–1845. pp.[ii].142+[ii].336+vi.240. [50,000.]

— — — Kurzes verzeichniss sämmtlicher vom anfange des jahres 1844 bis ende 1847 in Deutschland und den angrenzenden ländern gedruckter musikalien. . . . Zugleich als vorläufer des ersten ergänzungsbandes zur 3ten auflage des Handbuchs. Angefertigt von August Rausch. [1848]. pp.[ii].334. [10,000.]

[—] — — Erster [&c.] ergänzungsband. . . . Bearbeitet . . . von Adolph Hofmeister.

i. 1844–1851. 1852. pp.[iv].382. [17,500.]

ii. 1852–1859. 1860. pp.vi.470. [22,500.]

iii. 1860–1867. 1868. pp.[vi].562. [27,500.]

iv. 1868–1873. Herausgegeben . . . von

20

Friedrich Hofmeister. 1876. pp.[x].cxlvi. 576. [27,500.]

v. 1874–1879. 1881. pp.viii.cxli.684. [35,000.]

vi. 1880–1885. 1887. pp.[viii].cxcviii.774. [40,000.]

vii. 1886–1891. 1893. pp.viii.cclii.947. [60,000.]

viii. 1892–1897. 1900. pp.viii.319.1040. [70,000.]

ix. 1898–1903. 1906. pp.vii.335.1151. [65,000.]

x. 1904–1908. [1910]. pp.viii.494.951. [60,000.]

xi. 1909–1913. [1915]. pp.971.vi.218+viii. 431. [55,000.]

xii. 1914–1918. [1920–1921]. pp.581+vi.442. [32,500.]

xiii. 1919–1923. [1924–1925]. pp.v.996. [32,500.]

[continued as:]

Hofmeisters handbuch der musikliteratur.

xvii. 1924–1928. 1929. pp.800.408.xxiv. [47,500.]

xviii. 1929–1933. 1934–1935. pp.772+704. [40,000.]

xix. 1934–1940. 1943. pp.512. [52,500.]

no more published; vol.xix extends to Lincke in

the alphabetical part; vols.ii–xiii are described as 'Fünfter [&c.] band oder zweiter [&c.] ergänzungs-band'; this refers to the Verzeichniss &c., 1852 &c., below, of which these volumes are cumulations.

[CÉSAR GARDETON], Bibliographie musicale de la France et de l'étranger, ou répertoire général systématique de tous les traités et œuvres de musique vocale et instrumentale, imprimés ou gravés en Europe jusqu'à ce jour. 1822. pp.[v].608. [5000.]

C[ARL] F[ERDINAND] BECKER, Die tonwerke des XVI. und XVII. jahrhunderts oder systematisch-chronologische zusammenstellung der in diesen zwei jahrhunderten gedruckten musikalien. Leipzig 1839. pp.vi.coll.194.

—— Zweite ... ausgabe. 1855. pp.xiv.coll.360. [6000.]

JAHRBUCH für musik. Vollständiges verzeichniss der im jahre ... erschienenen musikalien, musikalischen schriften und abbildungen. Herausgegeben von Bartholf Senff. Leipzig.

[i]. 1842. pp.iv.108. [2500.]
[ii]. 1843. pp.iv.102. [3000.]
iii. 1844. pp.iv.108. [3000.]
iv. 1845. pp.iv.104. [3000.]
v. 1846. pp.iv.116. [3500.]

vi. 1847. pp.iv.116. [3500]
vii. 1848. pp.iv.116. [3500.]
viii. 1849. pp.iv.91. [2500.]
ix. 1850. pp.iv.112. [3500.]
x. 1851. pp.iv.123. [3500.]
xi. 1852. pp.iv.132. [4000.]
no more published.

KURZES verzeichniss sämmtlicher im jahre 1852 [&c.] in Deutschland und den angrenzenden ländern gedruckter musikalien, auch musikalischer schriften und abbildungen. Leipzig.

[i]. 1852. pp.110. [2750.]
[ii]. 1853. pp.142. [3500.]
[*continued as:*]

Verzeichniss [*afterwards:* Verzeichnis] sämmtlicher im jahre 1854 [&c.] in Deutschland und in den angrenzenden ländern [*afterwards:* im Deutschen reiche und in den ländern deutschen sprachgebietes; *afterwards:* sowie der für den vertrieb im Deutschen reiche wichtigen, im auslande] erschienenen musikalien, auch musikalischen schriften.

[iii]. 1854. pp.[ii].134. [3250.]
[iv]. 1855. Redigirt von Adolphe Hofmeister. pp.[ii].150. [3750.]
[v]. 1856. pp.[ii].160. [4000.]
[vi]. 1857. pp.[ii].158. [4000.]

[vii]. 1858. pp.[ii].166. [4250.]

[viii]. 1859. pp.[ii].170. [4250.]

ix. 1860. pp.[ii].194. [5000.]

x. 1861. pp.[ii].218. [5500.]

xi. 1862. pp.[ii].222. [5500.]

xii. 1863. pp.[ii].218. [5500.]

xiii. 1864. pp.[iv].212. [5500.]

xiv. 1865. pp.[ii].192. [5000.]

xv. 1866. pp.[iv].168. [4250.]

xvi. 1867. pp.[ii].182. [4500.]

xvii. 1868. pp.[ii].178. [4500.]

xviii. 1869. pp.[ii].190. [4750.]

xix. 1870. Bearbeitet von Franz Jost. pp.[iii.]
180. [4500.]

xx. 1871. Herausgegeben von Friedrich
Hofmeister. pp.[iii].240.lxxvi. [6000.]

xxi. 1872. pp.[ii].230.lxxxvi. [5750.]

xxii. 1873. pp.[ii].390.xcviii. [10,000.]

xxiii. 1874. pp.[ii].244.xcii. [6000.]

xxiv. 1875. pp.[iv]. lxxiii.298. [8000.]

xxv. 1876. pp.[iv].xxx.302. [8000.]

xxvi. 1877. pp.[iv].lxxxii.314. [8000.]

xxvii. 1878. pp.[iv].lxxvi.350. [10,000.]

xxviii. 1879. pp.[iv].lxxix.344. [9500.]

xxviii [*sic*, xxix]. 1880. pp.[iv].lxxxii.350.
[10,000.]

xxx. 1881. pp.[vi].lxxx.300. [7500.]

xxxi. 1882. pp.[vi].civ.400. [10,000.]
xxxii. 1883. pp.[vi].xciii.310. [7500.]
xxxiii. 1884. pp.[vi].xciv.342. [9000.]
xxxiv. 1885. pp.[v].ci.364. [9000.]
xxxv. 1886. pp.[v].xcix.352. [9000.]
xxxvi. 1887. pp.[vi].cv.402. [10,000.]
xxxvii. 1888. pp.[vii].cxxv.406. [10,000.]
xxxviii. 1889. pp.[vi].cxvii.412. [10,000.]
xxxix. 1890. pp.[vii].cxxvi.442. [11,000.]
xl. 1891. pp.[vii].cxxvii.442. [11,000.]
xli. 1892. pp.[vii].cxli.424. [11,000.]
xlii. 1893. pp.[viii].cl.420. [11,000.]
xliii. 1894. pp.[vii].cxlviii.441. [11,000.]
xliv. 1895. pp.[viii].cxliv.418. [11,000.]
xlv. 1896. pp.[viii].clxixx [*sic,* clxxix].514.
    [12,500.]
xlvi. 1897. pp.[viii].clxii.489. [12,500.]
xlvii. 1898. pp.[iv].71.215. [10,000.]
xlviii. 1899. pp.[iv].66.215. [10,000.]
xlix. 1900. pp.[iv].68.224. [11,000.]
l. 1901. pp.[iv].72.240. [12,000.]
li. 1902. pp.[iv].69.231. [12,000.]
lii. 1903. pp.[iv].68.220. [11,000.]
liii. 1904. pp.[iv].70.232. [12,000.]
liv. 1905. pp.[iv].69.236. [12,000.]
lv. 1906. pp.[iv].70.217. [11,000.]
lvi. 1907. pp.[iv].74.231. [12,000.]

lvii. 1908. pp.[iv].72.225. [11,000.]

lviii. 1909. pp.[vi].146.226. [11,000.]

lix. 1910. pp.[iv].144.218. [11,000.]

lx. 1911. pp.[iv].163.247. [12,000.]

lxi. 1912. pp.[iii].116.240. [12,000.]

lxii. 1913. pp.[ii].222.108+[iii].54. [11,000.]

lxiii. 1914. pp.[ii].185+[iii].128. [9000.]

lxiv. 1915. pp.[ii].144+[iv].116. [7000.]

lxv. 1916. pp.[ii].132+[iv].114. [7000.]

lxvi. 1917. pp.[ii].110+111–198. [5000.]

lxvii. 1918. pp.[ii].105+107–198. [5000.]

lxviii. 1919. pp.[ii].120+121–220. [6000.]

lxix. 1920. pp.[ii].163+165–297. [8000.]

lxx. 1921. pp.iv.272. [7000.]

lxxi. 1922. pp.iv.214. [6000.]

lxxii. 1923. pp.vi.196. [5000.]

lxxiii. 1924. pp.vii.304. [8000.]

lxxiv. 1925. pp.356. [9000.]

lxxv. 1926. pp.366. [10,000.]

lxxvi. 1927. pp.376. [10,000.]

lxxvii. 1928. pp.389. [10,000.]

[*continued as:*]

Hofmeisters jahresverzeichnis. . . . Verzeichnis sämmtlicher musikalien, musikbücher, zeit-schriften [&c.].

lxxviii. 1929. pp.366. [9000.]

lxxix. 1930. pp.400. [10,000.]

Music

lxxx. 1931. pp.316. [8000.]

lxxxi. 1932. pp.291. [7000.]

lxxxii. 1933. pp.296. [7000.]

lxxxiii. 1934. pp.272. [6000.]

lxxxiv. 1935. pp.339. [8000.]

lxxxv. 1936. pp.333. [8000.]

lxxxvi. 1937. pp.337. [8000.]

lxxxvii. 1938. pp.325. [8000.]

lxxxviii. 1939. pp.269. [7000.]

lxxxix. 1940. pp.222. [5000.]

xc. 1941. pp.217. [5000.]

xci. 1942. pp.163. [4000.]

[*continued as:*]

Jahresverzeichnis der deutschen musikalien und musikschriften. Deutsche bücherei.

xcii. 1943. pp.284. [6000.]

xciii. 1944. pp.196. [5000.]

xciv–xcvii. 1945–1948. pp.399. [10,000.]

xcviii. 1949. pp.468. [11,000.]

xcix. 1950. pp.322. [7500.]

c. 1951. pp.339. [8000.]

ci. 1952. pp.345. [8000.]

cii. 1953. pp.678. [10,000.]

ciii. 1954. pp.658. [10,000.]

civ. 1955. pp.603. [9500.]

cv. 1956. pp.716. [10,500.]

cvi. 1957. pp.377.258. [10,000.]

cvii. 1958. pp.391.260. [10,000.]
cviii. 1959. pp.375.260. [9500.]
cix. 1960. pp.   .264.
cx. 1961. pp.   .249.

in progress; vols.i–lxxxix were consolidated as the supplementary volumes to the third edition of Whistling, entered above.

CATALOGO delle opere pubblicate dall' I. r. stabilimento nazionale privilegiato di ... Tito di Gio. Ricordi in Milano. 1855. pp.xv.767. [28,500.]
— [another edition]. 1875. pp.viii.739. [40,000.]
— — Primo supplemento. 1875. pp.76. [500.]

ROB[ERT] EITNER, Verzeichniss neuer ausgaben alter musikwerke aus der frühesten zeit bis zum jahre 1800. [Monatshefte für musikgeschichte (vol.ii: beilage): Leipzig 1870]. pp.208. [7500.]
reissued in 1871 as an independent publication; substantial additions appear in the Monatshefte für musik-geschichte *(Berlin 1877), ix.*

ROBERT EITNER, Bibliographie der musik-sammelwerke des XVI. und XVII. jahrhunderts. Berlin 1877. pp.xi.964. [12,500.]

A[LFRED] MICHAELIS, Allgemeiner führer durch die musik-litteratur, unter besonderer berücksichtigung der werke lebender meister, sowie

wenig bekannter musikgattungen. Halle a. S.
1888. pp.viii.64. [1750.]

HENRY M. BROOKS, Olden time music. A compilation from newspapers and books. Boston 1888.
pp.xx.283. [650.]

CATALOGUE mensuel de toutes les publications
musicales de la France, la Belgique et la Suisse.
Première année, numéro 1[–10]. Vevey 1890–
1891. pp.290. [5000.]

JAMES DUFF BROWN, Guide to the formation of
a music library. Library association series (no.4):
1893. pp.[v].22. [500.]

[ ] BAUDOUIN-LALONDRE, Bibliographie musicale. Catalogue annuel de la musique et des
ouvrages techniques publiés en France en 1896.
1897. pp.iv.74. [580.]
[*continued as:*]
Annuaire de la musique.
 1897. pp.xlii.75. [6000.]
 1898. pp.384. [7000.]
 1899. pp.544. [7000.]
no more published.

JULIUS FUCHS, Kritik der tonwerke. . . . Band 1.
Die komponisten von Bach bis zur gegenwart. . . .
Abt. 1. Einteilung der komponisten nach dem
dauernden werte ihrer schöpfungen. Abt. 11.

Einteilung ausgewählter werke nach schwierig-
keitsgraden. (NB. Die vokalwerke sind noch
speziell nach stimmlagen geordnet). Abt. III.
Kritischer katalog. Leipzig 1897. pp.[viii].clii.400.
[25,000.]

no more published.

HAUPT-KATALOG des musikalien-verlags von
Johann André. Offenbach a. M.: 1900. pp.[ii].
xv.569. [16,000.]

includes the publications of the firm's predecessors.

LISTE des ouvrages adoptés dans les cours du
conservatoire de musique de Toulon. Toulon
[printed] 1900. pp.20. [300.]

[KARL] ALBERT GÖHLER, Verzeichnis der in den
frankfurter und leipziger messkatalogen der jahre
1564 bis 1759 angezeigten musikalien. Leipzig
1902. pp.[iii].20.64.96.34. [3715.]

FRANZ PAZDÍREK, Universal-handbuch der musikliteratur aller zeiten und völker. . . . . I. teil.
Inhalt: die gesamte, durch musikalienhandlungen
noch beziehbare musikliteratur aller völker. Wien
[1904–1910]. pp.xxix.420+xvi.1299+xvi.696+
xvi.531 + xvii.616 + xv.700 + xv.779 + xvi.208
+ xvi.532 + xv.728 + xv.1012 + xv.256.137 +
588.18 + xv.714 + xv.1239 + xvi.388 + xvi.356

+xvi.603+xvi.142. [500,000.]

teil 1 is complete; no more published; reissued in [1911] with a Paris imprint, as Manuel universel de la littérature musicale [*&c*].

G. SURTEES TALBOT, Graded lists of the music of the great composers. [Second edition]. Home music study union series (no.1): [1914]. pp.40. [2000.]

G. SURTEES TALBOT, Hints on the study of the great composers. . . . Comprising selected lists of the music of Handel [&c.]. Home music study union series (no.2): [1914]. pp.20. [1000.]

THE ATHENÆUM subject index to periodicals. . . . Music.

 1915. 1916. pp.12. [400.]
 1916. 1918. pp.22. [750.]
   [*continued as:*]
The subject index to periodicals. . . . H. Music. Library association.

 1917–1919. 1921. pp.[ii].coll.56. [1250.]
 1920. 1923. pp.[ii].coll.30. [750.]
 1921. 1924. pp.[ii].coll.26. [1250.]
 1922. 1925. pp.[ii].coll.28. [1250.]
subsequent issues were not published in sections.

MICHEL'ANGELO LAMBERTINI, Bibliophilie musicale. Les bibliothèques portugaises; essai de classi-

fication: les livres d'un amateur: cabinet iconographique. [Lisbon] 1918. pp.302. [2339.]
120 copies printed.

W. EDMUND QUARRY, Dictionary of musical compositions and composers. [1920]. pp.viii.192. [5250.]

LIONEL ROY MCCOLVIN, Music in public libraries. A guide to the formation of a music library, with select lists of music and musical literature. 1924. pp.150. [900.]

BOLLETTINO bibliografico musicale. Anno 1[–7]. [Milano] 1926–1933.

   i. 1952. pp.77.90.75.84. [1000.]
new series

PAUL COHEN, 'Musikdruck und -drucker zu Nürnberg im sechszehnten jahrhundert'. Erlangen 1927. pp.[iv].65. [443.]
reissued Nürnberg 1927.

TOBIAS NORLIND, Konzert- und opernlexikon. Stockholm [1928]. coll.192. [2000.]
A–Fall Jerusalems only; no more published.

CATALOGUE of the publications of the Plainsong & mediæval music society and of St. Mary's press, Wantage. Nashdom abbey: Burnham, Bucks. 1930. pp.12. [100.]

VERZEICHNIS der neudrucke alter musik. Staatliches institut für deutsche musikforschung: Leipzig:

> i. 1936. Herausgegeben von Walter Lott. pp.80. [750.]
> ii. 1937. pp.72. [700.]
> iii. 1938. pp.65. [600.]
> iv. 1939. pp.52. [500.]
> v. 1940. pp.43. [400.]
> vi. 1941. pp.37. [400.]
> vii. 1942. pp.25. [250.

covers the period to about 1800.

LIONEL R[OY] MCCOLVIN and HAROLD REEVES, Music libraries: their organization and contents, with a bibliography of music and musical literature. 1937–1938. pp.vii.239+vii.318. [7500.]

REICHSLISTE für musikbüchereien. Zusammengestellt . . . von der Reichstelle für das volksbüchereiwesen. Leipzig 1938. pp.80. [1500.]

ALFRED J[ULIUS] SWAN, The music director's guide to musical literature (for voices and instruments). Prentice-Hall musical series: New York 1941. pp.xii.164. [1500.]

MUSIC and musical appreciation. Fourth edition. National book council: Book list (no.85): 1942. pp.6. [300.]

Music

ANNA HARRIET HEYER, A check-list of publication of music. University of Michigan: School of music: Ann Arbor 1944. pp.[ii].xii.49. [250.]*
a United States union catalogue of standard series and collections.

ANDRÉ SOYER, Tableau chronologique et schématique des principaux compositeurs de musique nés après 1450 et morts avant 1944. Suivi d'un tableau synoptique mentionnant par écoles les œuvres les plus connues avec date de création. [1945]. [folding sheet]. [500.]

WILLIAM REDDICK, The standard musical repertoire, with accurate timings. Garden City, N.Y. 1947. pp.192. [2250.]

VASCO MARIZ, Dicionário bio-bibliográfico musical (brasileiro e internacional). Rio de Janeiro 1948. pp.252. [5000.]

WILLIAM C[HARLES] SMITH, A bibliography of the musical works published by John Walsh during the years 1695-1720. Bibliographical society: 1948. pp.[iv].xxxiv.216. [636.]

HAROLD BARLOW and SAM MORGENSTERN, A dictionary of musical themes. New York [1948]. pp.656. [10,000.]

THE MUSIC index. Detroit.

Music

i. 1949. [Edited by Florence Kretzschmar].
1950. pp.308. [6000.]
[ii]. 1950. 1951. pp.[viii].416. [8000.]*
[iii]. 1951. 1953. pp.[viii].505. [10,000.]*
[iv]. 1952. 1954. pp.[viii].483. [10,000.]*
in progress; only the annual cumulations are set out.

BOLLETTINO bibliografico musicale. Milano.
i. 1952. pp.77.89.75.84. [1000.]
in progress.

WILLI KAHL and WILHELM MARTIN LUTHER, Repertorium der musikwissenschaft. Musikschrifttum, denkmäler und gesamtausgaben in auswahl (1800–1950). Kassel &c. 1953. pp.viii.271. [2795.]

[W. HUGLO], Bibliographie grégorienne, 1935–1956. Solesmes &c. 1956. ff.[i].44. [500.]*

ALEC ROBERTSON, Music and musicians. Reader's guides (2nd ser., no.10): Cambridge 1956. pp.31. [150.]

S[ARA] YANCEY BELKNAP, Guide to the musical arts. An analytical index of articles and illustrations 1953–56. New York 1957. pp.iv.[1249]. [10,000.]

FOLKE LINDBERG, Catalogue of rare materials and first supplement. International association of music libraries: Radio commission: Stockholm 1959. ff.[ii].vi.185. [4500.]*

E[RIC] T[HOMAS] BRYANT, Music librarianship. A practical guide. 1959. pp.xi.503. [2000.]

[OVE BJØRNUM], Musik katalog. Et udvalg af aeldre og nyere musik. Dansk bibliografisk kontor: [Odense printed] 1959. pp.56. [900.]

HEINZ ZIRNBAUER, Der notenbestand der reichsstädtisch nürnbergischen ratsmusik. Eine bibliographische reconstruktion. Stadtbibliothek Nürnberg: Veröffentlichungen (no.1): Nürnberg 1959. pp.48. [200.]
covers the period 1500–1700.

FRANÇOIS LESURE, *ed.* Recueils imprimés, XVIᵉ–XVIIᵉ siècles. Répertoire international des sources musicales: München &c.

   i. Liste chronologique. 1960. pp.639. [1750.]
in progress.

WILHELM BUSCHKÖTTER, Handbuch der internationalen konzertliteratur. Berlin 1961. pp.374. [1250.]

МУЗЫКА. Государственная публичная библиотека имени Салтыкова-Щедрина: [Leningrad 1961]. pp.16. [60.]

ii. *Bio-bibliographies*
[*see also section 6 below*]

JOHANN GOTTFRIED WALTHER, Alte und neue

musicalische bibliothek, oder musicalisches lexicon, darinnen die musici . . . nebst ihren schrifften
und andern lebensumständen. Erffurt 1728. pp.
[viii].64. [150.]

a only; no more published.

— — [another edition]. Musicalisches lexicon,
oder musicalische bibliothec, darinnen . . . die
musici, welche so wol in alten als neuern zeiten,
ingleichen bey verschiedenen nationen, durch
theorie und praxin sich hervor gethan, und was
von jedem bekannt worden, oder er in schrifften
hinterlassen, . . angeführet. Leipzig 1732. pp.
[xiv].659.[ix]. [5000.]

a facsimile was published Kassel 1953, in the Documenta musicologica, *first series, no.iii.*

ERNST LUDWIG GERBER, Historisch-biographisches lexicon der tonkünstler, welches nachrichten
von dem leben und werken musikalischer schrift-
steller . . . enthält. Leipzig 1790–1792. pp.xvi.coll.
992+pp.[ii].xvi.86.coll.860. [10,000.]

— — Neues historisch-biographisches lexikon
[&c.]. 1812–1814. pp.xxxii.coll.974+pp.vi.coll.
824+pp.vi.coll.942+pp.[v].coll.844. [20,000.]

AL[EXANDRE ÉTIENNE] CHORON and F[RANÇOIS
JOSEPH MARIE] FAYOLLE, Dictionnaire historique

des musiciens. 1810–1811. pp.[iii].xcii.437+[iii].
471. [10,000.]

GIUSEPPE BERTINI, Dizionario storico-critico
degli scrittori di musica . . . di tutte le nazioni si'
antiche che moderne. Palermo 1814–1815. pp.
[vi].6.lvi.168 + [iii].8.236 + [iii].246 + [iii].125
[sic, 145].61.[sic, 51].[ii].xxxiv. [2000.]

A DICTIONARY of musicians, from the earliest
ages to the present time. 1824. pp.[iii].lxxii.401+
562. [10,000.]
— Second edition. 1827. pp.[ii].lxxii.401+
[iii].562. [10,000.]

F[RANÇOIS] J[OSEPH] FÉTIS, Biographie univer-
selle des musiciens et bibliographie générale de la
musique. Bruxelles 1835–1844. pp.ccliv.151+
viii.368 + [iii].372 + [iii].476 + [iii].529 + [iii].
513+[iii].625. [25,000.]
vols.i–iii were also issued with a Paris imprint and
vols.i–iv were reissued, Bruxelles 1837–1844.
— — Deuxième édition. Paris 1860–1865. pp.
[iii].xxxix.478 + [iii].484 + [iii].480 + [iii].491 +
[iii].480+[iii].496+[iii].548+[iii].527. [40,000.]
reissued 1866–1868 and 1875–1877.
— — — Supplément et complément. Publié
sous la direction de m. [François Auguste] Arthur

[Paroisse] Pougin. 1878–1880. pp.[iii].xv.480+
[v].691. [10,000.]

reissued in 1881.

— — — — Saggio di rettifiche ed aggiunte al
supplemento Fétis, vol.1 . . . riferibilmente a
maestri italiani e relative opere. Per Luigi Lianovosani [*pseud.* Giovanni Salvioli]. Milano &c.
[1878]. pp.40. [150.]

JAMES D[UFF] BROWN, Biographical dictionary
of musicians. With a bibliography of english
writings on music. Paisley &c. 1886. pp.viii.637.
[15,000.]

THEODORE BAKER, A biographical dictionary
of musicians. New York 1900. pp.vii.653.
[25,000.]

— — Supplement. 1905. pp.[ii].649–695.
[2000.]

— — Third [*sic*] edition, revised . . . by Alfred
Remy. 1919. pp.[xiv].1094. [40,000.]

— — Fourth [*sic*] edition. [Edited by Gustave
Reese and others]. 1940. pp.[xii].1234. [50,000.]

— — Baker's biographical [&c.]. Fifth [*sic*] edition. Completely revised by N. Slonimsky.
[1958]. pp.xvi.1855. [90,000.]

ROB[ERT] EITNER, Biographisch-bibliographi-
sches quellen-lexikon der musiker und musik-

gelehrten der christlichen zeitrechnung bis zur mitte des neunzehnten jahrhunderts. Leipzig 1900–1904. pp.480+[iii].480+[ii].480+[ii].480 + [ii].484 + [ii].480 + [ii].482 + [ii].482 + [ii].480 +[ii].479. [50,000.]

a facsimile was produced in 1947; and another Graz 1959, described as the '2. verbesserte auflage', to which was added in 1960, as 'band 11', a volume of 'nachträge und miscellanea'.

—— Miscellanea musicae bio–bibliographica. Musikgeschichtliche quellennachweise als nachträge und verbesserungen zu Eitners quellenlexikon. Herausgegeben von Hermann Springer, Max Schneider und Werner Wolffheim. Leipzig.

    i. 1912[–1913]. pp.[v].111. [1079.]

    ii. 1913–1914. pp.[ii].112. [1225.]

    iii. 1914–1916. pp.[ii].96. [1214.]

no more published; a specimen was issued in 1911.

——— Zweite . . . auflage. New York 1947. pp.435. [4500.]

A DICTIONARY of modern music and musicians. [General editor: A. Eaglefield-Hull]. 1924. pp. xvi.544. [20,000.]

covers the period from about 1880.

CARLO SCHMIDL, Dizionario universale dei musicisti. Milano [1926–] 1937–1938. pp.[ii].878 +[iv].788. [75,000.]

— — Supplemento. [1937–1938]. pp.[v].806. [40,000.]

H[ANS] J[OACHIM] MOSER, Musik lexikon. Berlin 1935. pp.[vii].1005. [15,000.]
— — Zweite auflage. 1943. pp.1102. [16,500.]
— — Vierte . . . auflage. 1955. pp.viii.723+ viii.725–1482. [17,000.]

JOSEPH DETHERIDGE, Chronology of music composers . . . 820 to 1810 [1937]. Birmingham 1936–1937. pp.xvi.144+vi.168. [large number.]
the compositions are described but not named.

LIST of selected books on foundations for a musical education. Corporation public libraries: Glasgow 1949. pp.16. [150.]

ALEXANDER WEINMANN, Chronologisch geordnete gesamtverzeichnisse der wichtigsten musikverlage aus der zeit zwischen 1770 und 1870. Beiträge zur geschichte des alt-wiener musikverlages (2nd ser.): Wien 1952 &c.
in progress.

iii. *Library and exhibition catalogues*

Africa, south

MUSIC. Natal society's library: [Pietermaritzburg 1918]. pp.[43]. [3000.]

Music

Austria

KATALOG der ausstellung des königreiches Grossbritannien und Irland. Internationale ausstellung für musik- und theaterwesen: Wien 1892. pp.[vi]. 47. [125.]

not limited to british music.

Belgium

CATALOGUE de la bibliothèque du Conservatoire royal de musique de Liége. Liége 1862. pp.63. [800.]

CATALOGUE de la bibliothèque de F[rançois] J[oseph] Fétis acquise par l'état belge. Bibliothèque royale: Bruxelles 1877. pp.xi.946. [6000.]

ALFRED WOTQUENNE, Catalogue de la bibliothèque du Conservatoire royal de musique. Bruxelles 1898–1912. pp.xi.535+[v].603+[viii]. 597+[viii].612. [16,809.]

EXPOSITION de documents musicaux (manuscrits — imprimés — estampes). Bibliothèque royale de Belgique: [Brussels 1955]. pp.23. [113.]

Brazil

EDIÇÕES raras de obras musicais. Coleção Teresa Cristina Marsa. Biblioteca nacional: [Rio de Janeiro 1955]. pp.24. [78.]

Music

Canada

A LIST of books of music and relating to music, which may be found in the College street circulating library of the Toronto public library system. 1915. pp.56. [1250.]

CATALOGUE of rare and modern books on history of music. Toronto [printed] [c.1930]. pp.24. [500.]

this appears to be a catalogue of the books in the possession of R. S. Williams and sons; not limited to history.

Denmark

K. SCHMIDT-PHISELDECK and H. TOPSØE-JENSEN, Musikalier. I. Udenlandsk musik. Hovedkatalog og 2 tillægslister. Statsbiblioteket: Fagkataloger (no.3): Aarhus 1926. pp.132.12.8. [2928.]

the first supplement is dated 1925.

— — Tillægsliste.

    iii. 1926. pp.10. [126.]
    iv. 1927. pp.12. [126.]
    v. 1927. pp.20. [329.]
    vi. 1928. pp.28. [483.]
    vii. 1928. pp.16. [219.]
    viii. 1929. pp.12. [107.]
    ix. 1929. pp.16. [162.]

x. 1930. pp.16. [68.]
contains index to Tillægsliste i–x.
xi. 1931. pp.18. [238.]
xii. 1932.
xiii. 1933.
xiv. 1934.
xv. 1935.
xvi. 1936.

KATALOG over dansk og udenlandsk musik og musiklitteratur. 2. udgave. Kommunebiblioteker: Kjøbenhavn 1932. pp.viii.158. [3750.]

France

[CHARLES] E[DMOND HENRI] DE COUSSEMAKER, Notice sur les collections musicales de la bibliothèque de Cambrai. 1843. pp.180.40. [500.]

[I. DELAS], Catalogue des livres composant la bibliothèque de la ville de Bordeaux. Musique. Bordeaux 1856. pp.xii.127. [1000.]

[JUSTE] ADRIEN [LENOIR] DE LA FAGE, Extraits du catalogue critique et raisonné d'une petite bibliothèque musicale. Rennes [1857]. pp.[iii].120.40. [100.]
covers the period 1500–1700; 100 copies printed.

CATALOGUE de la collection Cherubini . . . des

maîtres italiens, français, allemands, des XVIIIe et XIXe siècles. Œuvres dédiées ou offertes par eux à Cherubini. 1878. pp.20. [145.]

covers the period 1790–1842.

J[EAN] B[APTISTE] WECKERLIN, Bibliothèque du Conservatoire national de musique et de déclamation. Catalogue bibliographique . . . des principaux ouvrages de la réserve. 1885. pp.[iii].xxxi. 512. [500.]

covers the period to about 1700.

CATALOGUE d'une collection musicale et d'ouvrages divers légués par m. O. Thierry-Poux. Bibliothèque nationale: 1896. pp.59. [900.]

[JULES LAURENS *and others*], Catalogue de la collection musicale J.-B. [Jean Joseph Bonaventure] Laurens donnée à la bibliothèque d'Inguimbert. Carpentras [printed] 1901. pp.155. [2000.]

J[ULES ARMAND JOSEPH] ÉCHORCHEVILLE, Catalogue du fonds de musique ancienne de la Bibliothèque nationale. Société internationale de musique (section de Paris): 1910–1914. pp.[vii].243 + [iii].247 + [iii].243 + [iii].221 + [iii].243 + [iii]. 235+[iii].217+[iii].223. [20,000.]

covers the period to about 1800.

FRIEDRICH LUDWIG, Die älteren musikwerke der von Gustav Jacobstahl . . . begründeten bibliothek

Music

des "Akademischen gesangvereins" Strassburg. Strassburg 1913. pp.15. [250.]

L[IONEL] DE LA LAURENCIE and A[MÉDÉE] GASTOUÉ, Catalogue des livres de musique, manuscrits et imprimés, de la bibliothèque de l'Arsenal à Paris. Société française de musicologie: Publications (2nd ser., vol.vii): 1936. pp.xvii.185. [2000.]
covers the period to about 1800.

LISTE mensuelle des ouvrages entrés par achat, don ou échange. Bibliothèque nationale.

    1946. pp.24. [240.]
    1947. pp.14. [157.]
    1948. pp.58. [600.]
    1949. pp.71. [722.]
    1950. pp.53. [554.]
    1951. pp.32. [373.]
no more published.

[FRANÇOIS LESURE], Collection musicale André Meyer. Abbeville [printed] [1961]. pp.118. [1300.]

Germany

ERNST PFUDEL, Mittheilungen über die Bibliotheca rudolfina der Königl. ritter-akademie zu Liegnitz. I[–III]. Liegnitz 1777 [1776–1778]. pp. 130. [250.]

VERZEICHNISS des musikalischen nachlasses des

46

verstorbenen capellmeisters Carl Philipp Emanuel Bach. Hamburg 1790. pp.[ii].142. [1000.]

J[OHANN] FR[IEDRICH] TAEGLICHSBECK, Die musikalischen schätze der St. Katharinenkirche zu Brandenburg a. d. Havel. Ein beitrag zur musikalischen literatur des 16. und 17. jahrhunderts. Brandenburg 1857. pp.[ii].50. [69.]

VERZEICHNISS der in der leihanstalt für musikalische literatur von Alfred Dörffel ... enthaltenen bücher und musikalien. Leipzig 1861. pp.iii–viii.140. [2000.]

— — Erster nachtrag. 1890. pp.iv.125. [1500.]

N[ICOLAUS] M[ATTHIAS] PETERSEN, Verzeichniss der in der bibliothek der Königl. landesschule zu Grimma vorhandenen musikalien aus dem 16. und 17. jahrhundert. Grimma [1862]. pp.24. [63.]

JOS[EPH] MUELLER, Die musikalischen schaetze der Koeniglichen- und universitaets-bibliothek zu Koenigsberg in Pr., aus dem nachlasse Friedrich August Gotthold's. Bonn 1870. pp.[iv].431. [5000.]

covers the period to about 1800.

CARL ISRAËL, Die musikalischen schätze der Gymnasialbibliothek und der Peterskirche zu Frankfurt a. M. Programm des Städtischen gymnasiums: Frankfurt a. M. 1872. pp.[iv].120. [250.]

covers the period to about 1800.

DIE MUSIKALIEN der Grossherzoglichen hofbibliothek in Darmstadt. 1873.
— Supplement. 1874. pp.[ii].169. [3000.]

H[ANS] M[ICHAEL] SCHLETTERER, Katalog der in der Kreis- und stadtbibliothek, dem Staedtischen archive und der bibliothek des Historischen vereins zu Augsburg befindlichen musikwerke. Glogau [printed] [1878]. pp.xvi.138. [500.]

also issued as a Beilage *to the* Monatshefte für musikgeschichte, *Berlin 1878; covers the period 1500–1700.*

CARL ISRAËL, Uebersichtlicher katalog der musikalien der Ständischen landesbibliothek zu Cassel. [Zeitschrift des Vereins für hessische geschichte und landeskunde (n.s., supplement no.vii):] Cassel 1881. pp.viii.78. [750.]

covers the period 1500–1700.

EMIL BOHN, Bibliographie der musik-druckwerke bis 1700 welche in der Stadtbibliothek, der bibliothek des Academischen instituts fuer kirchenmusik und der Koeniglichen und universitaets-bibliothek zu Breslau aufbewahrt werden. Berlin 1883. pp.viii.450. [1250.]

Music

ALBERT QUANTZ, Die musikwerke der Kgl. universitäts-bibliothek in Göttingen. [Monatshefte für musikgeschichte (beilage): Leipzig 1883]. pp.47. [150.]

covers the period 1500–1700.

ROBERT EITNER, Katalog der musikaliensammlung des Joachimsthalschen gymnasium zu Berlin. Monatshefte für musikgeschichte (beilage): Berlin 1884. pp.106. [1500.]

covers the period 1700–1800.

[L.] OTTO KADE, Die älteren musikalien der stadt Freiberg in Sachsen. Monatshefte für musikgeschichte (vol.xx, beilage): Leipzig 1888. pp.vii. 32. [150.]

covers the period to about 1800.

[JOHANNES] EMIL [EDUARD BERNHARD] VOGEL, Die handschriften nebst den älteren druckwerken der musik-abtheilung. Die handschriften der Herzoglichen bibliothek zu Wolfenbüttel (achte abtheilung): Wolfenbüttel 1890. pp.viii.280. [989.]

covers the period to about 1800.

[ROBERT] EITNER and [L. OTTO] KADE, Katalog der musik-sammlung der Kgl. öffentlichen bibliothek zu Dresden (im Japanischen palais).

Monatshefte für musikgeschichte (beilage): Leipzig 1890. pp.[ii].150. [2000.]
covers the period to about 1700.

CARL STIEHL, Katalog der musik-sammlung auf der Stadtbibliothek. Lübeck [1893]. pp.[ii].60. [750.]

EDWIN MAYSER, Alter musikschatz. Mitteilungen aus der bibliothek des Heilbronner gymnasiums (vol.ii): Heilbronn 1893. pp.viii.82. [400.]
covers the period to about 1800.

[L.] OTTO KADE, Die musikalien-sammlung des Grossherzoglich Mecklenburg-Schweriner fürstenhauses aus den letzten zwei jahrhunderten. Schwerin 1893. pp.viii.484+[ii].424. [3000.]
—— Nachtrag. Der musikalische nachlass weiland ihrer königlichen hoheit der verwittweten frau erbgrossherzogin Auguste von Mecklenburg-Schwerin. 1899. pp.vii.142. [500.]

REINHARD VOLLHARDT, Bibliographie der musikwerke in der Ratsschulbibliothek zu Zwickau. Monatsheftn [*sic*] für musikgeschichte (beilage). Leipzig 1893-1896. pp.viii.300. [2000.]
covers the period 1500-1700.

[CARL FRIEDRICH PETERS and EMIL VOGEL], Katalog der musikbibliothek Peters. Leipzig 1894. pp. viii.168.iv.162. [7500.]

—— [another edition]. Band I. Bücher und schriften. Von Rudolf Schwartz. 1910. pp.iii–viii.227. [5000.]

no more published.

[PETER] GEORG [MAXIMILIAN] THOURET, Katalog der musiksammlung auf der Königlichen hausbibliothek im Schlosse zu Berlin. Leipzig 1895. pp.viii.357. [7500.]

FRIEDRICH KUHN, Beschreibendes verzeichnis der alten musikalien-handschriften und -druckwerke des Königlichen gymnasiums zu Brieg. Monatshefte für musikgeschichte (beilage): Leipzig [1896–]1897. pp.[iii].98. [600.]

covers the period to about 1800.

[RUDOLF JACOBS], Thematischer katalog der von Thulemeier'schen musikalien-sammlung in der bibliothek des Joachimsthal'schen gymnasiums zu Berlin. [Edited by Robert Eitner]. Monatshefte für musikgeschichte (beilage): Leipzig 1899. pp.[ii].110. [300.]

compiled in 1860; covers the period 1700–1800.

G. TISCHER and K. BURCHARD, Musikalienkatalog der hauptkirche zu Sorau N./L. Monatshefte für musikgeschichte (beilage): [Leipzig] 1902. pp.24. [400.]

covers the period 1600–1700.

Music

ERNST PRAETORIUS, Katalog der musikalien-
sammlung der Königl. gymnasialbibliothek in
Flensburg. Jahresbericht Ostern 1906: Beilage
(= Program 341): Flensburg 1905. pp.15. [125.]

AUSSTELLUNG: Schmuck und illustration von
musikwerken in ihrer entwicklung vom mittel-
alter bis in die neueste zeit. Kunstgewerbemuseum:
Frankfurt a. M. [1908]. pp.[vi].46. [279.]

KATALOG der sonderausstellung aus der musikbibliothek Paul Hirsch. Zweite musikfachausstellung: [Leipzig 1909]. pp.[36]. [40.]

[PAUL HIRSCH], Eine kleine bücherschau für die
teilnehmer an den hauptversammlungen der
Gesellschaft der bibliophilen [&c.]. . . . Führer
durch die ausstellung. [Frankfurt a. M. 1920].
pp.43. [214.]
300 copies privately printed.

[CARL HEINRICH MÜLLER], Verzeichnis der vom
Cäcilien-verein nach der Stadtbibliothek über-
führten handschriften und musikalien. [Frankfort
1924]. pp.2.8. [200.]*

[PHIL. THORN, ARMIN CLASEN and HANS SCHRÖ-
DER], Musikalisches schaffen und wirken aus drei
jahrhunderten. Sein fortleben in der gegenwart.
Ausstellung musikgeschichtlicher drucke, hand-

schriften und alter musikinstrumente. Gesellschaft der freunde des vaterländischen schul- und erziehungswesens: Ausschuss für musik: Hamburg 1925. pp.vi.89. [566.]

MUSIKBÜCHER. Zusammengestellt ... unter mitwirkung von hervorragenden fachleuten. Bücherverzeichnisse aus allen gebieten (no.xii): Leipzig [1925]. pp.66. [1500.]

MUSIKALISCHE handschriften, briefe und drucke. Sonderausstellung . . . für die tagung der Deutschen musikgesellschaft. Stadtgeschichtliches museum: [Leipzig 1925]. pp.[12]. [150.]

KATHI MEYER, Katalog der Internationalen ausstellung, musik im leben der völker. Frankfurt am Main 1927. pp.iii–viii.340. [2000.]

ROBERT [MARIA] HAAS, Die estensischen musikalien. Thematisches verzeichnis. Regensburg 1927. pp.232. [1000.]
covers the period to about 1800; on the collection of the Obizzi family, now in the Hofburg-Museum.

[KARL GUSTAV FELLERER], Die musikalischen schätze der Santinischen sammlung. Führer durch die ausstellung der universitäts-bibliothek. Münster i. Westf. 1929. pp.32. [170.]
now forms part of the university library of Münster

Music

WILHELM STAHL, Die musik-abteilung der Lübecker stadtbibliothek in ihren älteren beständen. Noten und bücher aus der zeit vom 12. bis zum anfang des 19. jahrhunderts. Stadtbibliothek der freien und Hansestadt Lübeck: Veröffentlichungen (vol.iv, part 2): Lübeck 1931. pp.62. [1000.]

[KARL HEINZ KÖHLER and EVELINE BARLITZ], Neuerwerbungen ausländischer musikliteratur. Deutsche Staatsbibliothek: Bibliographische mitteilungen (no.12 &c.): Berlin.
 1954–1955. . . . (no.12). pp.90. [600.]
 1956–1957. . . . (no.16). pp.120. [749.]

WILLI KAHL, Katalog der in der universitäts- und stadtbibliothek Köln vorhandenen musikdrucke des 16., 17. und 18. jahrhunderts. Beiträge zur rheinischen musikgeschichte (no.27): Köln 1958. pp.[ii].v.23. [118.]*

Great Britain

JOSEPH CALKIN, Catalogue of the library belonging to the Philarmonic Society, London. [c.1825]. pp.[ii].92. [500.]
 the British museum copy contains ms. additions.

A CATALOGUE of the musical library belonging to his majesty's Concert of ancient music, instituted in 1776, at the Rooms, Tottenham street, removed to the Concert room at the Opera house in 1795, and to the Rooms, Hanover square, in 1804. 1827. pp.[iii].65. [2000.]

CATALOGUE of music and musical literature contained in the library of St. Martin's hall. 1850. pp.viii.32. [1000.]

CATALOGUE of the Universal circulating musical library. [1853]. pp.x.576. [27,000.]
— Supplement. [1855]. pp.viii.577–888. [15,000.]
— Supplement. [1856]. pp.viii.889–1072. [8000.]
— Supplement III. 1861. pp.xx[*sic*, xi].1073–1342. [12,000.]

CATALOGUE of books and music in the library. Gresham college: 1872. pp.47. [750.]

THE EWING musical library. Catalogue of the Musical library of the late Wm. Ewing, esq., bequeathed to Anderson's university. Glasgow 1878. pp.[vii].256. [4000.]

[CATALOGUE of music. Accessions. British museum].
[i]. 1884. ff.452. [10,000.]
ii. 1886. ff.453–607. [4000.]

iii. 1888. ff.608–1320. [30,000.]
iv. 1889. ff.1321–1518. [7500.]
v. 1891. pp.1519–2467. [20,000.]
vi. 1894. pp.2469–3069. [15,000.]
vii. 1895. pp.3081–3373. [7500.]
viii. 1896. pp.227. [5000.]
ix. 1897. pp.539. [12,500.]
x. 1898. pp.372. [9000.]
xi. 1900. pp.572. [14,000.]
xii. 1902. pp.585. [14,000.]
xiii. 1903. pp.537. [12,500.]
xiv. 1904. pp.545. [12,500.]
xv. 1906. pp.518. [12,000.]
xvi. 1908. pp.580. [14,000.]
xvii. 1909. pp.616. [15,000.]
xviii. 1910. pp.539. [12,500.]
xix. 1912. pp.547. [12,500.]
xx. 1913. pp.578. [14,000.]
xxi. 1914. pp.391. [9000.]
xxii. 1915. pp.161. [4000.]
xxiii. 1916. pp.473. [11,000.]
xxiv. 1921–1922. pp.745. [17,500.]
xxv. 1924. pp.433. [10,000.]
xxvi. 1925. pp.249. [6000.]
xxvii. 1925. pp.233. [5500.]
xxviii. 1925. pp.169. [4000.]
xxix. 1926. pp.229. [5000.]

xxx. 1926. pp.173. [4000.]
xxxi. 1927. pp.195. [4500.]
xxxii. 1928. pp.212. [5000.]
xxxiii. 1929. pp.203. [5000.]
xxxiv. 1930. pp.208. [5000.]
xxxv. 1931. pp.204. [5000.]
xxxvi. 1932. pp.110. [2500.]
xxxvii. 1933. pp.157. [3500.]
xxxviii. 1934. pp.175. [4000.]
xxxix. 1935. pp.179. [4000.]
xl. 1936. pp.201. [5000.]
xli. 1937. pp.200. [5000.]
xlii. 1938. pp.200. [5000.]
xliii. 1939. pp.212. [5000.]
xliv. 1941. pp.168. [4000.]
xlv. 1942. pp.132+9. [3000.]
xlvi. 1943. pp.123. [2500.]
xlvii. 1944. pp.123. [2500.]
xlviii. 1946. pp.134. [3000.]
xlix. 1946. pp.168. [3500.]
l. 1947. pp.204.24. [4000.]
li. 1948. pp.206.16. [4000.]
lii. 1950. pp.171.28. [4000.]
liii. Music in the Hirsch library. [By Alexander Hyatt King and Charles Humphries].
1951. pp.438. [9000.]
liv. 1951. pp.241. [4000.]
lv. 1952. pp.336. [7000.]

lvi. 1953. pp.295. [5000.]
lvii. 1954. pp.243. [4000.]
lviii. 1955. pp.318. [6000.]
lix. 1955. pp.266. [5000.]
lx. 1956. pp.290. [5000.]
lxi. 1957. pp.319. [6000.]
lxii. 1958. pp.311. [6000.]
lxiii. 1959. pp.320. [6000.]
lxiv. 1960. pp.358. [7000.]
lxv. 1962. pp.452. [9000.]
lxvi. 1962. pp.253. [5000.]
lxvii. 1962. pp.310. [6000.]
lxviii. 1963. pp.272. [5000.]
lxix. 1964. pp.352. [7000.]

in progress.

CATALOGUE of musical works. Handsworth public library: West Bromwich [printed] 1886. pp.[ii].20. [500.]

DESCRIPTIVE catalogue of rare musical works, comprised in the library of John Bishop. Cheltenham [printed] [c.1890]. pp.iv.102. [3000.]

J[OHN] A[LEXANDER] FULLER-MAITLAND and A[RTHUR] H[ENRY] MANN, Catalogue of the music in the Fitzwilliam museum, Cambridge. 1893. pp.iii–viii.298. [2500.]

covers the period to about 1800.

Music

[JOHN POTTER BRISCOE], List of music and the literature of music. Free public libraries: Nottingham 1896. pp.12. [600.]

A CATALOGUE of music & musical literature in the central lending department of the Cambridge public free library. Cambridge [1897]. pp.20. [500.]

[WILLIAM BARCLAY SQUIRE], Catalogue of music. Recent acquisitions of old music (printed before the year 1800). British museum: 1899. pp.[ii].225. [4000.]

a copy in the British museum contains manuscript notes.

MUSIC, musical instruments and musicians list. Public libraries: Nottingham [c.1900]. pp.[7]. [550.]

WILLIAM BARCLAY SQUIRE, Musik-katalog der bibliothek der Westminster-abtei in London. Monatshefte für musikgeschichte (vol.xxxv: beilage): Leipzig 1903. pp.45. [600.]

covers the period to about 1800.

A. ROSENKRANZ, A catalogue of the Angelina Goetz library presented to the Royal academy of music. [1904]. pp.[viii].226. [3000.]

A SPECIAL loan exhibition of musical instruments, manuscripts, books . . . to commemorate the tercentenary of the granting . . . of a charter of incorporation to the Worshipful company of musicians in 1604. [1904]. pp.xxv.149. [1738.]

A CATALOGUE of ancient and modern books of music, mss., &c., &c., compiled from the general catalogue . . . of "The Henry Watson music library". Public free libraries: Manchester [1905]. pp.20. [257.]

[JAMES E. MATTHEW], Catalogue of a library of musical literature and music. [1906]. ff.[iii].214. 198.53. [7500.]*
a catalogue of the compiler's own library.

CATALOGUE of music. Museum: Warrington 1906. pp.16. [500.]
— Third edition. 1911. pp.[ii].19. [700.]

LIST of music and the literature of music. 4th edition. Public libraries: Nottingham 1906. pp.11. [750.]
— 6th edition. Catalogue of music [&c.]. 1914. pp.20. [1500.]

CATALOGUE of music and musical literature in the Central lending and reference departments. Public library: Edinburgh 1907. pp.48. [1750.]

CATALOGUE of music and musical literature in the Central library. Cardiff 1908. pp.vii.76. [1500.]

WILLIAM BARCLAY SQUIRE, Catalogue of printed music in the library of the Royal college of music. 1909. pp.[iii].368. [12,500.]

AN ILLUSTRATED catalogue of the music loan exhibition held . . . by the Worshipful company of musicians . . . 1904. 1909. pp.xxiv.354. [1250.]
covers the period to about 1800; 500 copies printed.

[PAUL HIRSCH], Katalog der sonderausstellung aus der musik-bibliothek Paul Hirsch. Zweite musikfachausstellung . . . zu Leipzig: 1909. pp. [32]. [40.]
covers the period to about 1800; the collection is now in the British museum; 200 copies printed.

[J. H. SHAW], Classified catalogue . . . of books on physical science (including music) in the lending library. Public library: Bury 1912. pp.60. [music: 500.]

W[ILLIAM] BARCLAY SQUIRE, Catalogue of printed music published between 1487 and 1800 now in the British museum. 1912. pp.iv.776+[ii].720.34. [30,000.]

— — Second supplement. Catalogue of printed music published before 1801. . . . By William C. Smith. 1940. pp.[iii].85. [1250.]
the first supplement forms part of the main work.

CATALOGUE of music and musical literature. Third edition. Public library: Chelsea 1914. pp.45. [2750.]
— Fifth edition. 1926. pp.53. [3250.]

MUSIC and musical subjects. List of books. Public libraries: Leyton 1915. pp.16. [600.]

G[ODFREY] E[RNEST] P[ELLEW] ARKWRIGHT, Catalogue of music in the library of Christ church. Oxford.

    i. Works of ascertained authorship. 1915. pp. xi.128. [2500.]
    ii. MS. works of unknown authorship. (i). Vocal. 1923. pp.xxxii.182. [800.]
no more published.

ALOYS HIFF, Catalogue of printed music published prior to 1801 now in the library of Christ church, Oxford. 1919. pp.iv.76. [500.]

GEO. A. STEPHEN, Music and musical literature ... in the Norwich public libraries. Norwich 1923. pp.60. [1250.]

MUSIC. A classified list of musical works and of musical literature. Public libraries: Class list (no.2): Fulham 1924. pp.44. [1250.]

[WILLIAM G. WILDING], Classified catalogue of music and literature of music. Finsbury public libraries: 1925. pp.x.234. [4000.]

JOHN WARNER, A list of music and books on music and musicians, etc. Public libraries: Subject lists (no.2): Newport 1925. pp.23. [600.]

HAND list of music in the lending department of the central public library. Newcastle-upon-Tyne 1926. pp.[vii].32. [1250.]

WILLIAM BARCLAY SQUIRE [part ii: HILDA ANDREWS], Catalogue of the King's music library. British museum: 1927–1929. pp.xi.143+x.277+[v].383. [8500.]

CATALOGUE of the Society's library. Plainsong & mediaeval music society: Burnham, Bucks. 1928. pp.39. [500.]

CATALOGUE of music and musical literature. Public library: St. Marylebone. 1930. pp.vi.85. [1500.]

J. A. CARR, Catalogue of music. Public libraries: Liverpool 1933. pp.vi.374. [7500.]

Music

CATALOGUE of music and musical literature. Northamptonshire county library: [s.l.] 1935. pp.17. [350.]

HANS GÁL, Catalogue of manuscripts, printed music and books on music up to 1850 in the library of the Music department at the university of Edinburgh (Reid library). Edinburgh &c. 1941. pp.xvii.78. [1500.]

KATHI MEYER and PAUL HIRSCH, Katalog der musikbibliothek Paul Hirsch. Band IV. Erstausgaben, chorwerke in partitur, gesamtausgaben, nachschlagewerke, etc., ergaenzungen zu bd. I–III. Cambridge 1947. pp.iii–xxiii.695. [1750.]
the library is now in the British museum.

MUSIC. Books and music recently added to the Manchester public libraries. Manchester 1952. pp.8. [200.]

CATALOGUE of an exhibition of music held in the King's library. British museum: [1953]. pp.[ii]. ii.52. [224.]*

CATALOG of the music library. Public libraries: Liverpool 1954. pp.[x].572. [17,500.]

K. C. HARRISON, Music. A list of music scores available in . . . the Eastbourne public libraries.

Music

[Eastbourne] 1956. pp.19. [900.]*

THE BRITISH union-catalogue of early music printed before the year 1801. A record of the holdings of over one hundred libraries throughout the British Isles. Editor: Edith B[etty] Schnapper. 1957. pp.xx.583+xx.585–1178. [45,000.]

W[ILFRED] C[ECIL] PUGSLEY and G. ATKINSON, Catalogue of music. A complete catalogue of the scores, miniature scores, recorded music and books dealing with the theory, history and criticism of music, in the Dagenham public libraries. Dagenham 1958. pp.299. [4000.]*

CATALOGUE of music scores. Public libraries: Bristol 1959. pp.[viii].305. [7500.]*

[UNITY SHERRINGTON], Hand-list of music published in some british and foreign periodicals between 1787 and 1848 now in the British museum. 1962. pp.80. [1500.]

MUSIC for groups. Northamptonshire county library: [Northampton] 1962. pp.38. [572.]

Hungary

ERICH H. MÜLLER, Die musiksammlung der bibliothek zu Kronstadt. Kronstadt 1930. pp.[iii]. 177. [1000.]

Music

Italy

CATALOGO della musica esistente presso Fortunato Santini in Roma nel palazzo de' principi Odescalchi. Roma 1820. pp.46. [500.]

now forms part of the university library of Münster.

CATALOGO delle opere di musica o ad essa relative che nel decennio sono state depositate nell'archivio della congrezione ed accademia di santa Cecilia di Roma. [Roma 1846]. pp.[ii].30. [1000.]

[LUIGI ARRIGONI], Organografia. . . . Autografia e bibliografia musicale della collezione Arrigoni Luigi. Milano 1881. pp.[viii].120. [652.]

200 copies privately printed.

[COUNT] EUGENIO DE' GUARINONI, Indice generale dell'archivio musicale Noseda. Milano [1890-] 1897. pp.xiv.420. [10,253.]

the Archivio forms part of the Reale conservatorio di musica, Milan.

CATALOGO della biblioteca del Liceo musicale di Bologna. Bologna.

    i. Teorica. Compilato da Gaetano Gaspari. Compiuto e pubblicato da Federico Parisini. [1888-]1890. pp.xxix.418. [5000.]

    ii-iv. Pratica. Compilato da G. Gaspari.

Compiuto . . . da F. Parisini [Luigi Torchi;
Raffaele Cadolini]. 1892–1905. pp.viii.573
+[v].389+viii.279. [10,000.]
v. Libretti d'opera in musica. Preparato . . .
Ugo Sesini . . . relaborando schede di
G. Gaspari. 1943. pp.xvi.561. [5000.]
incomplete; in progress?

MANOSCRITTI e libri a stampa musicati espositi
dalla Biblioteca nazionale di Torino. Esposizione
nazionale: Torino 1898. pp.24. [68.]
covers the period to about 1700.

CATALOGO sommario della esposizione grego-
riana aperta nella Biblioteca apostolica vaticana.
Studi e testi (vol.xiii): Roma 1904. pp.3–75. [191.]
*covers the period to about 1700; a corrected reprint
appeared in the same year.*

CATALOGO delle opere musicali teoriche e pra-
tiche di autori vissuti sino ai primi decenni del
secolo XIX, esistenti nelle biblioteche e negli archivi
pubblici e privati d'Italia. Associazione dei musico-
logi italiani: Parma [printed].
i. [1]. Città di Parma. [By Guido Gasperini
and Nestore Pellicelli (*sic*)]. [1909–]1911.
pp.viii.3–295. [1500.]
[i (2)]. Città di Reggio-Emilia. [Compila-

tori . . . Guido Gasperini . . . Nestore
Pelicelli (*sic*)], 1911. pp.[ii].24. [100.]

vii [*sic*, ii]. Città di Bologna. Archivio della
R. accademia filarmonica. [Biblioteca del-
l'avv. Raimondo Ambrosini; Archivio di
S. Petronio]. (Compilatore . . . Alfredo
Bonora [Emilio Giani]). 1910–1911[–1938].
pp.124. [1000.]
    incomplete.

iii. Città di Milano. Biblioteca ambrosiana.
Compilatore . . . Gaetano Cesari. 1910–
1911. pp.20. [100.]
    incomplete.

iv. [1]. Città di Firenze. Biblioteca del R.
istituto musicale. Compilatori . . . Riccardo
Gandolfi e . . . Carlo Cordara. 1910–1911.
pp.3–321. [2500.]

iv. [2]. Città di Pistoia. Archivio capitolare
della cattedrale. Compilatore . . . Umberto
de Laugier. 1936–1937. pp.vii.106. [1000.]

v. Città di Roma. [Biblioteca della R. accademia di s. Cecilia. Compilatore . . . Otello
Andolfi]. 1912–1913. pp.56. [300.]
    incomplete.

vi. [1]. Città di Venezia. Biblioteca Querini
Stampalia. [Museo Correr]. Compilatore
. . . Giovanni Concina. [?1913]–1914. pp.
113. [1000.]

vi. [2]. Città di Vicenza. [Biblioteca berto-
liana . . . de Sebastiano Rumor; Archivio
dalla cattedrale . . . da Primo Zanini]. 1923.
pp.[ii].48. [250.]

vii. Città di Genova. R. biblioteca universi-
taria. [Schedatore: Raffaele Bresciano].
[   ]. pp.[ii].21. [50.]

vii [sic]–viii. Città di Modena. R. biblioteca
estense. [Compilatore . . . Pio Lodi]. [1916–
1924]. pp.561. [2500.]

ix. Città di Ferrara. Biblioteca comunale. [By
Emanuele Davia and Alessandro Lom-
bardi]. 1917. pp.[iii].40. [150.]

x. [1]. Città di Napoli. Archivo dell'Oratorio
dei Filippini. [Compilatore . . . Salvatore di
Giacomo]. 1918. pp.xiv.108. [1750.]

x. [2]. Città di Napoli. Biblioteca del R.
conservatorio di musica di s. Pietro a
Majella. Compilatori . . . Guido Gasperini
. . . Franca Gallo. [1918–]1934. pp.viii.696.
[6000.]

xi. Città di Assisi. Biblioteca comunale.
Compilatore . . . Francesco Pennacchi.
1921. pp.xvi.45.viii. [250.]

xii. Città di Torino. R. biblioteca nazionale.
[Compilatore . . . Attilio Cimbro (Alberto
Gentili)]. 1928. pp.38. [250.]

xiii. Biblioteche e archivi della città di Pisa. Compilatore . . . Pietro Pecchiai. 1932–1933[-1935]. pp.3–90. [750.]

xiv. Città di Verona. Biblioteca della Soc. accademica filarmonica di Verona. Fondo musicale antico. Compilatore ... Giuseppe Turrini. 1935–1936. pp.viii.54. [350.]

the title and imprint vary; no more published.

INDICE di alcuni cimeli esposti appartenenti alla biblioteca del R. istituto [musicale "Luigi Cherubini"]. Firenze 1911. pp.32. [99.]

[TAMMARO] DE MARINIS, I libri di musica della contessa Sofia Coronini Fagan salvati a Gorizia nel settembre 1916. Milano 1919. pp.xv.61. [263.]

[FRANCESCO VATIELLI and LUIGI TORRI], Mostra bibliografica musicale. Primo congresso internazionale di bibliografia e bibliofilio: Bologna 1929. pp.3–90. [348.]

[MARIANGELA DONÀ], La musica nelle biblioteche milanesi. Mostra di libri e documenti. Biblioteca nazionale braidense: Milano [1953]. pp.xii.56. [131.]

Japan

CATALOGUE of the W. H. Cummings' collection in the Nanki music library. [Tokyo] 1925.

pp.[iii].iv.70. [500.]
covers the period 1600–1800.

LIST of acquisition [*sic*]. Musashino college of music: Library: Tokyo.★

    i. 1957–1958. pp.[iii].43. [750.]
    ii. [1958–1959]. pp.[iv].91. [1250.]
    iii. 1959–1960. pp.[iv].113. [1500.]
    iv. 1960–1961. pp.[iv].119. [1500.]
    v. 1961–1962. pp.[iv].193. [2000.]
    vi. 1962–1963. pp.[iv].151. [1750.]
in progress.

LITTERAE rarae liber primus. Musashino academia musicae: Biblioteca: Tokio 1962. pp.[v].142. [600.]

Mexico

MÚSICA, libros y composiciones. Biblioteca Benjamín Franklin: México 1944. ff.23. [290.]★

Netherlands

CATALOGUS van de bibliotheken der Maatschappij tot bevordering der toonkunst en der Vereeniging voor Noord-Nederlands muziekgeschiedenis. Amsterdam 1884. pp.iv.146.xxii. [3000.]

CATALOGUS der musiekbibliotheek van D[aniel]

Music

F[rançois] Scheurleer. 's-Gravenhage 1893. pp. [xi].567. [5000.]

120 copies privately printed.

— Vervolg. 1903. pp.[xi].357. [4000.]

— 2de Vervolg. 1910. pp.[viii].217. [2500.]

— — Muziekhistorisch museum van d^r D. F. Scheurleer. Catalogus van de muziekwerken en de boeken over muziek. 1923–1925. pp.xi.399+ viii.465+[ii].166. [7500.]

200 copies printed; the collection is now the property of the city of The Hague.

Poland

JÓSEF REISS, Książki o muzyce od XV do XVII wieku w Bibljotece jagiellońskiej. Część druga. Kraków 1934. pp.32. [80.]

500 copies printed.

KATALOG mikrofilmów muzycznych. Biblioteka narodowa: Stacja mikrofilmowa i zakład muzyczny: Warszawa.

i. 1956. pp.251. [2250.]

in progress?

KATALOG dubletów. Catalogue of music-books, printed music and periodicals for exchange. Biblioteka Pánstwowej wyższej szkoly muzycznej: Katowice 1962. pp.[i].58. [750.]

Music

Portugal

PRIMEIRA parte do index da livraria de mvsica do mvyto alto, e poderoso rey dom Ioão o IV. [Lisbon] 1649. pp.[xix].525. [4000.]

— [type facsimile edited by Joaquim de Vasconcellos, with an added editorial volume bearing the title:] El-rey d. João o 4to. Porto 1900–1905. pp.[xix].527+[ii].xxxi.368. [4000.]

CATALOGUE des livres rares composant la bibliothèque musicale d'un amateur. Porto 1898. pp. [ii].190. [1567.]
the collection was that of Joaquim de Vasconcellos.

INVENTÁRIO dos inéditos e impressos musicais. Fasciculo 1. Universidade: Biblioteca: Publicações: Coimbra 1937. pp.xv.59.47. [300.]

MANUEL JOAQUIM, Vinte livros de música polifónica do Paço ducal de Vila Viçosa. Fundação da Casa de Bragança: Lisboa 1953. pp.xxxi.301. [20.]

Spain

FELIP PEDRELL, Catàlech de la biblioteca musical de la Diputació de Barcelona ... Vol.I. Barcelona 1908–1909. pp.3–331+3–383. [1271.]
500 copies printed.

J[OHN] B[RANDE] TREND, Catalogue of the music

in the Bibliotheca medinaceli, Madrid. New York &c. 1927. pp.[iii].485–554. [250.]
covers the period to about 1800.

HIGINIO ANGLÉS and JOSÉ SUBIRÁ, Catálogo musical de la Biblioteca nacional de Madrid. Consejo superior de investigaciones científicas: Instituto español de musicología: Catálogos de la música antigua conservada en España (vol.i–iii): Barcelona 1946–1951. pp.iii–xix.491 + xvi.292 +xxiii.412. [2000.]

Sweden

RAFAEL MITJANA [and ÅKE DAVIDSSON], Catalogue critique et descriptif des imprimés de musique des XVIᵉ et XVIIᵉ siècles conservés à la bibliothèque de l'université royale d'Upsala. Upsala 1911–1951. pp.viii.vii.coll.502+pp.168+ 204. [700.]

ÅKE DAVIDSSON, Catalogue critique et descriptif des imprimés de musique des XVIᵉ et XVIIᵉ siècles conservés dans les bibliothèques suédoises, excepté la bibliothèque de l'université royale d'Upsala. Studia musicologica upsaliensia (vol.i): Upsala 1952. pp.471. [534.]

ÅKE LELLKY, Katalog över orkester- och körverk, tillgängliga för utlåning från Kungl. musikaliska

akademiens bibliothek och Sveriges orkester-
föreningars riksförbunds centralbibliothek. Kung-
liga musikaliska akademie: Bibliothek: Publikationer (vol.i): Stockholm 1953. pp.148. [1800.]

—— Supplement nr.1[–7] (1954–1960). pp.
[ii].39. [350.]*

Switzerland

JULIUS RICHTER, Katalog der musik-sammlung
auf der universitäts-bibliothek in Basel. Monatshefte für musikgeschichte (beilage): Leipzig 1892.
pp.[v].104. [1000.]
covers the period to about 1700.

[EDGAR REFARDT], Katalog der musikabteilung
der Oeffentlichen bibliothek der universität Basel
und der in ihr enthaltenen schweizerischen musikbibliothek. Erster band. Musikalische kompositionen. Basel 1925. pp.xi.141. [5000.]
not limited to swiss music.

INTERNATIONALE musik-ausstellung. Luzern
1938. pp.100.8. [550.]

GEORG WALTER, Katalog der gedruckten und
handschriftlichen musikalien des 17. bis 19. jahrhunderts im besitze der Allgemeinen musikgesellschaft Zürich. Zürich 1960. pp.vii.145.
[3500.]

75

Music

United States

CATALOGUE of music, including musical compositions and works relating to music and musicians. Carnegie free library: Alleghany, Pa. 1899. pp.12. [300.]

FINDING-LIST of music. Free public library: Worcester, Mass. 1906. pp.92. [1500.]

CATALOGUE of the Allen A. Brown collection of music in the Public library of the city of Boston. Boston [1908–]1910–1915. pp.viii.574+[iv].576+[iv].332. [50,000.]
— Supplement [1908–1916]. 1916. pp.[iv].438. [12,500.]

MUSICAL library owned by Rafael Joseffy. Piano compositions, orchestral parts and scores, chamber music, vocal scores. [New York c.1920]. pp.61. [1600.]

MUSIC. Catalog of the collection of instrumental and vocal scores in the Chicago public library. Chicago 1923. pp.vi.269. [7500.]
— Supplement I. 1926. pp.39. [1000.]

ANNA HARRIET FRYER, A check-list of publications of music. University of Michigan: School of music: Ann Arbor 1944. pp.[ii].xii.49. [200.]*

Music

a union catalogue of selected periodicals, historical collections, and large collected works.

EDYTHE N. BACKUS, Catalogue of music in the Huntington library printed before 1801. San Marino, Cal. 1949. pp.ix.773. [2500.]

NATHAN VAN PATTEN, Catalogue of the memorial library of music, Stanford university. Stanford 1950. pp.xiii.310. [1226.]

JOAQUIN NIN-CULMELL and MARY L. RICHMOND, Four centuries of music. An exhibit. Williams college: Chapin library: Williamstown, Mass. 1950. pp.32. [150.]

AN EXHIBIT of music and materials on music, early and rare. Graduate college [&c.]: Iowa City 1953. pp.vii.39. [100.]

ANNA HARRIET MEYER, A bibliography of contemporary music in the music library, North Texas state college. Denton 1955. ff.[ii].128. [2000.]*

THE PRINTED note. 500 years of music printing and engraving. Toledo museum of art: [Toledo 1957]. pp.144. [188.]*
an exhibition catalogue.

Music

6. Countries &c.

Africa

CATALOGUE of music in the Strange collection of Africana. Public library: Johannesburg 1944. pp.[iii].118. [859.]
— Supplement. 1945. ff.[ii].21. [200.]*

F[REDERICK] Z[IERVOGEL] VAN DER MERWE, Suid-afrikaanse musiekbibliografie 1787–1952. Pretoria 1958. pp.410. [4500.]

DARIUS L. THIEME, African music. A briefly annotated bibliography. Library of Congress: Washington 1964. pp.xxvi.55. [597.]

America, latin
[see also *Spain*]

SELECT list of references on indian music and dances. Library of Congress: Washington 1911. ff.4. [31.]*

LIST of latin american musical compositions . . . which can be purchased in the United States. Pan american union: Washington. 1932. ff.[i].25. [750.]*
— Second edition. 1933. ff.[iv].60. [1000.]

GILBERT CHASE, Partial list of latin american

music obtainable in the United States, with a supplementary list of books and phonograph records. Pan american union: Music division: Music series (no.1): Washington 1941. ff.[i]–iii.36. [500.]*

—— Third edition. Compiled by Leila Fern Thompson. 1948. ff.[i].ii.57.iii.17. [1000.]*

GILBERT CHASE, Bibliography of latin american folk music. Library of Congress: Division of music: [Washington] 1942. ff.[i].iii.pp.iv–ix.145. [1143.]*

GILBERT CHASE, A guide to latin american music. Library of Congress: Music division: Latin american series (no.5): Washington [1943]. pp.xiii.274. [2699.]

LEILA FERN, Selected references in english on latin american music. A reading list. Pan american union: Music division: Music series (no.13): Washington 1944. ff.iii.20. [100.]*

COMPOSITORES de América. Datos biográficos y catálogos de sus obras. Unión panamericana: Sección de música: Washington.*

    i. 1955. pp.[iii].98. [1000.]
    ii. 1956. pp.155. [1500.]
    iii. 1957. pp.[iii].119. [1000.]

iv. 1958. pp.164. [1500.]
v. 1959. pp.107. [1000.]
vi. 1960. pp.116. [1000.]

LATIN AMERICAN orchestral music available in the
United States. Pan american union: Washington
[1956]. pp.[iv].80. [1000.]*

Arabic

HENRY GEORGE FARMER, The arabic musical
manuscripts in the Bodleian library. 1935. pp.18.
[17.]

HENRY GEORGE FARMER, The sources of arabian
music: a bibliography of arabic mss. which deal
with the theory, practice and history of arabian
music. Glasgow bibliographical society: Records
(vol.xiii): Glasgow 1939. pp.iii–xvi.99. [302.]
*reissued independently in 1940 with a slightly
different subtitle.*

Argentina

ALBERT T[HOMAS] LUPER, The music of Argen-
tina. Pan american union: Music division: Music
series (no.5): Washington 1942. ff.[iii].30. [325.]*

Austria

FR. BÜSING, Verzeichniss aller im jahre 1860 in
Oesterreich erschienenen musikalien. Oesterrei-

Music

chischer catalog (part vi): Wien 1861. pp.[iii].34.
[1000.]

the rest of the Catalog *is by F. Andriessen.*

FÜHRER durch die ausstellung, Ein jahrhundert
wiener musikleben. Gesellschaft der musikfreunde: Wien [1912]. pp.28. [300.]
— [another edition]. [1937]. pp.28. [300.]

CONSTANTIN SCHNEIDER, [Führer durch die]
Musikausstellung im Salzburger Dom. Salzburg
[1928]. pp.40. [448.]

OESTERREICHISCHE musikbibliographie. Verzeichnis der österreichischen neuerscheinungen
auf dem gebiete der musik. Bearbeitet von der
Österreichischen nationalbibliothek. Verein der
österreichischen buch-, kunst-, musikalien-, zei-
tungs- und zeitschriftenhändler: Wien.

    i. 1949. pp.104. [1058.]
    ii. 1950. pp.96. [921.]
    iii. 1951. pp.105. [1024.]
    iv. 1952. pp.78. [735.]
    v. 1953. pp.134. [1486.]
no more published.

PRAKTISCHE musik (auswahl). Oesterreichische
bibliographie: Sonderheft: Wien.

    1958. pp.52. [543.]
    1959. pp.48. [470.]

Music

1960. pp.48. [469.]
in progress?

ALEXANDER WEINMANN, Verzeichnis der verlags-
werke des musikalischen magazins in Wien, 1784–
1802, "Leopold Koželuch". Beiträge zur geschichte des alt-wiener musikverlages: Wien
[1950]. pp.31. [500.]*

Basque

[JOSÉ] ANTONIO DE DONOSTIA, Essai d'une bibliographie musicale basque. [Centre basque & gascon
d'études régionales: Cahiers (no.ii):] Bayonne
1932. pp.36. [100.]

Belgium [see also *France*]

RENÉ VANNES, Dictionnaire des musiciens–compositeurs. Petits dictionnaires des lettres et des arts
en Belgique (vol.x): Bruxelles [1947]. pp.445.
[6000.]

KAREL DE SCHRIJVER, Bibliografie der belgische
toonkunstenaars sedert 1800. Leuven 1958. pp.152.
[1000.]

Brazil

VASCO MARIZ, Dicionário bio-bibliográfico
musical, brasileiro e internacional. Rio de Janeiro
1948. pp.[xi].252. [2000.]

Music

Bulgaria

БЪЛГАРСКИ музаикален книгопис. Тримесечен библиографски бюлетин за новоизлязла литература по музика и ноти. Български библиографски институт: София.

  i. 1958. pp.[ii].iv.46+[ii].58+[ii].46+[ii].70. [1634.]

  ii. 1959. pp.[ii].46+[ii].58+[ii].34+[ii].78. [1612.]

  iii. 1960. pp.[ii].46+[iii].54+[ii].38+[ii].66. [1474.]

  iv. 1961. pp.[ii].44+[ii].42+[ii].38+[ii].58 [1468.]

  v. 1962. pp.[ii].42+[ii].58+[ii].44+[ii].60. [1616.]

  vi. 1963. pp.[ii].48+[ii].44+[ii].40+[ii].56. [1525.]

in progress; each issue is accompanied by a select leaflet entitled Publications musicales et musicologiques, parues en Bulgarie.

Byzantine

[AMÉDÉE GASTOUÉ], Introduction à la paléographie musicale byzantine. Catalogue des manuscrits de musique byzantine de la Bibliothèque nationale de Paris et des bibliothèques publiques de France. [Société internationale de musique: 1907]. pp.ix.103. [150.]

Music

Canada

A LIST of canadian music. Canadian federation of music teachers associations: Toronto [1946]. pp.[ii].23. [1500.]

CATALOGUE of canadian composers. Canadian broadcasting corporation: [Toronto] 1947.

— Revised . . . edition. Edited by Helmut Kallmann. [1952]. pp.254. [5000.]

Chile

[RAMÓN ARMINIO LAVAL], Bibliografía musical. Composiciones impresas en Chile y composiciones de autores chilenos publicadas en el extranjero. Segunda parte, 1886–1896. Biblioteca nacional: Santiago de Chile 1898. pp.89. [335.]
the first part was not published.

China

GLEN W[ILLIAM] BAXTER, An index to the Ch'in ting tz'u p'u. Harvard-Yenching institute: Cambridge [Mass.] 1951. ff.viii.71. [1321.]*

TSAI-PING LIANG, *ed.* Bibliography on chinese music. Chinese national music association: Taipei 1956. pp.49.[xxvii]. [368.]

Czechoslovakia

JAN VÁCLAV ROZUM, Seznam českých knih,

Music

obrazů a hudebních výtvorů. Praze 1854. pp.240. [2750.]

BIBLIOGRAFICKÝ katalog ČSR. České hudebniny. Praha.

    1955. pp.80.[iv]. [421.]
    1956. pp.viii.74. [360.]
    1957. pp.65. [329.]
    1958.   [501.]
    1959. pp.viii.85. [428.]
    1960. pp.viii.86. [428.]
    1961. pp.viii.64. [370.]
    1962. pp.viii.56. [362.]
in progress.

Denmark

K. SCHMIDT-PHISELDECK, Musikalier. II. Dansk musik. Statsbiblioteket i Aarhus: Fagkataloger (no.3): 1929. pp.186. [3675.]
—— 2. . . . udgave. 1951.

JÜRGEN BALZER, Bibliographie des compositeurs danois. Dansk komponist-forening: Copenhague 1932. pp.64. [1100.]

DANSK musikfortegnelse. Musikhandlerforeningen: København.

    1934–1939.
    1940–1942. pp.102. [3500.]

Music

Finland

INGEBORG LAGERCRANTZ, Lutherska kyrkovisor.
1. Finländska musikhandskrifter från 1500– och
1600–talen. Lutherska litteraturstiftelsens Svenska
publikationer (no.2): Helsingfors 1948–   . pp.
[iv].256+   .

France

BIBLIOGRAPHIE musicale [française]. Catalogue
des nouvelles œuvres musicales françaises. Commission [Chambre syndicale] du commerce de
musique.

    i. 1875. pp.168. [6000.]

    ii. 1876. pp.169–338. [6000.]

    iii. 1877. pp.339–466. [4000.]

    iv. 1878. pp.100. [4000.]

    v. 1879. pp.84. [3000.]

    vi. 1880. pp.72. [3000.]

    vii. 1881. pp.64. [2500.]

    viii. 1882. pp.72. [2500.]

    ix. 1883. pp.68. [2500.]

    x. 1884. pp.64. [2500.]

    xi. 1885. pp.65–136. [2500.]

    xii. 1886. pp.76. [3000.]

    xiii. 1887. pp.64. [2500.]

    xiv. 1888. pp.64. [2500.]

    xv. 1889. pp.56. [2500.]

xvi. 1890. pp.16.16.20.20. [3000.]
xvii. 1891. pp.16.12.12.16. [2500.]
xviii. 1892. pp.16.12.12.12. [2000.]
xix. 1893. pp.12.12.12.12. [1000.]
xx. 1894. pp.12.12.12.12. [1000.]
xxi. 1895. pp.16.16.16.12. [2000.]
xxii. 1896. pp.16.12.16.20. [2000.]
xxiii. 1897. pp.28.24.32.26. [3000.]
xxiv. 1898. pp.32.26.18.18. [2500.]
xxv. 1899. pp.32.32.32.28. [3000.]
xxvi. 1900. pp.32.32.24.24. [3000.]
xxvii. 1901. pp.24.20.24.28. [2500.]
xxviii. 1902. pp.24.22.24.24. [2500.]
xxix. 1903. pp.20.24.20.16. [2000.]
xxx. 1904. pp.26.23.24.   .
xxxi. 1905.
xxxii. 1906.
xxxiii. 1907. pp.   .18.14.20.
xxxiv. 1908. pp.20.22.   .16.
xxxv. 1909. pp.   .20.   .20.
xxxvi. 1910. pp.18.   .16.2–17.
xxxvii. 1911. pp.20.19.14.13. [2000.]
xxxviii. 1912. pp.   .   .   .15.
xxxix. 1913. pp.16.17.14.15. [2000.]
xl. 1914.

*no more published; the first three numbers are en-
titled only* Catalogue des nouvelles œuvres musicales françaises.

[EMMANUEL] HENRI [PARENT] DE CURZON, État sommaire des pièces et documents concernant le théâtre et la musique, conservés aux Archives nationales. 1899. pp.28. [large number.]

MANUAL of modern french music, including the modern belgian school. [1917]. pp.60. [2000.]

CATALOGUE de la section française. Exposition internationale La musique dans la vie des nations: 1927. pp.173. [800.]

CATALOGUE détaillé de la bibliothèque de l'ancienne société des compositeurs. [c.1930]. ff.[ii].69. 5.12. [500.]*

AMÉDÉE GASTOUÉ [and others], La musique française du moyen âge à la révolution. Catalogue. Bibliothèque nationale: 1934. pp.[vi].vi.196. [483.] *an exhibition catalogue.*

HENRI GOUGELOT, Catalogue des romances françaises parues sous la révolution et l'empire. Melun.
    [i]. Les recueils de romances. 1937. pp.77. [284.]
    [ii]. Les romances séparées. 1943. pp.231.

LISTE des œuvres musicales entrées par dépôt

légal, acquisition ou don. année 1. 1945. pp.120. [1188.]

includes some foreign works; continued, for french publications only, as:
Bibliographie de la France. Supplément C. Musique.

  1946. pp.140. [1440.]
  1947. pp.244. [3353.]
  1948. pp.104. [960.]
  1949. pp.64. [640.]
  1950. pp.80. [800.]
  1951. pp.80. [800.]
  1952. pp.96. [960.]
  1953. pp.80. [800.]
  1954. pp.120. [1120.]
  1955. pp.80. [795.]
  1956. pp.92. [845.]
  1957. pp.64. [622.]
  1958. pp.68. [624.]
  1959. pp.88. [776.]
  1960. pp.52. [396.]
  1961. pp.132. [1060.]
  1962. pp.76. [607.]
  1963. pp.84. [648.]
in progress.

ANDRÉ BOLL, *ed.* Répertoire analytique de la

musique française des origines à nos jours. [1948].
pp.[ii].300. [5000.]

ROBERT WANGERMÉE, Les maîtres de chant, des
XVIIe et XVIIIe siècles à la collégiale des ss. Michel
et Gudule à Bruxelles. Académie royale de Bel-
gique: Classe des beaux-arts: Mémoires: Collection in-8° (ser.2, vol.iv, part 1): Bruxelles 1950.
pp.310. [200.]

CARI JOHANSSON, French music publishers' catalogues of the second half of the eighteenth century. Kungl. musikaliska akademie: Bibliotek:
Publikationer (vol.ii): Stockholm 1955. pp.xiii.
228+facsimiles. [200.]

Germany
[see also section 5, above]

FELIX JOSEPH LIPOWSKY, Baierisches musiklexi-
kon. München 1811. pp.x.338 [*sic*, 438]. [1000.]

[CARL] KOSSMALY and CARLO [*pseud.* CARL
HEINRICH HERZEL], *edd.* Schlesisches tonkünstlerlexicon. Breslau 1846–1847. pp.332. [2500.]

BARON CARL [FRIEDRICH HEINRICH WILHELM
PHILIPP JUSTUS] VON LEDEBUR, Tonkünstlerlexicon
Berlin's von den ältesten zeiten bis auf die gegen-
wart. Berlin 1861. pp.iv.704.iv. [1750.]

Music

[GUIDO ADLER, *ed.*], Fach-katalog der musik-historischen abtheilung von Deutschland und Oesterreich-Ungarn, nebst anhang: musikvereine, concertwesen und unterricht. Internationale ausstellung für musik- und theaterwesen: Wien 1892. pp.xvi.596. [2500.]

[PETER] GEORG [MAXIMILIAN] THOURET, Führer durch die fachausstellung der deutschen militär-musik. Wien [1892]. pp.44. [150.]

LA MARA [*pseud.* MARIE LIPSIUS], Verzeichnis der compositionen &c. von Carl Maria v. Weber, Franz Schubert, Felix Mendelssohn, Robert Schumann, Frederic Chopin, Franz Liszt und Richard Wagner. Leipzig [*c.*1900]. pp.86. [1250.]

CATALOGUE of german music exhibited at the St. Louis world's fair. German publisher's agency: New York [1904]. pp.[ii].86. [5000.]

THEODOR MÜLLER-REUTER, Lexikon der deutschen konzertliteratur. Leipzig 1909. pp.xxii.626. [469.]

— — Nachtrag zu band 1. 1921. pp.viii.238. [203.]

the supplement deals with Beethoven, Brahms, Haydn.

DIE MUSIK Hamburgs im zeitalter Seb. Bachs.

Ausstellung . . . in gemeinschaft mit dem Hamburgischen staatsarchiv und dem Hamburgischen museum für kunst und gewerbe veranstaltet von der Hamburger staats- und universitäts-bibliothek. Hamburg 1921. pp.viii.84. [900.]

PAUL COHEN, 'Musikdruck und -drucker zu Nürnberg im sechszehnten jahrhundert'. Erlangen 1927. pp.[iv].65. [443.]
reissued Nürnberg 1927.

ERICH H[ERMANN] MUELLER [VON ASOW], Deutsches Musiker-lexikon. Dresden 1929. pp.viii.coll. xvi.1644. [50,000.]
— Zweite ausgabe. Kürschners deutsches [&c.]. 1954. pp.xiv.coll.1702. [50,000.]

ALFRED ERDMANN WERNER BÖHME, Pommersches musikschrifttum in 15 jahren nachkriegszeit (1918–1932). Greifswald [1932]. pp.9. [400.]

JOHANNES HÜBNER, Bibliographie des schlesischen musik- und theaterwesens. Historische kommission für Schlesien: Schlesische bibliographie (vol.vi.2): Breslau 1934. pp.xv.280. [music: 2306.]

GEORG KINSKY, Erstlingsdrucke der deutschen tonmeister der klassik und romantik. Wien 1934. pp.21. [100.]

a copy in the British museum contains manuscript notes, probably by the author.

AUS ZWEI jahrhunderten deutscher musik. Preussische staatsbibliothek: Berlin 1935. pp.52. [205.]

REICHSLISTE für musikbüchereien. Reichsstelle für das volksbüchereiwesen: Leipzig 1938. pp.80. [1500.]
includes some foreign music.

CURT RÜCKER, Thüringens musikkultur im schrifttum. Ein handweiser. Weimar 1938. pp. [ii].46. [350.]

GEORG DRAUD, Verzeichnisse deutscher musikalischer bücher 1611 und 1625. In originalgetreuem nachdruck herausgegeben von Konrad Ameln. Bonn [1957]. pp.xi.545–563.733–759.[ii]. [750.]
consists of facsimiles of relevant parts of the author's Bibliotheca librorum germanicorum classica, *1611 and 1625.*

[ADAM BERNHARD GOTTRON], Tausend jahre mainzer musik. Katalog der ausstellung. Gutenberg-museum: Kleiner druck (no.63): Mainz 1957. pp.32. [138.]

BONNER katalog. Verzeichnis der urheberrechtlich geschützten musikalischen werke mit revers-gebundenem aufführungsmaterial. Deutscher musikverleger-verband: Bonn [1959]. pp.xi.326. [15,000.]

[SIEGFRIED KÖHLER, *ed.*], Komponisten und musikwissenschaftler der Deutschen Demokratischen Republik. Verband deutscher komponisten und musikwissenschaftler: Berlin [1959]. pp.200. [1500.]

[HEINZ ZIRNBAUER], Nürnberger musik zwischen gotik und barok. Stadtbibliothek: Ausstellungs-katalog (no.10): Nürnberg 1959. pp.[24]. [207.]

IRMTRUD PETERS, Theater, rundfunk und musik in Bremen. Eine bibliographie. Herausgegeben von Rolf Engelsing. Bremische bibliographie (vol.2): Bremen 1963. pp.65. [540.]

Great Britain

ANDREW DEAKIN, Musical bibliography. A catalogue of the musical works, . . . published in England during the fifteenth, sixteenth, seventeenth and eighteenth centuries. Birmingham 1892. pp.[x].68. [850.]

JAMES D[UFF] BROWN and STEPHEN S[AMUEL]

STRATTON, British musical biography: a dictionary of musical artists, authors and composers, born in Britain and its colonies. Birmingham 1897. pp. [iii].iv.463. [10,000.]

ANDREW DEAKIN, Outlines of musical bibliography: a catalogue of early music and musical works printed or otherwise produced in the British Isles. . . . Part I. Birmingham 1899. pp.112. [500.]
extends to 1650 only; no more published.

FRANK KIDSON, British music publishers, printers and engravers: . . . from queen Elizabeth's reign to George the fourth's, with select bibliographical lists of musical works printed and published within that period. [1900]. pp.xii.231. [1000.]

ROBERT STEELE, The earliest english music printing. A description and bibliography of english printed music to the close of the sixteenth century. Bibliographical society: Illustrated monographs (no.xi): 1903. pp.xi.109. [200.]
one of the British museum copies contains ms. additions by the author.

JEFFREY PULVER, A biographical dictionary of old english music. 1927. pp.xii.537. [2000.]
covers the period to about 1700.

Music

THE MUSIC seller reference book.
  1927–1928. pp.192. [5000.]
  [1928–1929]. pp.308. [4000.]
  [1930–1931]. pp.360. [5000.]
  [1931–1932]. pp.292. [4000.]
  [1932–1933]. pp.272. [4000.]
  [1933–1934]. pp.256. [3000.]
  [1934–1935]. pp.248. [3000.]
  [1935–1936]. pp.144. [4000.]
a bibliography of sheet music, published in England no more published.

CATÁLOGO general de la biblioteca del centro de música del Consejo británico. Buenos Aires [1946]. pp.iii–xiv.273. [4000.]

C. L. CUDWORTH, Thematic index of english eighteenth-century overtures and symphonies. Royal musical association: Proceedings (vol. lxxviii, appendix): 1953. pp.ix.xxxv. [158.]

[JACK ALLAN WESTRUP *and others*], English music. Guide to an exhibition. Bodleian library: Oxford 1955. pp.40. [101.]

L[EONARD] D[OUGLAS] GIBBIN, The music trader's guide to works by twentieth century british composers together with the names of their publishers, comprising instrumental works, songs, text books and manuals. [1956]. pp.132. [12,500.]

Music

THE BRITISH catalogue of music. Council of the British national bibliography.

 1957. General editor: A. J. Wells. pp.150. [1500.]

  1958. pp.176. [2000.]

  1959. pp.161. [2000.]

  1960. pp.176. [2000.]

  1961. pp.175. [2000.]*

  1962. pp.vii.173. [2000.]*

  1963. pp.vii.154. [2000.]*

in progress.

BRITISH orchestral music. Volume one of the catalogue of works by members of the Composers' guild of Great Britain. [1958]. pp.56. [1000.]

Hungary

IZABELLA K. DEDINSZKY, Zeneművek, 1936–40. Orszagos Széchényi könyvtar: Az 1936–40 évkör magyar szakkönyvészete: Budapest 1944. pp.v. 286. [3500.]

Italy

GAETANO GASPARI, Ragguagli biografici e bibliografici dei musicisti bolognesi del secolo XVII e delle loro opere a stampa. Modena 1880. pp. [ii].49–79. [15.]

ADOLFO BERWIN and ROBERT HIRSCHFELD, Fach-katalog der abtheilung des königreiches Italien. Internationale ausstellung für musik und theaterwesen: Wien 1892. pp.viii.294. [3000.]

IDA NAZARI, Bibliographia musicalis italica. Anno I [nos.1–5]. Bibliographia universalis: Roma 1897. pp.(ff.)71. [350.]
no more published.

[CARLO FRATI], Manoscritti e libri a stampa musicati esposti dalla Biblioteca nazionale di Torino. Esposizione nazionale: Torino 1898. pp.24. [36.]

JOSEPH KILLING, Kirchenmusikalische schätze der bibliothek des abbate Fortunato Santini. Ein beitrag zur geschichte der katholischen kirchenmusik in Italien. Düsseldorf [1910]. pp.[v].516. [5000.]
previously published in part as a dissertation, Münster i. W. 1908; the collection now forms part of the university library of Münster.

ALBERTO DE ANGELIS, L'Italia musicale d'oggi. Dizionario dei musicisti. Roma 1918. pp.373. [5000.]
—— Terza edizione. 1927. pp.557. [10,000.]

CATALOGO della sezione italiana. Esposizione

internazionale La mvsica nella vita dei popoli' Francoforte. Roma 1927. pp.161. [508.]

[ANITO MONDOLFO], Mostra bibliografica di musica italiana dalle origini alla fine del secolo XVIII. Reale biblioteca nazionale Centrale: Firenze 1937. pp.103. [226.]

CATALOGO. Mostra bibliografica dei musicisti cremonesi: dal rinascimento all'ottocento. Biblioteca governativa e libreria civica: Cremona 1949. pp.47. [137.]

CLAUDIO SARTORI, Dizionario degli editori musicali italiani (tipografi, incisori, librai-editori). Biblioteca di bibliografia italiana (no.xxxii): Firenze 1958. pp.219. [2000.]

EXHIBIT of contemporary italian music in the United States of America 1959. Cremona [1958]. pp.181. [1500.]

MARIANGELA DONÀ, La stampa musicale a Milano fino all'anno 1700. Biblioteca di bibliografia italiana (vol.xxxix): Firenze 1961. pp.ix. 170. [400.]

CLAUDIO SARTORI, Catalogo del fondo musicale nella biblioteca comunale di Assisi. Biblioteca musicae (vol.I, part 1): Milano 1962. pp.3–452. [2000.]

Music

Japan

LIST of references on japanese music. Library of Congress: Washington [?1905]. ff.3. [15.]*

Jews

JULIUS SACHS, Der jüdische musikalien-katalog. Die wichtigsten werke jüdischer komponisten. Breslau 1936. pp.96. [3000.]

THEO[PHIL] STENGEL and HERBERT GERIGK, Lexicon der Juden in der musik, mit einem titelverzeichnis jüdischer werke. Institut der NSDAP zur erforschung der judenfrage: Veröffentlichungen: Berlin [1943]. coll.404. [7500.]

BIBLIOGRAPHY of instrumental and vocal music. Jewish music council: New York 1946. pp.[ii].18. [700.]*

BIBLIOGRAPHY of articles and books on jewish music. National jewish music council: New York 1947. ff.[i].7.2. [100.]*

BIBLIOGRAPHY of jewish instrumental music. Jewish music council: New York [1949]. pp.[ii]. 16. [300.]*

— 1949–1950 addenda. [1951]. ff.8. [125.]*

ALFRED SENDREY, Bibliography of jewish music. New York 1951. pp.xli.404. [10,682.]

Music

[HANS KRIEG], Musicological jewish works by Hans Krieg. Amsterdam [c.1955]. ff.2. [50.]*

Netherlands

ALPHONSE [JEAN MARIE ANDRÉ] GOOVAERTS, Histoire et bibliographie de la typographie musicale dans les Pays-Bas. Académie royale de Belgique: Mémoires: Collection in-8° (vol.xxix, no.7): Bruxelles 1880. pp.[iv].608. [1415.]
reissued independently, Anvers 1880.

G. H. VAN ECK, Katalogus van, in Nederland verschenen muziekuitgaven, benevens boek- en plaatwerken, betreffende: de toonkunst. 's-Gravenhage 1889–1890. pp.[iii].191 + [viii].lxxv. [5000.]
the punctuation of the titlepage has been followed; the second volume, containing a classified index, is entitled Handboek der nederlandsche muzieklitteratuur.

D[ANIEL] F[RANÇOIS] SCHEURLEER, Bijdragen tot een repertorium der nederlandsche muziekliteratuur. . . . Deel I. [Vereeniging voor nederlandsche muziekgeschiedenis:] Amsterdam 1902. pp.[ii]. 154. [1750.]

J[AN] W[ILLEM] ENSCHEDÉ, Nederlandsche musicalia. Vereeniging voor Noord-Nederlands muziekgeschiedenis [1911: Centrale vereeniging voor

openbare leeszalen en bibliotheken: De boekzaal:
Monografiën voor boek en bibliotheekwezen:]
Amsterdam [1911: Zwolle].

    1908. pp.[vii].56. [1000.]
    1909. pp.[vii].60. [1000.]
    1910. pp.[viii].52. [1000.]
    1911. pp.[vi].40. [750.]
no more published.

J. H. LETZER, Muzikaal Nederland, 1850–1910.
Bio-bibliographisch woordenboek van nederlandsche toonkunstenaars en toonkunstenaressen,
alsmede van schrijvers en schrijfsters op musiek-
literarisch gebied. . . . Tweede uitgaaf. Utrecht
1913. pp.[iii].201.9. [5000.]

[SALOMON ADRIAN MARIA BOTTENHEIM], Catalogus van de bibliotheek der Vereeniging voor
nederlandsche muziekgeschiedenis. Amsterdam
1919. pp.[viii].274. [2500.]

S[ALOMON ADRIAN MARIA] BOTTENHEIM, De
nederlandsche afdeeling op de internationale
muziek-tentoonstelling (Musik im leben der völker) te Frankfort. . . . Catalogus. [s.l. 1927]. pp.22.
[250.]

NEDERLANDSCH muziekleven, 1600–1800. Ge-

Music

meentemuseum: 's-Gravenhage 1936. pp.124.
[737.]
an exhibition catalogue.

Norway

CARL WARMUTH, Katalog over norsk musik-
forlag og norske komponisters værker udkomme
i udlandet. Christiania [1887]. pp.[iv].64. [2500.]

Poland

ALBERT SOWIŃSKI, Les musiciens polonais et
slaves anciens et modernes. 1857. pp.xi.600. [3000.]
—— [another edition]. Słownik muzyków
polskich dawnych i nowoczesnych. Paryż 1874.
pp.lx.436.[16]. [2500.]

ALFRED NOSSIG, Katalog der polnischen abteilung der Internationalen musik- und theaterausstellung. Wien 1892. pp.ix.84. [200.]

KATALOG wystawy zbiorów teatralnych i
muzycznych. Bibljoteka narodowa: Katalogi
wystaw (vol.iii): Warszawa 1934. pp.[viii].155.
[music: 376.]

KORNEL MICHAŁOWSKI, Bibliografia polskiego
piśmiennictwa muzycznego. Materiały do bibliografii muzyki polskiej (vol.iii): [Kraków 1955].
pp.280. [1837.]

Music

BIBLIOGRAFIA polskich czasopism muzycznych. Pod redakcją Tadeusza Strumiłły. [Cracow] 1955 &c.

in progress.

Portugal [see also *Spain*]

JOAQUIM [ANTONIO DA FONSECA E] DE VASCONCELLOS, Os musicos portuguezes. Biographia-bibliographia. Porto 1870. pp.xxxvi.291+312. [5000.]

ERNESTO VIEIRA, Diccionario biographico de musicos portuguezes. Historia e bibliographia da musica em Portugal. Lisboa 1900. pp.[vii].560+496.xxii. [2500.]

JOSÉ MAZZA, Dicionario biográfico de músicos portugueses. [Edited by José Augusto Alegria]. Occidente: Supplemento: [Lisbon 1945   ]. pp.104. [250.]

Russia

N[IKOLAI] M[IKHAILOVICH] LISOVSKY, Обозрѣніе литературы по театру и музикѣ за 1889–1891 гг. С.-Петербургъ 1893. pp.62. [334.]
25 copies printed.

НОТНАЯ ЛЕТОПИСЬ 1 [&c.] год. Государственная центральная книжная палата РСФСР: Москва 1931–

Music

[*continued as:*]

летопись музыкальной литературы. Все-
сонзная книмная палата.

1946. pp.26.32.34.34. [1362.]
1947.
1948.
1949.
1950.
1951.
1952.
1953. pp.57.55.34.58. [1473.]
1954.
1955. pp.88.73.82.314. [2417.]
1956. pp.82.107.76. .
1957. pp.120.118.108.406. [3287.]
1958. pp.122.126.181.172.181. [3397.]
1959. pp.126.152.111.178.200. [3440.]
1960. pp.136.172.140.194.222. [3976.]
1961. pp.172.165.143.196.214. [4186.]
1962. pp.182.136.152.192.160. [4111.]
1963. pp.183.137.156.207.154. [4280.]

in progress.

ALEXANDRA VODARSKY-SHIRAEFF, Russian composers and musicians. New York 1940. pp.158.
[3000.]

RUSSIA. A check list preliminary to a basic
bibliography of materials in the russian language.

Music

Part VIII. Theatre and music [prior to 1918]. Library of Congress: Reference department: Washington 1944. ff.[i].23. [398.]★

LIST of soviet music publications available in the United States of America. National council of american-soviet friendship: New York 1945. ff.[iv].73. [1250.]

B[ORIS LVOVICH] VOLMAN, Русские печатные ноты XVIII века. Ленинград 1957. pp.294. [300.]

LITERATUR unserer bibliothek zur themengruppe bildende und darstellende kunst, musik im sowjetkommunistischen einflussbereich. Gesamteuropäisches studienwerk: Bibliothek: Auswahlverzeichnis (no.xii): Vlotho 1958. ff.[ii].86. [750.]★

V. A. LURE, Обзор литературы выпущенной краеведческими музеями РСФСР за 1953–1959 гг. Научно-исследовательский институт музееведения: Москва 1960. pp.113.

Scotland

DAVID BAPTIE, Musical Scotland, being a dictionary of scottish musicians from about 1400. ... To which is added a bibliography of musical publications connected with Scotland from 1611. Paisley 1894. pp.iv.219. [2500.]

Music

Slavonic. see *Poland* and *Russia*

Slovakia

JURAJ POTÚČEK, Súpis slovenských hudobnín a literatúry o hudobníkoch. Bratislava 1952. pp.437. [6000.]

——[another edition]. Súpis slovenských hudobnoteoretických prác, knižné, publikácie, študie, člaňki, kritiky a referáty. Slovenská akadémia vied: Bratislava 1955. pp.471. [7000.]

Spain

BALTASAR SALDONI [Y REMENDO], Diccionario biográfico-bibliográfico de efemérides de musicos españoles. Madrid 1868–1881. pp.343+595+437 +447. [2500.]

JUAN F[ACUNDO] RIAÑO [Y MONTERO], Critical & bibliographical notes on early spanish music. 1887. pp.viii.154. [250.]

[SALVADOR SANPERE Y MIQUEL and G. ROCA Y SANPERE], Katalog der ausstellung des königreiches Spanien. Internationale ausstellung für musik- und theaterwesen: Wien 1892. pp.95. [1250.]

FELIPE PEDRELL, Diccionario biográfico y bibliográfico de músicos y escritores de música espa-

ñoles, portugueses é hispano-americanos. Barcelona [1894–]1897. pp.xix.715. [10,000.]
A–F only; no more published.

MANUAL of modern french music. . . . With a supplementary catalogue of modern spanish music. [1917]. pp.60. [spanish: 250.]

HIGINIO ANGLÉS, La musica española desde la edad media hasta nuestros días. Catálogo de la exposición histórica. Diputación provincial de Barcelona: Biblioteca central: [Barcelona] 1941. pp.84. [500.]

GUÍA de la exposición de música antigua española, siglos IX a XVIII. Biblioteca nacional: [Madrid 1958]. pp.[8]. [115.]

Sweden

UPPSLAGSBOK för svenska musikhandeln. Linköping.

 1896–1900. Utgifven af John Lindqvist. pp.[iii].115. [5000.]
 1901–1905. pp.[iii].124. [5000.]
 1906–1910. pp.[iii].114. [5000.]
 1911–1915.
 1916–1920.
 1921–1925.

Music

1926–1930.

1931–1935. pp.[iii].152. [7500.]

CARL [MARTIN M:SON] NISSER, Svensk instrumentalkomposition 1770–1830. Nominalkatalog: Stockholm [1943]. pp.467. [3000.]

ÅKE DAVIDSSON, Svensk musiklitteratur. En förteckning. Svensk musikhandlare föreningen: Stockholm 1946. pp.[ii].22. [250.]

ÅKE DAVIDSSON, Bibliografi över svensk musiklitteratur, 1800–1945. Uppsala 1948. pp.viii.215. [5432.]

[EDVIN KALLSTENIUS], Swedish orchestral works. Annotated catalogue. Stockholm [1949]. pp.85. [50.]

SVENSK musikförteckning. Nr 1. Redigerad av Bibliografiska institutet vid Kungl. biblioteket i Stockholm. Svenska musikhandlareförening: Stockholm 1956. pp.18. [500.]
no more published.

ÅKE DAVIDSSON, Studier rörande svenskt musiktryck före år 1750. Studia musicologica upsaliensia (no.v): Uppsala 1957. pp.167. [124.]

Switzerland

GEORGE BECKER, La musique en Suisse depuis les

temps les plus reculés jusqu'à la fin du dixhuitième siècle. Notices historiques, biographiques et bibliographiques. Genève 1874. pp.[iv].191. [250.]

KARL NEF, Schriften über musik und volksgesang. Centralkommission für schweizerische landeskunde: Bibliographie der schweizerischen landeskunde (section v.6d): Bern 1908. pp.xii.151. [3000.]

MUSIK. Werke der mitglieder des Schweizerischen tonkünstlervereins veröffentlicht von 1848–1925. Schweizerische landesbibliothek: Bern 1927. pp.viii.154. [5000.]

EDGAR REFARDT, Historisch-biographisches musiker lexikon der Schweiz. Leipzig &c. 1928. pp.xv.355. [3000.]

United States

CATALOGUE of copyright entries. . . . Part 3 [5]: Musical compositions. Treasury department [1906 &c.: Library of Congress: Copyright office]: Washington 1891 &c.
in progress.

O[SCAR] G[EORGE THEODORE] SONNECK, Bibliography of early secular american music. Washington 1905. pp.x.194. [2000.]
200 copies privately printed.

— — A bibliography of early secular american music [18th century]. . . . Revised and enlarged by William Treat Upton. Library of Congress: Music division: 1945. pp.xvi.617. [3000.]

FRANK J. METCALF, American psalmody or titles of books, containing tunes, printed in America from 1721 to 1820. Heartman's historical series (no.27): New York 1917. pp.54. [750.]
81 copies printed.

CLAIRE REIS, American composers of today. International society for contemporary music (United States section): New York 1930. pp.[vi]. 54. [500.]
— — Second edition. American composers. A record of works written between 1912 and 1932. 1932. pp.[viii].132. [1250.]

ALBERT G[EORGE] RAU and HANS T[HEODORE] DAVID, A catalogue of music by american Moravians, 1742–1842, from the archives of the Moravian church at Bethlehem, Pa. Moravian seminary and college for women: Bethlehem 1938. pp.120. [350.]

HARRY DICHTER and ELLIOTT SHAPIRO, Early american sheet music . . . 1768–1889. Including a directory of early american music publishers. New York 1941. pp.xxxi.287. [800.]

Music

BIO-BIBLIOGRAPHICAL index of musicians in the
United States of America from colonial times.
Pan american union: Music section: Washington
1941. pp.[ii].xxiii.439. [12,500.]★
 *'from' is used in the sense of 'since'; the so-called
'second edition' of 1956 is a reprint.*

LIBRARY of american music scores. U.S. Office
of war information: [Washington 1944–1945].
ff.[i].33+5+3. [1250.]★

HERMENE WARLICK EICHHORN and TREVA WIL-
KERSON MATHIS, North Carolina composers, as
represented in the holograph collection. University of North Carolina: Women's college: Greens-
boro, N.C. 1945. pp.39. [500.]

WISCONSIN composers. Wisconsin federation of
music clubs: [Beloit 1948]. pp.88. [4000.]

DANIEL I[GNATIUS] MCNAMARA, The ASCAP
[American society of composers, authors and
publishers] biographical dictionary of composers,
authors, and publishers. New York [1948]. pp.
vii.483. [12,500.]
 — — Second edition. [1952]. pp.xi.636.
[15,000.]

CATALOGUE of scores in the music section of the
American library. United States information
service: 1950. pp.[iii].40. [500.]★

JULIUS MATTFELD, Variety music cavalcade, 1620–1950. A chronology of vocal and instrumental music popular in the United States. New York [1952]. pp.xviii.637. [2000.]

BOOKS on music in the United States. United States information service: Library: [c.1955]. pp. [ii].11. [200.]

JOHN EDMUNDS and GORDON BOELZNER, Some twentieth century american composers. A selective bibliography. Public library: New York 1959. pp.58. [1500.]

7. *Works on music*

[*bibliographies in which are set out both music and works on music are entered in section 5 above and are not repeated here; see also section 3, above.*]

[JOHANN SIGMUND GRUBER], Litteratur der musik oder anleitung zur kentnis der vorzüglichen musikalischen bücher. Herausgegeben von einem liebhaber der musik. Nürnberg 1783. pp.56. [300.]

— — Zweite . . . auflage. Frankfurt &c. 1792. pp.[iv].122.[xx]. [750.]

JOHANN SIGMUND GRUBER, Beyträge zur litteratur der musik. Nürnberg 1785. pp.116. [iv]. [750.]

—— [supplement]. Zweytes stück. Frankfurt &c. 1790. pp.74. [400.]

JOHANN NICOLAUS FORKEL, Allgemeine litteratur der musik oder anleitung zur kenntniss musikalischer bücher, welche von den ältesten bis auf die neuesten zeiten bey den Griechen, Römern und den meisten neuern europäischen nationen sind geschrieben worden. Leipzig 1792. pp.xxiv.540. [4000.]

PIETRO LICHTENTHAL, Dizionario e bibliografia della musica. Milano 1826. pp.ix.368+302+xix. 327+548. [7500.]
a french translation of 1839 is limited to the dictionary.

CARL FERDINAND BECKER, Systematisch-chronologische darstellung der musikalischen literatur von der frühesten bis auf die neueste zeit. Leipzig 1836. pp.vi.coll.572.pp.572–605. [10,000.]
—— Nachtrag. 1839. pp.vi.coll.196. [2000.]

CARL FERDINAND BECKER, Alphabetisch und chronologisch geordnetes verzeichniss einer sammlung von musikalischen schriften. Ein beitrag zur literaturgeschichte der musik. Zweite

. . . ausgabe . . . von dem besitzer der sammlung. Leipzig 1846. pp.26. [1120.]

P[AUL] SCUDO, L'année musicale [La musique en l'année] ou revue annuelle . . . des publications littéraires relatives à la musique.

    i. 1860. pp.380. [100.]
    ii. 1861. pp.431. [100.]
    iii. 1862. pp.361. [100.]
no more published.

ADOLPH BÜCHTING, Bibliotheca musica oder verzeichniss aller in bezug auf die musik in den letzten 20 jahren . . . im deutschen buchhandel erschienenen bücher und zeitschriften, mit ausschluss der liederbücher wie überhaupt der musikalien. Nordhausen 1867. pp.85. [750.]

[WILHELM EFFENBERGER], Musikalischer wegweiser für musiker und musikfreunde. Die musik-literatur Deutschlands in den jahren 1857–1871, umfassend bücher und zeitschriften auf dem gesammtgebiete der musik. . . . Vierte . . . ausgabe. Leipzig 1872. pp.26.19. [1250.]

CARL ENGEL, The literature of national music. 1879. pp.[v].108. [500.]

BIBLIOTECA musicale del prof. P[ietro] Canal in

Music

Crespano Veneto. Bassano [printed] 1885. pp.3–
104. [1152.]
includes some early music.

ROBERT EITNER, Bücherverzeichnis der musikliteratur aus den jahren 1839 bis 1846, im anschluss
an Becker und Büchting. Monatshefte für musikgeschichte (beilage): Leipzig 1885. pp.89. [1000.]

JAMES E. MATTHEW, The literature of music.
Book-lover's library: 1896. pp.x.281. [500.]

[F. P.], The year's literature . . . being a concise
record of the [musical] literature of the year. 1896.
pp.16. [100.]
no more published.

RUSSELL STURGIS, Annotated bibliography of
fine art. . . . Music. By Henry Edward Krehbiel.
American library association: Annotated lists:
Boston 1897. pp.v.89. [music: 300.]

LUISA LACÁL, Diccionario de la música, técnico,
histórico, bio-bibliográfico. Madrid 1899. pp.
viii.600. [12,500.]

ARTHUR LOW BAILEY, Bibliography of biography of musicians in english. University of
the state of New York: State library bulletin
(Bibliography no.17): [Albany] 1899. pp.493–576.
[1250.]

Music

HENRY TENNYSON FOLKARD, Music and musicians. A list of books and pamphlets relating to the history, biography, theory and practice of music. Public library: Wigan 1903. pp.44. [1500.]
50 copies printed.

[CARL FREDRIK HENNERBERG], Katalog övfer Kungl. musikaliska akademiens bibliotek. II. Literatur. (Musikteori, musikhistoria m.m.). A Nominalafdeling. Stockholm 1910. pp.[v].136. [3000.]

INTERNATIONAL anthology of musical books (England, France, Germany and Italy). [1910]. pp.iv.129.v–xx. [3000.]

COELESTINUS VIVELL, Initia tractatuum musices ex codicibus editorum. Graecii 1912. pp.viii.352. [8500.]

JULIA GREGORY, Catalogue of early books on music (before 1800). . . . Prepared under the direction of O[scar] G[eorge Theodore] Sonneck. Library of Congress: Washington 1913. pp.4. [ii].5–312. [1850.]
a copy in the Newberry library, Chicago, contains ms. notes and additions, together with a record of the holdings of the Newberry library, Yale university library and other libraries.

———— Supplement (books acquired by the

Music

library 1913–1942). Hazell Bartlett. With a list of books on music in chinese [by Kuang-ch'ing Wu] and japanese [by Shio Sakanishi]. 1944. pp. iv.143. [500.]

KÁLMÁN ISOZ, Zenei kéziratok. 1. kötet. Zenei levelek. A Magyar nemzeti múzeum könyvtáránok címjegyzéke (vol.vi): Budapest 1921–1924. pp.96+97–208+xvi.209–392. [1449.]

ADOLF ABER, Handbuch der musikliteratur in systematisch-chronologischer anordnung. Kleine handbücher der musikgeschichte nach gattungen (vol.xiii): Leipzig 1922. pp.xx.coll.696.pp.[ii]. [9000.]

EDGAR REFARDT, Verzeichnis der aufsätze zur musik in den nichtmusikalischen zeitschriften der universitätsbibliothek Basel. Leipzig 1925. pp. xviii.106. [3000.]

THEATERGESCHICHTE, bearbeitet von Friedrich Michael. Musikwissenschaft, bearbeitet von Rudolf Schwartz. Jahresberichte des Literarischen zentralblattes über die wichtigsten wissenschaftlichen neuerscheinungen des gesamten deutschen sprachgebietes (1924, vol.xiii): Leipzig 1925. pp. 99. [music: 150.]

GREGORI M[ARÍA] SUNYOL, Assaig de repertori

bibliogràfic musical. Abadia de Montserrat 1925. pp.3–52. [800.]

ERIC BLOM, A general index to modern musical literature in the English language . . . including periodicals for the years 1915–1926. [1927]. pp. xi.159. [4000.]

WILHELM STAHL, Musik-bücher der Lübecker stadtbibliothek. Stadtbibliothek der freien und Hansestadt Lübeck: Veröffentlichung (vol.iv, part I): Lübeck 1927. pp.42. [750.]
a select catalogue of writings on music.

KATHI MEYER and PAUL HIRSCH, Katalog der musikbibliothek Paul Hirsch. I. Theoretische drucke bis 1800. Berlin 1928. pp.[iv].299. [680.]
the library is now in the British museum.

MUSIC and musical appreciation. A selected list of books . . . compiled by the Faculty of music. Second edition. [National book council: Book list] (no.85): 1928. pp.[4]. [100.]

BOLLETTINO bibliografico musicale. Letteratura musicale. Catalogo. No.1[–12]. 1928–1933.

CATALOGUE of the Nanki music library. Part I. Musicology. Tokyo 1929. pp.[viii].373.25. [3000.]

KARL TH. BAYER, Musikliteratur. Ein kritischer

führer für bibliothekare. Stadtbibliothek: Volks-
bücherei-zentrale: Arbeiten (no.ii): Berlin 1929.
pp.191. [1000.]

A CATALOGUE of books relating to music in the
library of Richard Aldrich. New York 1931.
pp.viii.435. [3000.]
200 copies printed.

GEORGY [PAVLOVICH] ORLOV, Музыкальная
литература. Ленинградская филармония:
Ленинград 1935. pp.xii.224. [948.]

LIST of books on music. National association
of schools of music: Bulletin (no.3): [*s.l.*] 1935.
pp.[ii].57. [1350.]
— Supplement.
    i. . . . (no.6): 1936. pp.20. [300.]
    ii. . . . (no.11): 1939. pp.30. [500.]
    iii. . . . (no.15): 1941. pp.31. [500.]

ALFRED [DENIS] CORTOT and FREDERICK GOLD-
BECK, Traités & autres ouvrages théoriques des xvᵉ,
xvɪᵉ, xvɪɪᵉ & xvɪɪɪᵉ siècles. Catalogue. Bibliothèque Alfred Cortot (vol.i): [*s.l.* 1936]. pp.xi.212.
[800.]
325 copies printed; no more published.

BIBLIOGRAPHIE des musikschrifttums. Staatliches

institut [Institut] für deutsche musikforschung:
Leipzig [Frankfurt a. M.].

> i. 1936. Herausgegeben . . . von [Emil] Kurt
> Taut. pp.438. [10,000.]
>
> ii. 1937. pp.vii.333. [5980.]
>
> iii. 1938. Herausgegeben . . . von Georg Kar-
> städt. pp.ix.215. [4432.]
>
> iv. 1939. pp.viii.157. [3180.]
>
> [v]. 1950–1951. Herausgegeben ... von Wolf-
> gang Schmieder. 1954. pp.xi.247. [5648.]
>
> vii. 1952.
>
> viii. 1953.
>
> ix. 1954.
>
> x. 1955.

in progress; not published for 1940–1949.

[EMIL] KURT TAUT, Verzeichnis der in allen
kulturländern im jahre 1937 erschienenen bücher
und schriften über musik, mit einschluss der neu-
auflagen und uebersetzungen. Jahrbuch der musikbibliothek Peters (1937, supplement): Leipzig
1938. pp.107–187. [2500.]

READERS' guide to books on music. Library
association: County libraries section [no.19]: 1938.
pp.32. [900.]

RUTH E. BRADLEY, Background readings in

music. Reading for background (no.7): New York 1938. pp.32. [250.]

PERCY A[LFRED] SCHOLES, A list of books about music in the english language. 1939. pp.[ii].64. [2500.]

A BIBLIOGRAPHY of periodical literature in musicology and allied fields and a record of graduate theses accepted. American council of learned societies: Committee on musicology: Washington.

    i. 1938–1939. Assembled . . . by D[onald] H[ayes] Daugherty. pp.xiv.135. [1000.]*
    ii. 1939–1940. Assembled . . . by H. D. Daugherty, Leonard Ellinwood and Richard S. Hill. 1943. pp.xvii.150. [940.]
no more published.

KATALOG der musikwissenschaftl. bibliothek von Friedrich Ludwig. Göttingen [c.1940]. ff.[iv].222. [3250.]*
includes some music.

EDWARD N[EIGHBOR] WATERS, Books on music. A list of recent titles suggested for consideration for army libraries. War department: Special service division: Army library service: Washington 1942. pp.[ii].32. [425.]*

ANNUAL communications bibliography: motion pictures — radio — music. . . . Supplement to volume one, Hollywood quarterly. Berkeley &c. 1946. pp.[v].59. [1250.]
no more published.

[ERLING WINKEL], Musik. Musikfilosofi, musikteori, musikhistorie, biografi. Statsbiblioteket i Aarhus: Fagkataloger (no.4): Aarhus 1946. pp.197. [3000.]

HUBERT [JAMES] FOSS, Books about music. National book league: Reader's guide: 1947. pp. 12. [50.]
the bibliography proper is by William Arthur Munford.

HAROLD GLEASON and ALBERT T[HOMAS] LUPER, A bibliography of books on music and collections of music selected from works in the english language, generally available in the United States, with emphasis on those recently published. [*s.l.* 1948]. ff.[ii].47. [650.]*

READERS' guide to books on composers. Library association: County libraries section: [Readers' guide (new series, no.5): 1949]. pp.32. [450.]

VINCENT H. DUCKLES and H. S. NICEWONGER,

Guide to reference materials on music. University of California: Berkeley 1949. pp.iv.35. [319.]

THE MUSIC index. Detroit.
 i. 1949. [Edited by Florence Kretzschmar]. 1950. pp.308. [6000.]
 [ii]. 1950. 1951. pp.[viii].416. [8000.]*
 [iii]. 1951. 1953. pp.[viii].505. [10,000.]*
 iv. 1952. pp.[viii].483. [10,000.]
 v. 1953. pp.[viii].459. [10,000.]*
 vi. 1954. pp.[x].581. [12,500.]*
 vii. 1955. pp.[x].552. [12,500.]*
 viii. 1956. pp.[x].570. [12,500.]*
 ix. 1957. pp.[xi].705. [15,000.]*
 x. 1958. pp.[xii].577. [12,500.]*
 xi. 1959. pp.[xii].706. [15,000.]*
 xii. 1960. pp.[xii].748. [15,000.]*
 xiii. 1961. pp.[x].903. [17,500.]*
in progress; only the annual cumulations are set out.

MUSIC. An annotated book list. Standing conference of county music committees: 1950. pp.20. [150.]

R[OBERT] D[ONALDSON] DARRELL, Schirmer's guide to books on music and musicians. A prac-

tical bibliography. New York [1951]. pp.xxxviii. 402. [4500.]
limited to books in print, for the most part in english.

HANS [THEODORE] DAVID [*and others*], A list of doctoral dissertations in musicology and allied fields. Music teachers national association [&c.]: Denton, Texas 1951. ff.[i].41. [325.]*
limited to the universities of the United States and Canada.

INFORMATIONS bibliographiques et documentation sur la musique, à l'intention des bibliothèques publiques. Direction des bibliothèques de France: 1952. pp.[i].ii.64. [1000.]

JAMES B. COOVER, A bibliography of music dictionaries. Bibliographical center for research: Special bibliographies (no.1): Denver 1952. pp.vi.81. [811.]

CUMULATED index of record reviews. Music library associations: Washington.
    i. 1948–1950. 1952. pp.128. [1300.]
in progress.

HELEN WENTWORTH AZHDERIAN, Reference works in music and music literature in five libraries of Los Angeles county. Music library association: Southern California chapter: Los Angeles 1953. pp.x.313. [4563.]*

WILLI KAHL and WILHELM MARTIN LUTHER, Repertorium der musikwissenschaft. Musikwissenschaft, denkmäler und gesamtausgaben in auswahl (1800–1950). Mit besitzvermerken deutscher bibliotheken. Kassel &c. 1953. pp.viii.271. [2795.]

WOLFGANG SCHMIEDER, Bibliographie des musikschrifttums, 1950–1951. Institut für musikforschung, Berlin: Frankfurt a. M. 1954. pp.xii. 247. [5648.]

JEAN LEGUY, Catalogue bibliographique des livres de langue française sur la musique. 1954. pp.60. [2500.]

BIBLIOGRAPHIE des musikschrifttums. Institut für musikforschung Berlin: Frankfurt a. M.
 1950–1951. Herausgegeben . . . von Wolfgang Schmieder. 1954. pp.xii.247. [5648.]
 1952–1953. 1956. pp.xii.269. [5788.]
 1954–1955. 1957. pp.xv.318. [6965.]
 1956–1957. 1961. pp.xv.310. [7187.]
in progress.

Music

ЛИТЕРАТУРА о музыке. Библиографический указатель. Всесоюзная книжная палата: Москва.
> 1948–1953. [By Sofya Lvovna Uspenskaya
> *and others*]. 1955. pp.344. [3658.]
> 1954–1956. 1958. pp.276. [3342.]
> [*continued as:*]
Советская литература [&c.].
> 1957. 1959. pp.183. [1967.]

MUSIC. Public libraries: [Nottingham 1956].
pp.[ii].40. [1000.]
a list of books and periodicals on music.

KARL HEINZ KÖHLER and EVELINE BARTLITZ, Neuerwerbungen ausländischer musikliteratur 1954–
1955. Deutsche staatsbibliothek: Bibliographische
mitteilungen (no.12): Berlin 1956. pp.90. [750.]
— — 1956–1957. . . . (no.16). pp.120. [729.]

GUSTAVE REESE, Fourscore classics of music
literature. A guide to selected original sources on
theory and other writings on music not available
in english. New York [1957]. pp.xviii.91. [80.]

JACQUES CHAILLEY [*and others*], Précis de musicologie. Université de Paris: Institut de musicologie:
1958. pp.iii–xxiv.432. [3000.]

Music

CARL GREGOR, DUKE OF MECKLENBURG, Bibliographie einiger grenzgebiete der musikwissenschaft. Bibliotheca bibliographica aureliana (vol.
65): Baden-Baden 1962. pp.199. [3519.]

ÅKE DAVIDSSON, Bibliographie der musiktheo-
retischen drucke des 16. jahrhunderts. Bibliotheca
bibliographica aureliana (no.ix): Baden-Baden
1962. pp.99. [750.]

RICHARD SCHAAL, Verzeichnis deutschsprachiger
musikwissenschaftlicher dissertationen, 1861–
1960. Gesellschaft für musikforschung: Musikwissenschaftliche arbeiten (no.19): Kassel 1963. pp.
167. [2819.]

Dramatic music. see **Opera**

8. Folk and primitive music

LIST of works in the New York public library
relating to folk songs, folk music, ballads, &c.
[New York 1907]. pp.40. [1250.]

JULIUS MATTFELD, The folk music of the western
hemisphere. A list of references in the New York
public library. New York 1925. pp.74. [900.]

DOUGLAS H. VARLEY, African native music. An
annotated bibliography. Royal empire society:
Bibliographies (no.8): 1936. pp.117. [1500.]

128

Music

JULIO ESPEJO NUÑEZ, Bibliografía básica de arqueología andina. v. Música precolombina. Lima 1956. pp.12. [152.]

HANS FISCHER, Schallgeräte in Ozeanien. . . . Mit . . . einer ethnographisch-musikologischen bibliographie. Collection d'études musicologiques (vol. 36): Strasbourg &c. 1958. pp.179. [2500.]

BRUNO NETTL, A bibliographic essay on primitive, oriental, and folk music. Reference materials in ethnomusicology. Detroit studies in music bibliography (no.1): [Detroit] 1961. pp.[v].47. [125.]

9. Instrumental music
[see also **Chamber music.**]

HAUPTKATALOG des Musikalien-leih-instituts von Otto Hentze in Hamburg. Band I. Instrumentalmusik und musik für pianoforte, orgel und harmonium. Hamburg 1873. pp.[v].709. [34,620.].

A. ROSENKRANZ, Novello's catalogue of orchestral music. A manual of the orchestral literature of all countries. 1902. pp.204. [5012.]

SELECTIONS from the repertoire of the Queen's hall orchestra which can be performed with an orchestra of 76 performers. Hampstead [printed] 1906. pp.42. [1163.]

OSCAR GEORGE THEODORE SONNECK, Orchestral music (class M 1000–1268). Catalogue. Scores. Library of Congress: Washington 1912. pp.663. [4000.]

WILHELM ALTMANN, Orchester-literatur-katalog. Verzeichnis von seit 1850 erschienenen orchester-werken (symphonien, suiten, symphonischen dichtungen, ouverturen, konzerten für solo-instrumente und orchester) nebst angabe der hauptsächlichsten bearbeitungen. Leipzig 1919. pp.vii.198. [10,000.]

— Zweite . . . auflage. Leipzig 1926. pp.vii.227. [8500.]

— — II. band. Neuerscheinungen 1926 bis 1935 und nachträge. 1936. pp.xvii.187. [5000.]

LIONEL DE LA LAURENCIE, Inventaire critique du fonds Blancheton de la bibliothèque du Conservatoire de Paris. Société française de musicologie: Publications (2nd ser., vols.i–ii): 1930–1931. pp. 3–107.19+3–112.35. [301.]
covers the period 1700–1800.

[DAVID DUBINSKY], The Edwin A. Fleisher music collection [vol.ii: collection of orchestral

music] in the Free library of Philadelphia. Philadelphia 1933–1945. pp.xxii.493+[iii].501–1055. [4560.]
privately printed.

KATHI MEYER and PAUL HIRSCH, Katalog der musikbibliothek Paul Hirsch. III. Instrumental- und vokalmusik bis etwa 1830. Frankfurt a. M. 1936. pp.[iv].362. [1193.]
the library is now in the British museum.

HOFMEISTERS orchester-bibliothek. Ein verzeichnis von werken wertbeständiger orchestermusik für das sinfoniekonzert und das unterhaltungskonzert. [Second edition]. Leipzig [1937]. pp.174. [6000.]

ORCHESTRAL works: symphonies, overtures, suites, concertos, ballets, intermezzi, and miscellaneous compositions. Mapleson music library: Catalogue (no.1): [New York 1940]. [1350.]*

CATALOG of orchestral compositions in library of Michigan music project. Work projects administration: Lansing [c.1940]. ff.41. [800.]

CATALOG of band selections in library of Michigan music project. Work projects administration: Lansing [c.1940]. ff.9. [200.]*

CATALOGUE of instrumental music. Newberry

library: Armed services music loan section: Chicago 1943. ff.57.21. [2500.]*

CATALOGUE of orchestral music in the collections of the Musical library. Circulation department . . . New York public library. [New York 1943]. ff.[iii].134. [47.]*

RAYMOND BURROWS and BESSIE C. REDMOND, Symphony themes. New York [1942]. pp.295. [100.]

A COLLECTION of instrumental music of the 16th–18th centuries & madrigals of the 16th & 17th centuries. Smith college: [Northampton, Mass. *c.*1950]. ff.11. [250.]*
   a list of copies, now in the possession of Smith college, made by Alfred Einstein.

CECILIA DRINKER SALTONSTALL and HANNAH COFFIN SMITH, Catalogue of music for small orchestra. Music library association: Washington 1947. pp.267. [998.]

CLAUDIO SARTORI, Bibliografia della musica strumentale italiana stampata in Italia fino al 1700. Biblioteca di bibliografia italiana (vol.xxiii): Firenze 1952. pp.xxiv.652. [1000.]

INSTRUMENTAL and orchestral music. Notting-

Music

hamshire county library: [Nottingham] 1954. pp.
32. [600.]

CATALOGUE of miniature and orchestral scores
in the Central lending library. Bradford 1956.
pp.44. [1250.]

SETS of orchestral music. Surrey county library:
Book list (no.24): [Esher] 1960. pp.[iv].41. [500.]*

CATALOGUE of finnish orchestral and vocal compositions. Teosto: Helsinki 1961. pp.88. [1250.]

10. *Miniature scores*

REFERENCE book of miniature scores with thematic list of the symphonies and chamber music
works of the great masters. [Fifth edition]. [1936].
pp.43.[xxx]. [2500.]

HANDLIST of miniature scores. City libraries:
Music section: Newcastle-upon-Tyne 1953. pp.34.
[750.]

MINIATURE scores. Nottinghamshire county
library: [Nottingham] 1954. pp.24. [500.]

CATALOGUE of miniature and orchestral scores
in the Central lending library. Bradford 1956.
pp.44. [1250.]

Music

[RAYMOND UPTON], Index of miniature scores. British availability. 1956. pp.120. [2500.]

EDGAR REFARDT, Thematischer katalog der instrumentalmusik des 18. jahrhunderts in den handschriften der universitätsbibliothek Basel. Schweizerische musikforschende gesellschaft (2nd ser., vol.6): Bern [1957]. pp.59. [500.]

KEITH G[EORGE] E[LLIOTT] HARRIS, A catalogue of miniature and full orchestral scores in Yorkshire libraries. Library association: Reference, special and information section: Yorkshire group: Bradford 1960. pp.200. [1500.]*

VINCENT [HARRIS] DUCKLES and MINNIE ELMER, Thematic catalog of a manuscript collection of eighteenth-century italian instrumental music in the university of California, Berkeley, music library. Berkeley &c. 1963. pp.[x].403. [1000.]*

11. *Music for the blind*

LIST of music for the blind . . . in the circulating department of the New York public library. [New York 1906]. pp.7. [350.]

CATALOGUE de musique éditée en braille à l'usage des aveugles. Société d'impression et de

reliure du livre pour les aveugles: 1921. pp.51.
[1500.]

12. *Music printing*

ALPHONSE [JEAN MARIE ANDRÉ] GOOVAERTS,
Notice biographique et bibliographique sur Pierre
Phalèse, imprimeur de musique à Anvers au
XVIe siècle. Bruxelles 1869. pp.82. [200.]

ALPHONSE GOOVAERTS, Histoire et bibliographie
de la typographie musicale dans les Pays-Bas.
Anvers 1880. pp.[iv].608. [1415.]

FRANK KIDSON, British music publishers,
printers and engravers: . . . from queen Elizabeth's
reign to George the fourth's, with select bibliographical lists of musical works printed and
published within that period. [1900]. pp.xii.231.
[1000.]

ROBERT STEELE, The earliest english music
printing. A description and bibliography of
english printed music to the close of the sixteenth
century. Bibliographical society: Illustrated monographs (no.xi): 1903. pp.xi.109. [200.]
*one of the British museum copies contains ms. addi-
tions by the author.*

A CATALOGUE of one hundred works illustrating
the history of music printing from the fifteenth

to the end of the seventeenth century in the library
of Alfred Henry Littleton. 1911. pp.40. [100.]

A GUIDE to the exhibition in the King's library
illustrating the history of printing, music-printing
and bookbinding. British museum: 1913. pp.180.
[music: 46.]

PAUL COHEN, 'Musikdruck und -druker zu
Nürnberg im sechszehnten jahrhundert'. Erlangen
1927. pp.[iv].65. [443.]
reissued Nürnberg 1927.

HANS ULRICH LENZ, Der berliner musikdruck
von seinen anfängen bis zur mitte des 18. jahrhunderts. Lippstadt [printed] 1932. pp.117. [126.]
reissued Kassel 1932.

CATALOGUE of music available in black line
print. Public library: New York 1935. [20.] [60.]

J[EAN] A[UGUSTE] STELLFELD, Bibliographie des
éditions musicales plantiniennes. Académie royale
de Belgique: Classe des beaux-arts: Mémoires:
Collection in-8° (vol.v, no.3): Bruxelles 1949.
pp.248. [21.]

13. *Musical notation*

[SIR EDWARD MAUNDE THOMPSON], A guide to
the manuscripts and printed books illustrating the
progress of musical notation exhibited in the

Music

Department of manuscripts and the King's library. British museum: 1885. pp.20. [158.]

KATALOG einer kleinen sammlung wertvoller musikalien und bücher, als beitrag zur geschichte der musikalischen notation vom frühen mittelalter bis zur gegenwart ausgestellt von der firma Leo Liepmanssohn. Musik-fachausstellung: [Berlin 1906]. pp.24. [77.]

14. Sacred music

VERZEICHNISS, lateinischer und italiänischer kirchen-musiken an motetten, hymnen und liedern, psalmen, magnificat, sanctus, kyrie, missen und passions-oratorien sowohl in partitur als in stimmen, alle in manuscript desgleichen an präambulis, fugen, fugetten, versetten und interludiis ... sonatinen, sonaten und concerten vor die orgel, gedruckt und in kupfer gestochen; welche bey Bernh. Christoph Breitkopf und sohn in Leipzig ... zu bekommen sind. Leipzig 1769. pp.24. [250.]
reissued in 1781.

MUSICA sacra. Vollständiges verzeichniss aller seit dem jahre 1750–1867[–1871] gedruckt erschienenen [werke heiliger tonkunst]. Erfurt.

[i]. Compositionen für die orgel, lehrbücher

für die orgel, schriften über orgelbaukunst.
1867. pp.56. [2000.]
— Nachtrag. 1872. pp.16. [500.]

ii. Choralbücher, liturgien, schriften über
liturgie, choral- und gemeindegesang, sowie sonstiger diesen gegenstand betreffen-
der werke. 1872. pp.48. [1500.]

iii. Oratorien, messen, cantaten und andere
werke der kirchenmusik im clavierauszuge
oder mit begleitung der orgel. 1872. pp.26.
[1000.]

VEREINS-CATALOG ... die von dem Referenten-
collegium des Cäcilien-vereins für alle länder
deutscher zunge in den "Vereins-catalog" aufgenommenen kirchenmusikalischen oder kirchenmusik bezüglichen werke enthaltend. [Regens-
burg 1876–1905]. pp.524+296+256+160+92+
32+22+36. [3300.]

F[RANZ] X[AVER] HABERL, Bibliographischer und
thematischer musikkatalog des Päpstlichen kapell-
archives im Vatikan zu Rom. Monatshefte für
musik-geschichte (vol.xx, beilage): Leipzig 1888.
pp.xii.184. [269.]

WALTER HOWARD FRERE, Bibliotheca musico-
liturgica. A descriptive handlist of the musical &
latin-liturgical mss. of the middle ages preserved

in the libraries of Great Britain and Ireland. Plainsong and mediæval music society [vol.ii: Nashdom abbey]: [1894–] 1901–1932. pp.[vii].164.[xlix]+ xvii.189. [1031.]

300 copies printed; vol.i was reissued with the imprint of Nashdom abbey; a copy in the Bodleian library contains ms. notes.

FIRST list of services. Church music society. 1900. pp.4. [50.]

CATHOLIC church music. Breitkopf & Härtel: [1903]. pp.116. [1500.]

LIST of music approved for use in the catholic churches and chapels of Scotland. Church music commission for Scotland: Edinburgh 1906. pp.44. [150.]

LIST of approved church music for the archdiocese of Westminster. 1907. pp.vii.104. [1500.]

CARL ROULAND, Katalog des musik-archives der St. Peterkirche in Wien. Wien 1908. pp.[viii].84. [2000.]

JOSEPH KILLING, Kirchenmusikalische schätze der bibliothek des abbate Fortunato Santini. Ein beitrag zur geschichte der katholischen kirchenmusik in Italien. Düsseldorf [1910]. pp.[v].516. [5000.]

previously published in part as a dissertation, Münster i. W. 1908; the collection now forms part of the university library of Münster.

RAFAEL MITJANA, Catalogue critique et descriptif des imprimés de musique des XVIe et XVIIe siècles conservés à la bibliothèque de l'université royale d'Upsala. . . . Tome I. Musique religieuse, I. Upsala 1911. pp.viii.vii.coll.502. [243.]
the second and third volumes contain supplements on sacred music.

FRANK J. METCALF, American psalmody or titles of books, containing tunes, printed in America from 1721 to 1820. Heartman's historical series (no.27): New York 1917. pp.54. [750.]
81 copies printed.

CATALOGUE and reference book of approved music for the services of the catholic church. [1920]. pp.[iii].36. [1000.]

CARL SÜSS, Kirchliche musikhandschriften des XVII. und XVIII. jahrhunderts. Katalog . . . herausgegeben von Peter Epstein. Stadtbibliothek: Frankfurt a. M. 1926. pp.xiv.224. [1600.]

JOSEF ALBERT HÜNTEMANN, Die messen der Santini-bibliothek zu Münster i. W. . . . Inaugural-

Music

dissertation . . . München. Quakenbrück [printed] 1928. pp.[ii].vii.72. [775.]

MAX SCHREIBER, Kirchenmusik von 1500–1600. Originaldrucke und manuskripte chronologisch zusammengestellt. Birkeneck [printed] 1932. pp. [vii].88. [2000.]

—— 1600–1700. 1934. pp.[vii].184. [5000.]

KARL ERICH ROEDIGER, Die geistlichen musik-handschriften der universitäts-bibliothek Jena. Universitätsbibliothek: Claves jenenses (vol.iii): Jena 1935. pp.xi.139+[ii].210. [550.]

HANS MARQUARDT, Die stuttgarter chorbücher unter besonderer behandlung der messen. Studien zum erhaltenen teil des notenbestandes der Württembergischen hofkapelle des 16. jahrhunderts. Tübingen 1936. pp.[iii].82. [50.]

HERBERT BOYCE SATCHER, A bibliography of church music and allied subjects. Diocese of Pennsylvania: Commission on music: [Philadelphia] 1949. pp.24. [400.]

CLAUDIO SARTORI, La cappella musicale del duomo di Milano. Catalogo delle musiche dell'archivio. [Milano 1957]. pp.369. [3500.]

CLAUDIO SARTORI, Assisi. La Cappella della

basilica di s. Francesco. 1. Catalogo del fondo musicale nella biblioteca comunale di Assisi. Bibliotheca musicae (no.i): Milano 1962. pp.452. [2500.]

15. *Teaching of music*

ANNE E. PIERCE, Good references on teaching music in elementary schools. Office of education: Bibliography (no.41): Washington 1935. pp.[ii]. 10. [60.]

THEMATIC catalogue of educational music. Royal schools of music: [1936]. pp.64. [1000.]
—— [second edition]. [1950]. pp.80. [1000.]

ARNOLD M[ILROY] SMALL, *ed.* Bibliography of research studies in music education, 1932–1944. Music educators' national conference: Committee on research in music education: [Iowa City 1944]. pp.55. [1500.]
—— [second edition]. Bibliography . . . 1932–1948. By William S. Larson. Chicago [1949]. pp.119. [3000.]

THEMATIC catalogue of educational music. Associated board of the royal schools of music: [1951]. pp.80. [1000.]
— [another edition]. 1963. pp.60. [1000.]

THEMATIC catalogue of educational music.

Associated board of the royal schools of music: [1957]. pp.60. [1000.]

Vocal music. see **Opera**

16. *Miscellaneous*

ERNST CHALLIER, Special-handbuch. Ein alphabetisches geordnetes verzeichniss sämmtlicher gemischter potpourris (fantasien, quodlibets), melodramatischer werke (mit pianofortebegleitung), werke für die linke hand, werke mit begleitung von kinderinstrumenten. Berlin 1883. pp.40. [1240.]

—— Erster nachtrag. 1887. pp.41–52. [350.]

—— Zweiter nachtrag. 1890. pp.53–60. [150.]

[PETER] GEORG [MAXIMILIAN] THOURET, Führer durch die fachausstellung der deutschen militärmusik. Wien [1892]. pp.44. [150.]

KURZES verzeichnis der tabulatur-drucke in der bibliothek dr. Werner Wolffheim, für Martin Breslauer . . . zusammengestellt. [*s.l.* 1921]. pp.[8]. [30.]

limited to the period down to 1747; twenty copies privately printed.

HANS ERDMANN, G. BECCE and L. BRAV, Allgemeines handbuch der film-musik. Berlin &c. [1927].

MUSIC and morale in wartime. A suggested list of songs for community singing, short list of music of some of the allied nations, bibliography on music and war. State of Indiana: Department of public instruction: Bulletin (no.139): [Indianapolis] 1943. pp.16. [225.]

SYDNEY NORTHCOTE, Music in social service. National council of social service: Books advice service: Annotated book list (no.i): [1946]. pp.11. [75.]

RUTH NEEDHAM, Music in bible history; a bibliography. Fuller theological seminary: Fuller library bulletin (no.30): Pasadena, Col. 1956. pp.12. [75.]

ANN PHILIPS BASART, Serial music. A classified bibliography of writings on twelve-tone and electronic music. University of California: Bibliographic guides: Berkeley &c. 1961. pp.xiii.151. [823.]*

Opera, dramatic music. [*see also* **Drama** *and* **Vocal music.**]

[*handbooks consisting of long summaries of operatic plots are excluded.*]

1. *General*

[DUKE LOUIS CÉSAR DE LA BAUME LE BLANC DE

145

LA VALLIÈRE], Ballets, opera, et autres ouvrages lyriques, par ordre chronologique depuis leur origine. 1760. pp.[viii].300. [1750.]

FERDINAND GLEICH, Wegweiser für opernfreunde. Erläuternde besprechung der wichtigsten auf dem repertoire befindlichen opern. . . . Zugleich mit einem nach den stimmgattungen geordneten verzeichnisse . . . geeigneter opernstücke zum gebrauch für dilettanten. Leipzig 1857. pp. viii.224. [225.]

MUSICA theatralis, d. i. vollständiges verzeichniss sämmtlicher, seit dem jahre 1750 bis zu ende des jahres 1863 im deutschen und auswärtigen handel gedruckt erschienener, opern-clavier-auszüge mit text, und sonstiger, für die bühne bestimmter musikwerke. Erfurt 1864. pp.56. [2000.]

FÉLIX CLÉMENT and PIERRE LAROUSSE, Dictionnaire lyrique ou histoire des opéras, contenant l'analyse et la nomenclature de tous les opéras et opéras-comiques représentés en France et à l'étranger depuis l'origine de ce genre d'ouvrages jusqu'à nos jours. [1867–1870]. pp.xv.765. [15,000.]

— — — Deuxième supplément. [1873]. pp. [iv].767–824. [1250.]

— — — Troisième supplément. [1877]. pp.[ii]. 825–880. [1000.]

— — — Quatrième supplément. [1880]. pp. [ii].881–955. [1250.]

the first supplement forms part of the main work, which was reissued, with the addition of the supplements, under the title of Dictionnaire des opéras, *in [1881].*

— — — Dictionnaire des opéras. . . . Revu et mis à jour par [François Auguste] Arthur [Paroisse] Pougin. [1897]. pp.xvi.1180. [22,500.]

— — — — Supplément. 1904. pp.[iii].1181–1293. [2000.]

replaces two earlier supplements, paged 1181–1196 and 1181–1263; the complete work was reprinted (the supplement reissued) in [1905].

LUIGI LIANOVOSANI [*pseud.* GIOVANNI SALVIOLI], Bibliografia melodrammatica. Milano [1878]. pp.44. [61.]

[DAMIANO MUONE], Libretti di melodrammi &c. presentati all'esposizione musicale in Milano dal cav. Damiano Muone. Milano 1881. pp.12.

GIOVANNI PALOSCHI, Piccolo dizionario delle opere teatrali rinomate. Milano &c. [1884]. pp.83. [1000.]

— — Quarta edizione. [1898]. pp.171. [2000.]

[KARL WILHELM JULIUS] HUGO RIEMANN, Opernhandbuch. Repertorium der dramatisch-musika-

lischen litteratur. Leipzig [1881–]1887. pp.[viii].
743. [17,500.]

———— II. Supplement. 1893. pp.747–862. [3500.]
the first supplement forms part of the main work.

ALBERT SCHAEFER, Historisches und systematisches verzeichnis sämmtlicher tonwerke zu den
dramen Schillers, Goethes, Shakespeares, Kleists
und Körners. Leipzig 1886. pp.viii.192. [100.]

EMERICH KASTER, Neuestes und vollständigstes
tonkünstler- und opern-lexicon. Berlin 1889. pp.
vi.64.
Aagesen–Azzoni only; no more published.

CARLO DASSORI, Opere e operisti. Dizionario
lirico 1541–1902. Elenco nominativo universale
dei maestri compositori di opere teatrali. Genova
1903. pp.977. [15,406.]

OSCAR GEORGE THEODORE SONNECK, Dramatic
music (class M 1500, 1510, 1520). Catalogue of full
scores. Library of Congress: Washington 1908.
pp.170. [1250.]

JOHN TOWERS, Dictionary-catalogue of operas
and operettas which have been performed on the
public stage. Morgantown, W.Va. 1910. pp.1046.
[27,500.]

Opera

OSCAR GEORGE THEODORE SONNECK, Catalogue of opera librettos printed before 1800. Library of Congress: Washington 1914. pp.[ii].1172+[ii].1173–1674. [17,000.]

[MAURITZ HJALMAR ALFRED EUGEN BOHEMAN], Katalog öfver kungl. musikaliska akademiens bibliotek. I. Operapartitur. Klavérutdrag ur operor, operetter, sångspel. Stockholm 1905. pp. 46. [1250.]

GIUSEPPE ALBINATI, Piccolo dizionario di opere teatrali, oratori, cantate, &c. Milano &c. [1913]. pp.[iv].327. [4000.]

ROLAND HOLT, A list of music for plays and pageants. New York &c. 1925. pp.xii.93. [300.]

WALDEMAR RIECK, Opera plots. An index to the stories of operas, operettas, etc., from the sixteenth to the twentieth century. Public library: New York 1927. pp.[iii].102. [3500.]

KATHI MEYER and PAUL HIRSCH, Katalog der musikbibliothek Paul Hirsch. Veröffentlichungen &c. Band II. Opern-partituren. Berlin 1930. pp. [vi].335. [976.]
300 copies printed; the library is now in the British museum.

GOTTH[OLD] E[PHRAIM] LESSING, Handbuch des opernrepertoirs. Danzig 1934. loose leaf. [200.]

—— [another edition]. London &c. 1952. pp. iii–xv.393. [375.]

WILHELM ALTMANN, Katalog der seit 1861 in den handel gekommenen theatralischen musik (opern, operetten, possen, musik zu schauspielen usw.). Ein musikbibliographischer versuch. Wolfenbüttel 1935. pp.384. [10,000.]
A–Siegmund only; no more published.

ALFRED LOEWENBERG, Annals of opera, 1597–1940. Compiled from the original sources. Cambridge 1943. pp.xxiv.879. [3500.]

—— Second edition. Societas bibliographica: Genève 1955. pp.xvi.coll.1440+pp.[iv].coll.1441–1758. [3750.]

GAETANO GASPARI and UGO SESINI, Catalogo della biblioteca del Liceo musicale di Bologna. . . . Libretti d'opera in musica. Bologna 1943. pp.xvi.561. [5000.]
incomplete; no more published.

CATALOGUE of miscellaneous opera scores etc., including works presented by Gerald Cooper, E. J. Dent, mrs Rosa Newmarch. Sadler's wells theatre: 1947. ff.5. [100.]*

Opera

CATALOGUE of opera scores, libretti, books, etc. presented to Sadler's wells by John Gordon. 1947. ff.33. [700.]*

CATALOGUE of operas in vocal score lent to Sadler's wells by messrs L. Novello & co. ltd. 1947. ff.18. [500.]*

LIST of operas and operettas for schools and youth clubs. National operatic & dramatic association: [1957]. pp.[ii].8. [35.]*

2. Countries

Argentina

ALFREDO FIORDA KELLY, Cronologia de las operas, dramas líricos, oratorios, himnos, etc. cantados en Buenos Aires. Buenos Aires 1934. pp.83. [380.]

Austria

ALEXANDER VON WEILEN, Zur Wiener theatergeschichte. Die vom jahre 1629 bis zum jahre 1740 am Wiener hofe zur aufführung gelangten werke theatralischen charakters und oratorien. Wien 1901. pp.[ii].140. [1053.]

ALBERT JOSEF WELTNER, ALOIS PRZISTAUPINSKY and FERDINAND GRAF, Das Kaiserlich-königliche hof-operntheater in Wien. Statistischer rückblick

Opera

... 25. Mai 1869 bis 30. April 1894. Wien 1894. pp.xxxix.232. [400.]

ALOIS PRZISTAUPINSKY, 50 Jahre wiener opern-theater. Eine chronik ... 25. Mai 1869–30. April 1919. [Vienna] 1919. pp.130. [700.]

ANTON BAUER, Opern und operetten in Wien. Verzeichnis ihrer erstaufführungen in der zeit von 1629 bis zur gegenwart. Gesellschaft zur heraus-gabe von denkmälern der tonkunst in Österreich: Wiener musikwissenschaftliche beiträge (vol.2): Graz &c. 1955. pp.xii.156. [4856.]

Belgium

ARTHUR DE GERS, Historique complet du Théâtre royal d'Anvers 1834–1914. Deuxième édition revue et corrigée. Anvers [1914]. pp.[118].61[ii]. [375.]

ARTHUR DE GERS, Théâtre royal de la Monnaie, 1856–1926. Bruxelles 1926. pp.104. [350.]

Czechoslovakia

V. and J. HORNOVÁ, Česka zpěvohra. S histo-rickým úvodem dra. Zd. Nejedlého. Praha [1903]. pp.xvi.340. [100.]

France

J. B. COLSON, Manuel dramatique, ou détails

essentiels sur 240 opéras comiques . . . formant le fonds du répertoire des théâtres de France, et sur 100 vaudevilles pris, dans ceux qui ont obtenu le plus de succès à Paris. Bordeaux 1817. pp.xvi.239. 336.207. [340.]

ALBERT DE LASALLE, Histoire des Bouffes parisiens. 1860. pp.[iv].124. [82.]
limited to 1855–1860.

F[ÉLIX] CROZET, Revue de la musique dramatique en France, contenant . . . notices . . . de tous les opéras ou opéras-comiques qui ont été représentés en France. Grenoble 1866. pp.477. [1250.]
— — Supplément. 1872. pp.39. [100.]

THÉODORE [DUFAURE] DE LAJARTE, Bibliothèque musicale du Théâtre de l'opéra. Catalogue. [1876–]1878. pp.[iii].376+[iii].352. [2000.]

ALBERT DE LASALLE, Mémorial du Théâtre-lyrique. Catalogue raisonné des . . . opéras qui y ont été représentés . . . avec des notes biographiques et bibliographiques. 1877. pp.[iii].108. [182.]

ALBERT SOUBIES, Soixante-sept ans à l'Opéra en une page . . . (1826–1893). Paris 1893. pp.viii.24. [175.]

ALBERT SOUBIES, Soixante-neuf ans à l'Opéra-

comique en deux pages . . . 1825–1894. Paris 1894.
pp.x.30. [575.]

ALBERT SOUBIES, Histoire du Théâtre-lyrique,
1851–1870. Paris 1899. pp.vii.61. [175.]

ALBERT SOUBIES, Le Théâtre-italien de 1801 à
1913. Paris 1913. pp.[iv].iv.186.iv. [250.]

J[ACQUES] G[ABRIEL] PROD'HOMME, L'Opéra
(1669–1925). . . . Répertoire. . . . Bibliographie.
1925. pp.xvi.167. [1225.]

M[ADELEINE] HORN-MONVAL, Répertoire bibliographique des traductions et adaptations françaises
du théâtre étranger, du XVe siècle à nos jours.
Tome III. 1: Théâtre italien. 2: Opéras italiens
(livrets). 1960. pp.180. [2152.]

Germany

HERBERT GRAF, Das repertoire der öffentlichen
opern- und singspielbühnen in Berlin seit dem
jahre 1771. Berlin.

  i. Kochische gesellschaft deutscher schau-
      spieler (1771–75) und Döbbelinsches thea-
      ter in der Behrenstrasse (1775–86). 1934.
      pp.48. [137.]
no more published.

GUSTAV FRIEDRICH [MARTIN AUGUST] SCHMIDT,

Opera

Neue beiträge zur geschichte der musik und des theaters am herzoglichen hofe zu Braunschweig-Wolfenbüttel. . . . Erste folge. Chronologisches verzeichnis der in Wolfenbüttel, Braunschweig, Salzthal, Bevern und Blankenburg aufgeführten opern, ballette und schauspiele (komödien) mit musik bis zur mitte des 18. jahrhunderts nach den vorhandenen textbüchern, partituren . . . quellen-urkunden. München 1929. pp.[iii].ff.30. [557.]

WALTER SCHULZE, Die quellen der hamburger oper (1678–1738). Eine bibliographisch-statistische studie. Bibliothek der Hansestadt Hamburg: Mitteilungen (vol.iv): Hamburg 1938. pp.x.170. [200.]

FELIX VON LEPEL, Die italienischen opern und opernaufführungen am kurfürstlichen hofe zu München (1654–1787). Berlin 1953. pp.20. [200.]

Great Britain

RICHARD NORTHCOTT, Records of the Royal opera, Covent garden, 1888–1921. 1921. pp.95. [150.]

Hungary

A. MAGY. KIR. OPERAHÁZ, 1884–1909. Adatok a színház huszonötéves történetéhez. Budapest 1909. pp.423. [220.]

Opera

A MAGYAR királyi operaház évkönyve 50 éves fennállása alkalmából. [Budapest 1934]. pp.183. [440.]

Italy

General

D. J. MERAS, Calendario lírico italiano. Madrid 1878.

TADDEO WIEL, I codici musicali contariniani del secolo XVII nella R. biblioteca di San Marco in Venezia. Venezia 1888. pp.xxx.121. [120.]

ADOLFO BERWIN and ROBERT HIRSCHFELD, Fach-katalog der abtheilung des Königreiches Italien. Internationale ausstellung für musik und theater-wesen: Wien 1892. pp.viii.204. [opera: 1500.]

GIOVANNI and CARLO SALVIOLI, Bibliografia universale del teatro drammatico italiano, con particolare riguardo alla storia della musica italiana.... Volume primo. Venezia [1894–]1903. pp.ix.coll.936.56. [10,000.]
A–Czarina only; no more published.

ALFRED WOTQUENNE, Catalogue de la biblio-thèque du Conservatoire royal de musique de Bruxelles. . . . Annexe I. Libretti d'opéras et

Opera

d'oratorios italiens du XVIIe siècle. Bruxelles 1901. pp.[iii].191. [450.]

250 copies printed.

GUIDO BUSTICO, Il teatro musicale italiano. Guide bibliografiche: Roma 1924. pp.3–82. [500.]

Bologna

[ALESSANDRO MACHIAVELLI], Serie cronologica de' drammi recitati su de' pubblici teatri di Bologna dall'anno . . . 1600 sino al corrente 1737. Opera de' signori Soci filopatri di Bologna. Bologna 1737. pp.94.

CRONOLOGIA di tutti gli spettacoli rappresentati nel Gran teatro comunale di Bologna dalla solenne sua apertura 14 maggio 1793 a tutto l'autunno del 1880. Bologna 1880. pp.248. [550.]

CORRADO RICCI, I teatri di Bologna nei secoli XVII e XVIII. Bologna 1888. pp.xxiii.736. [1000.]

Cittadella

GIUSEPPE PAVAN, Il teatro di Porta bassanese in Cittadella. Serie cronologica degli spettacoli. Cittadella 1901. pp.16. [100.]

GIUSEPPE PAVAN, Il Teatro sociale di Cittadella. Serie cronologica degli spettacoli musicali. Vicenza 1908. pp.[xi].16.

Opera

Florence

GIUSEPPE PAVAN, Saggio di cronisteria teatrale fiorentina. Serie cronologica delle opere rappresentate al Teatro degli immobili in via della Pergola [in Florence] . . . nei secoli XVII e XVIII. Milano &c. [1901]. pp.24. [300.]

Genoa

TAVOLA cronologica di tutti i drammi, o sia opere in musica recitate nei teatri del Falcone e di Sant'Agostino da cento anni addietro, cioè dall'anno 1670 al 1771. Genova &c. 1771.

REMO GIAZOTTO, Il melodramma a Genova nei secoli XVII & XVIII. Con gli elenchi completi dei titoli, dei musicisti, dei poeti e degli attori di quei componimenti rappresentati tra il 1652 e il 1771 &c. Genova 1941. pp.79. [250.]
the larger part of the edition was destroyed in an air raid.

Lucca

ULDERICO ROLANDI, Spettacoli musicali per la funzione delle "tasche" in Lucca. Milano 1932. pp.3–51. [100.]

Mantua

ERNESTO LUI, I cento anni del Teatro sociale di

158

Opera

Mantova (1822–1922). Cronistoria. Mantova 1922. pp.v.175. [1200.]

Milan

G[IUSEPPE] C[HIAPPORI], Serie cronologica delle rappresentazioni drammatico-pantomimiche poste sulle scene dei principali teatri di Milano d'all'autunno 1776 sino all'intero autunno 1818. Milano 1818. pp.336. [1000.]

— — Continuazione [seconda (terza) continuazione].

    1818–1819. 1829. pp.78. [100.]
    1819–1820. 1821. pp.196. [100.]
    1820–1824. 1825. pp.[ii].288. [250.]

LUIGI ROMANI, Teatro della Scala. Cronologia di tutti gli spettacoli rappresentati in questo teatro dal suo aprimento fino ad oggi. Milano 1862. pp.xxxix.165.

RAPPRESENTAZIONI liriche date al R. Teatro alla Canobbiana in Milano (1779–1871). Melodrammi, nomi de' maestri, poeti, esecutori principali. [Varese] 1871.

POMPEO CAMBIASI, Rappresentazioni date nei RR. Teatri di Milano (1778–1872). Milano 1872. pp.120.

Opera

—— La Scala (1778–1906). . . . 5ª edizione 1906. pp.xlii.523.

deals with the Canobbiana and the Scala.

Modena

ALESSANDRO GANDINI, Cronistoria dei teatri di Modena dal 1539 al 1871. . . . Continuata da Luigi Francesco Valdrighi e Giorgio Ferrari-Moreni. Modena 1873.

G. FERRARI-MORENI and V. TARDINI, Cronistoria dei teatri di Modena dal 1873 a tutto il 1881. Modena 1883. pp.268. [50.]

Naples

FRANCESCO FLORIMO, La scuola musicale di Napoli e i suoi conservatorî, con uno sguardo sulla storia della musica in Italia. Tomo IV. = Elenco di tutte le opere in musica rappresentate nei teatri di Napoli dal 1651 al 1881. Napoli 1881. pp.xxiv.609. [3000.]

Padua

A. PALLEROTTI [*pseud.* ANTONIO PITTARELLO], Spettacoli melodrammatici e coreografici rappresentati in Padova nei teatri Obizzi, Nuovo e del Prato della Valle dal 1751 al 1892. Padova 1892. pp.72. [750.]

Opera

Parma

PAOLO-EMILIO FERRARI, Spettacoli drammatico-musicali e coreografici in Parma dal'anno 1628 all'anno 1883. Parma 1884. pp.vii.383. [500.]

Reggio

[PROSPERO FANTOZZI], Catalogo delle rappresentazioni in musica esposte nei teatri di Reggio dal 1701 al 1825. [Reggio] 1826. pp.32.

Sardinia

ULDERICO ROLANDI, Libretti e librettisti di Sardegna. Cagliari 1939. pp.28. [100.]

Turin

PAOLO BREGGI, Serie degli spettacoli rappresentati al Teatro regio di Torino dal 1688 al presente. Torino 1872. pp.81. [250.]

GIACOMO SACERDOTE, Teatro regio di Torino. Cronologia degli spettacoli rappresentati dal 1862 al 1890. Torino 1892. pp.181. [400.]

Varese

POMPEO CAMBIASI, Teatro di Varese, 1776–1891. . . . Serie delle opere e dei balli. Milano [1891]. pp.52. [175.]

Opera

Venice

[GIOVANNI CARLO BONLINI], Le glorie della poesia e della musica contenute nell'esatta notizia de'. teatri della città di Venezia e nel catalogo purgatissimo de' drami musicali quivi sin' hora rapresentati. Padoa 1731. pp.267. [500.]
the Bibliothèque nationale copy contains additions in ms.

ANTONIO GROPPO, Catalogo di tutti i drammi per musica recitati ne' teatri di Venezia dall'anno 1637, in cui ebbero principio le pubbliche rappresentazioni de' medesimi sin all'anno presente 1745. ... Con tutti gli scenarj, varie edizioni, ed aggiunte fatte a' drammi stessi. Venezia [1745]. pp.151.31. [811.]

—— Aggiunta al catalogo dei drammi dalla primavera dell'anno 1745 fino all'autunno dell'anno 1752. [Venezia 1753]. pp.31.

[GIOVANNI SALVIOLO], La Fenice, gran teatro di Venezia. Serie degli spettacoli dalla primavera 1792 a tutto il Carnovale 1876. Milano &c. [1876.] pp.61. [600.]

LIVIO NISO GALVANI [*pseud.* GIOVANNI SALVIOLO], I teatri musicali di Venezia nel secolo XVII (1637–1700). Memorie storiche e bibliografiche. Milano 1878. pp.195. [600.]

Opera

TADDEO WIEL, I teatri musicali veneziani del settecento. Catalogo delle opere in musica rappresentate nel secolo XVIII in Venezia (1701–1800). Venezia 1897. pp.lxxx.16–600. [1274.]

GIUSEPPE PAVAN, Teatri musicali veneziani. Il teatro San Benedetto (ora Rossini). Catalogo cronologico degli spettacoli (1755–1900). Venezia 1917. pp.78.

Netherlands

ALFRED LOEWENBERG, Early dutch librettos and plays with music in the British museum. Aslib: 1947. pp.30. [100.]

Poland

KORNEL MICHAŁOWSKI, Opery polskie. Materiały do bibliografii muzyki polskiej (vol.i): Krakow 1954. pp.277. [1000.]

Russia

VLADIMIR VASILEVICH STASOV, Русскія и иностранныя оперы исполнявшіяся на императорскихъ театрахъ въ Россіи въ 18-мъ и 19-мъ столѣтіяхъ. С.-Петербургъ 1898. pp.43. [750.]

R[OBERT] ALOYS MOOSER, Opéras, intermezzos, ballets, cantatas, oratorios joués en Russie durant

Opera

le XVIIIe siècle. Genève 1945. pp.iii–xi.175. [650.]
—— 2e édition. 1955. pp.xiv.170. [800.]

United States

A LIST of books on the operas announced for production at the Boston opera house ... MCMXI–MCMXII, in the Public library. Boston 1911. pp. [v].49. [500.]

JULIUS MATTFELD, A hundred years of grand opera in New York 1825–1925. New York 1927. pp.107. [500.]

Yugoslavia

HRVATSKA opera (1870–1920). Izdala Uprava Narodnogo kazalista. Zagreb 1920. pp.75. [300.]

3. *Miscellaneous*

ULDERICO ROLANDI, Riflessi oraziani nei libretti per musica. Roma 1938. pp.[ii].91. [275.]

Vocal music.

[bibliographies primarily of literary interest are entered under Poetry.]

Vocal Music

1. *General*

HAUPTCATALOG des Musikalien-leih-instituts von Otto Hentze in Hamburg. Band 2. Vocalmusik. Hamburg 1874. pp.v.387. [14,621.]

[CATALOGUE of music. Words. British museum].
[i]. 1884. ff.112. [2500.]
ii. 1886. ff.113–145. [750.]
no more published.

'STUDENTSÅNGER'. Tillegnade akademiska sångföreningen of O. W. Helsingfors 1895. pp.4. [110.]

PIERRE AUBRY, Esquisse d'une bibliographie de la chanson populaire en Europe. Essais de musicologie comparée: 1905. pp.39. [500.]

LIST of works in the New York public library relating to folk songs, folk music, ballads, etc. [New York 1907]. pp.40. [1250.]

F. BENTLEY NICHOLSON, List of songs, duets, and vocal methods in the Henry Watson music library. Public libraries: Music lists (no.3): Manchester 1913. pp.[ii].294. [5000.]

Vocal Music

J. A. CARTLEDGE, List of glees, madrigals, part-songs, etc. in the Henry Watson music library. Public libraries: Music lists (no.4): Manchester 1913. pp.200. [3500.]

G. SCHIRMER, INC., New singing teacher's guide. A classified list of vocal music for the use of singer and teacher. [New York] 1922. pp.xiii.231. [7500.]

KATHI MEYER and PAUL HIRSCH, Katalog der musikbibliothek Paul Hirsch. III. Instrumental- und Vokalmusik bis etwa 1830. Frankfurt a. M. 1936. pp.[iv].362. [1193.]
300 copies printed; the library is now in the British museum.

ORCHESTRAL accompaniments to excerpts from grand & light operas, oratorios, cantats, concert songs, etc. Mapleson music library: Catalogue (no.2): [New York c.1942]. pp.77. [3200.]*

HAROLD BARLOW and SAM MORGENSTERN, A dictionary of vocal themes. New York [1950]. pp. vi.547. [8000.]

JOHN MERRILL KNAPP, Selected list of music for men's voices. Princeton 1952. pp.xi.165. [3000.]

HANDLIST of vocal scores. City libraries: Music section: Newcastle-upon-Tyne 1954. pp.[iii].40. [700.]

VOCAL music. Nottinghamshire county library: [Nottingham] 1954. pp.33. [600.]

HANDLIST of songs. Public library: Music section: [Newcastle-upon-Tyne] 1955. pp.[ii].49. [750.]

CHORAL music. Nottinghamshire county library: [Nottingham] 1957. pp.40. [750.]

BERTON COFFIN, Singer's repertoire. Second edition. New York 1960.*
    i. Coloratura soprano, lyric soprano and dramatic soprano. pp.321. [9000.]
    ii. Mezzo soprano and contralto. pp.222. [6000.]
    iii. Lyric and dramatic tenor. pp.210. [6000.]
    iv. Baritone and bass. pp.223. [6000.]

SETS of vocal music. Surrey county library: Book list (no.22): [Esher] 1960. pp.[iv].44. [1250.]*

2. Countries

America

MELLINGER EDWARD HENRY, A bibliography for

the study of american folk-songs, with many titles of folk-songs (and titles that have to do with folk-songs) from other lands. [1936]. pp.[vi].142. [2500.]

[LEILA FERN], Selected list of collections of latin american songs and references for guidance in planning fiestas. Pan american union: Music division: Washington 1942. ff.4. [25.]*

— — Third edition. . . . with addenda. Selected list of latin american song books [&c.]. 1943. ff.12. [60.]*

Australia

HUGH ANDERSON, Australian song index 1828–1956. Black bull chapbooks (no.7): Ferntree Gully 1957. pp.20. [300.]

Bulgaria

ANTON P. STOILOV, Показалецъ напечатанитѣ прѣзъ XIX вѣкъ български народни пѣсни. Българска библиотека (vols.xi, xiv): София 1916–1918. pp.xxiii.288+vii.359. [1064.]

Denmark

ALFRED NIELSEN, Sang-katalog. Alfabetisk stikords-fortegnelse over de paa danske, norske og svenske forlag indtil udgang af 1912 udkomne sange. Dansk musikhandler-forenings forlag: København 1916. pp.[iii].667. [34,000.]

—— Anden del (afsluttet med udgangen af 1922). Med et tillæg: sange af danske, finske, norske og svenske komponister udkomne udenfor de fire nordiske lande. 1924. pp.[viii].360. [19,000.]

Finland

CATALOGUE of finnish orchestral and vocal compositions. Teosto: Helsinki 1961. pp.88. [1250.]

France

ALEXIS SOCARD, Livres populaires. Noëls et cantiques imprimés à Troyes depuis le XVIIe siècle jusqu'à nos jours. 1865. pp.[vi].136. [100.]
200 copies printed.

EDWARD SCHWAN, Die altfranzösischen liederhandschriften, ihr verhältniss, ihre entstehung und ihre bestimmung. Berlin 1886. pp.viii.275. [2000.]

CONSTANT PIERRE, Les hymnes et chansons de la révolution. Aperçu général et catalogue. Ville de Paris: Publications relatives à la révolution française: 1904. pp.[vii].xiv.1040. [2337.]

[P.] DE BEAUREPAIRE-FROMENT, Bibliographie des chants populaires français. 1906. pp.41. [500.]

—— Troisième édition. [1910]. pp.xciii.186. [1500.]

A[NDRÉ] GAIRAL DE SÉRÉZIN, Les belles chansons. Répertoire de . . . chansons publiées séparément en petit format (musique et chant). Lyon [printed] [*c*.1926]. pp.32. [1200.]

WERNER RUST, Die chansons-sammlung der universitätsbibliothek Greifswald. Bibliographisch und inhaltsgeschichtlich dargestellt. Aus den schätzen der universitätsbibliothek (vol.iv): Greifswald 1929. pp.45. [168.]

ANDRÉ CHENAL and [A. ROSAT], Les meilleures chansons. Répertoire analytique de dix-huit cents œuvres de choix pour familles, sociétés, patronages. [By] André Chenal et le Chercheur. 1933. pp.317. [1800.]

EDMOND DUMÉRIL, Lieds et ballades germaniques traduits en vers français. Essai de bibliographie critique. Bibliothèque de la Revue de littérature comparée (vol.xcix): 1934. pp.292. [1516.]

J[OSEPH] OLLIVIER, Catalogue bibliographique de la chanson populaire bretonne. Quimper 1941. pp.lxviii.452. [1154.]

BIBLIOGRAPHIE sommaire des manuels et recueils de chant. Secrétariat d'état à l'enseignement technique, à la jeunesse et aux sports: 1952. pp.12. [80.]

FRIEDRICH GENNRICH, Bibliographie der ältesten französischen und lateinischen motetten. Summa musicae medii aevi (vol.ii): Darmstadt 1957. pp. lii.125. [1219.]

CATALOGUE 1949. Bibliothèque théâtrale, partitions pour chorales. Ligue de l'enseignement: Fédération départementale des œuvres laïques de la Vienne: Poitiers [1959]. pp.52. [500.]

Germany

F[RANZ] L[UDWIG] SCHUBERT, Wegweiser in der gesangs-literatur für den solo- und chorgesang. Leipzig 1861. pp.[ii].94. [1000.]

ROBERT SCHAAB, Führer durch die literatur des männergesanges. Leipzig [1863]. pp.[iv].38. [500.]
— — Dritte . . . auflage. [1873]. pp.[iv].78. [1500.]

FRANZ XAVER HABERL, Alphabetisches und sach-register sämmtlicher im katalog des Allgemeinen deutschen Cäcilienvereins aufgenommenen musi-kalien. Regensburg [printed] [1876]. pp.[iv].48. [2000.]

ERNST CHALLIER, Grosser lieder-katalog. Ein

alphabetisch geordnetes verzeichniss sämmtlicher
einstimmiger lieder mit begleitung des pianoforte, sowie mit begleitung des pianoforte und
eines oder mehrerer anderer instrumente. Berlin
1885. pp.1016. [100,000.]

— — Nachtrag. Berlin [Giessen].

   i. 1885–1886. pp.1017–1053. [3500.]

   ii. 1886–1888. pp.1055–1115. [5000.]

   iii. 1888–1890. pp.1115–1194. [6500.]

   iv. 1890–1892. pp.1195–1289. [7000.]

   v. 1892–1894. pp.1291–1382. [7000.]

   vi. 1894–1896. pp.1383–1466. 6500.]

   vii. 1896–1898. pp.1467–1568. [8000.]

   viii. 1898–1900. pp.1571–1675. [8000.]

   ix. 1900–1902. pp.1677–1803. [10,000.]

   x. 1902–1904. pp.1805–1926. [10,000.]

   xi. 1904–1906. pp.1927–2043. [10,000.]

   xii. 1906–1908. pp.2045–2146. [8000.]

   xiii. 1908–1910. pp.2149–2241. [7500.]

   xiv. 1910–1912. pp.2243–2330. [6500.]

   xv. 1912–1914. pp.2331–2415. [6500.]

*no more published; supplements xiii–xv have the
additional title* Lexikon des liedes.

SPECIAL-KATALOG der fachausstellung des män-
nergesangvereines "Schubertbund" in Wien bei
der Internationalen ausstellung für musik- und
theaterwesen. [Vienna 1892]. pp.40. [1000.]

EMIL BOHN, Fünfzig historische concerte in Breslau, 1881–1892. Nebst einer bibliographischen beigabe: Bibliothek des gedruckten mehrstimmigen weltlichen deutschen liedes vom anfange des 16. jahrhunderts bis ca. 1640. Breslau 1893. pp.vii.188. [700.]

ERNST CHALLIER, Grosser duetten-katalog. Ein alphabetisch geordnetes verzeichniss sämmtlicher zweistimmiger lieder mit begleitung. Giessen 1898. pp.118. [10,000.]

— — Erster nachtrag. 1901. pp.121–139. [1500.]

— — Zweiter nachtrag. 1906. pp.141–162. [2000.]

— — Dritter nachtrag. 1911. pp.163–182. [1500.]

the third supplement has the additional title of Lexikon des liedes, teil II.

ERNST CHALLIER, Grosser männergesang-katalog. Ein alphabetisch geordnetes verzeichniss sämmtlicher männer-chöre mit und ohne begleitung. Giessen 1900. pp.648. [60,000.]

— — Hilfs-register. 1901. pp.45.

— — Zweiter nachtrag. 1902. pp.649–724. [7000.]

— — Dritter nachtrag. 1905. pp.725–819. [9000.]

Vocal Music

— — Vierter nachtrag. 1907. pp.821–905. [8000.]

— — Fünfter nachtrag. 1909. pp.907–962. [6000.]

— — Sechster nachtrag. 1912. pp.963–1022. [5000.]

the first supplement forms part of the main work; the fourth–sixth supplements bear the additional title of Lexikon des liedes, *teil IV.*

MAX FRIEDLANDER, Das deutsche lied im 18. jahrhundert. Stuttgart &c. 1902. pp.lx.384+viii. 360+[v].632. [798.]

ERNST CHALLIER, Grosser chor-katalog. Ein alphabetisch geordnetes verzeichniss sämmtlicher gemischter chöre mit und ohne begleitung. Giessen 1903. pp.343. [30,000.]

— — Erster nachtrag. 1905. pp.345–384. [3000.]

— — Zweiter nachtrag. 1910. pp.385–438. [4000.]

— — Dritter nachtrag. 1913. pp.439–482. [4000.]

RAPHAEL MOLITOR, Deutsche choral-wiegen-drucke. Regensburg &c. 1904. pp.ix.77. [200.]

PAUL HEITZ, Unbekannte ausgaben geistlicher und weltlicher lieder . . . gedruckt von Thiebold

Berger (Strassburg 1551–1584). Strassburg 1911. pp.27.ff.76. [76.]
400 copies printed.

GUSTAV JUNGBAUER, Bibliographie des deutschen volksliedes in Böhmen. Beiträge zur deutsch-böhmischen volkskunde (vol.xi): Prag 1913. pp.xlvii.576. [2711.]

EDMOND DUMÉRIL, Lieds et ballades germaniques traduits en vers français. Essai de bibliographie critique. Bibliothèque de la Revue de littérature comparée (vol.xcix): 1934. pp.292. [1516.]

GEORG SCHÜNEMANN, Führer durch die deutsche chorliteratur. Reichsmusikkammer: Amt für chorwesen und volksmusik: Wolfenbüttel.
    i. Männerchor. 1935. pp.379. [5000.]
    ii. Gemischter chor. 1936. pp.234. [3500.]
no more published.

F. MÜNGER, Protestantische choräle und choralgebundene orgelmusik. Der organist (beilage): Zürich 1938. pp.16. [250.]

ERICH VALENTIN, *ed.* Handbuch der chormusik. Arbeitsgemeinschaft deutscher chorverbände: Regensburg [1953–1958]. pp.643+525. [15,000.]

ROBERT WHITE LINKER, Music of the minnesinger and early meistersinger. A bibliography.

University of North Carolina: Studies in the germanic languages and literatures (no.32): Chapel Hill 1962. pp.xvi.80. [550.]

Great Britain

INDEX to Warren's Collection of catches, canons, glees, and madrigals [1763-1794], together with the Vocal harmony [*c*.1765]. 1836. pp.[iii].23. [806.]

EDWARD F[RANCIS] RIMBAULT, Bibliotheca madrigaliana. A bibliographical account of the musical and poetical works published in England during the sixteenth and seventeenth centuries, under the titles of madrigals, ballets, ayres, canzonets, etc. etc. 1847. pp.xvi.88. [2000.]
reissued c.1900 with a different titlepage.

[WILLIAM HENRY HUSK], Catalogue of the library of the Sacred harmonic society. 1853. pp.xii.131. [1147.]
— — Supplement. 1855. pp.viii.60. [350.]
— — [another edition]. 1862. pp.xv.320. [2331.]
— — [another edition]. 1872. pp.iii–xx.400. [2923.]
— — — Supplement. 1882. pp.40. [208.]
Husk's copy, the 1853, 1855, 1872 volumes containing his voluminous notes, is in the British museum.

CATALOGUE of organ music, also sacred music with english words. Novello's catalogus (nos. 1–2): 1866. pp.160. [4000.]

[JOHN FREDERICK RANDALL STAINER *and others*]. Catalogue of english song books forming a portion of the library of sir John Stainer. With appendices of foreign song books, collections of carols, books on bells, &c. 1891. pp.107. [750.]
privately printed.

MINNIE EARL SEARS, Song index. Standard catalog series: New York 1926. pp.xxxiv.650. [12,000.]
— — Supplement. 1934. pp.xl.367. [7000.]

CATALOGUE of the Society's library. Plainsong & mediaeval music society: Burnham, Bucks. 1928. pp.39. [500.]

CATALOGUE of the publications of the Plainsong & mediaeval music society and of St. Mary's press, Wantage. Nashdom abbey: Burnham, Bucks. 1930. pp.12. [100.]

CYRUS LAWRENCE DAY and ELEANORE BOSWELL MURRIE, English song-books, 1651–1702. A bibliography, with a first-line index of songs. Bibliographical society: 1940. pp.xxi.440. [4150.]

CATALOGUE of choral music. Newberry library: Armed services music loan section: Chicago 1943. ff.13.*

MUSIC and morale in wartime. A suggested list of songs for community singing [&c.]. State of Indiana: Department of public instruction: Bulletin (no.139): [Indianapolis] 1943. pp.16. [225.]

VIC FILMER, Vic Filmer's guide to buskers. Names the key, first chord, and starting note. [Second edition]. [1944]. pp.24. [300.]

A COLLECTION of instrumental music of the 16th–18th centuries & madrigals of the 16th & 17th centuries. Smith college: [Northampton, Mass. *c.*1950]. ff.11. [250.]*
a list of copies, now in possession of Smith college, made by Alfred Einstein.

E. A. WHITE, An index of english songs contributed to the journal of the Folk song society, 1899–1931, and its continuation the Journal of the English folk dance and song society to 1950. Edited . . . by Margaret Dean Smith. English folk dance & song society: 1951. pp.xv.58. [1500.]

CATALOGUE of choral works performed by societies affiliated to the National federation of

music societies during the period between its
inauguration in 1936 and the year 1953. Second...
edition. National federation of music societies:
1953. pp.72. [500.]

C. L. CUDWORTH, Thematic index of english
eighteenth-century overtures and symphonies.
Royal musical association: Proceedings (vol.
lxxviii, appendix): 1953. pp.ix.xxxv. [158.]

CATALOGUE of choral works performed by
societies affiliated to the National federation of
music societies ... between ... 1936 and ... 1949.
[1954]. pp.63. [250.]

PRINTED music in the library of the Madrigal
society. An excerpt from . . . the catalogue of
accessions of printed music. British museum:
Department of printed books: 1955. pp.252–266.
[300.]

LUTHER A. DITTMER, The Worcester fragments.
A catalogue raisonné and transcription. American
institute of musicology: Musicological studies and
documents (no.2): [Rome] 1957. pp.185. [109.]

Hungary

PAL ERDÉLYI, Énekes könyveink a XVI. és XVII.
században. Budapest 1899. pp.75. [256.]

Vocal Music

Ireland

COLM O LOCHLAINN, Anglo-irish song-writers since Moore. Bibliographical society of Ireland: Publications (vol.vi, no.i): Dublin 1950. pp.[ii]. 24. [200.]

Italy

CATALOGO dei soli, duetti, trii e concerti per il violino chi [sic] si trovano in manuscritto nella officina musica di Breitkopf in Lipsia. [Leipsic] 1762. pp.48. [750.]

CATALOGO delle arie, duetti, madrigali e cantate, con stromenti diversi e con cembalo solo, che si trovano in manuscritto nella officina musica di Breitkopf in Lipsia. [Leipsic] 1765. pp.38. [500.]

[JOHANNES] EMIL [EDUARD BERNHARD] VOGEL, Bibliothek der gedruckten weltlichen vocalmusik Italiens aus den jahren 1500–1700, enthaltend die litteratur der frottole, madrigale, canzonette, arien, opern, etc. Stiftung von Schnyder von Wartensee: Berlin 1892. pp.xxiv.530+[iii].597. [40,000.]

a facsimile was published, Hildesheim 1962; a new edition, revised by Alfred Einstein, is in progress in Notes (*Washington 1945 &c.*), *2nd ser.ii &c.*

Vocal Music

Jews

BIBLIOGRAPHY of instrumental and vocal music.
Jewish music council: New York 1946. pp.[ii].18.
[700.]*

BIBLIOGRAPHY of jewish vocal music. National
jewish music council: New York [1948]. pp.36.
[600.]*

— 1949–50 addenda. [1951]. ff.17. [250.]*

Latin

FRIEDRICH GENNRICH, Bibliographie der ältesten
französischen und lateinischen motetten. Summa
musicae medii aevi (vol.ii): Darmstadt 1957. pp.
lii.125. [1219.]

REPERTORIUM organorum recentioris et motetorum vetustissimi stili. Summa musicae medii aevi
(vol.vii &c.): Langen.

   i. II. Friedrich Ludwig, Handschriften in
     mensuralnotation. Die quellen der motet-
     ten ältesten stils. Besorgt von Friedrich
     Gennrich. . . . (vol.vii): 1961. pp.[vi].347–
     457.183–315. [299.]
  ii. Musikalisches anfangs-verzeichnis des
     nach tenores geordneten repertorium. . . .
     (vol.viii): 1962. pp.[v].71. [515.]

Vocal Music

Negro

INDEX to Negro spirituals. Public library: Cleveland 1937. ff.[v].149. [1800.]*

Netherlands

D[ANIEL] F[RANÇOIS] SCHEURLEER, Nederlandsche liedboeken. Lijst der in Nederland tot het jaar 1800 uitgegeven liedboeken. Frederik Mullerfonds: 's-Gravenhage 1912. pp.xi.321. [3887.]

—— Eerste supplement. 1923. pp.[viii].120. [600.]

Russia

V[IKTOR] M[IKHAILOVICH] SIDELNIKOV, Русская народная песня. Библиографический указатель, 1735–1945 гг. Институт мировой литературы им. А. М. Горького: Москва 1962. pp.171. [3000.]

Scotland

CECIL HOPKINSON and C[ECIL] B[ERNARD] OLDMAN, Haydn's settings of scottish songs in the collections of Napier and Whyte. Edinburgh 1954. pp.[ii].87–120. [221.]
20 copies privately printed.

Spain

JOSÉ MARÍA SBARBI, Monografía sobre los refranes, adagios y proverbios castellanos y las obras ó fragmentos que expresamente tratan de ellos en nuestra lengua. Madrid 1891. pp.415. [600.]

F. RUBIO PIQUERAS, Códices polifónicos toledanos. Estudio crítico de los mismos. Toledo [1925]. pp.79. [34.]

Sweden and Finland

ARVID HULTIN, Luettelo helsingin yliopiston kirjaston arkkikirjallisuudesta. Helsingin yliopiston kirjaston julkaisuja (vol.xii): Helsinki 1929–1932. pp.xxiii.299+x.688+xvi.285. [5000.]

NYARE svenska orkester- och körverk. Katalog. Förening svenska tonsättare: [Stockholm 1937]. pp.57. [800.]

— Fjärde upplagan. 1944. pp.78. [1500.]

United States

CHECK-LIST of recorded songs in english language in the Archive of american folk song to July, 1940. Library of Congress: Music division: Washington 1942. pp.[v].216+[ii].217–456+[ii]. 138. [10,000.]*

DRINKER library of choral music presented to the Association of american choruses by dr. Henry S[andwith] Drinker. Association of american choruses: [Princeton 1943]. pp.[ii].vii.53. [300.]

Vocal Music

ARTHUR KYLE DAVIS, Folk-songs of Virginia. A descriptive index and classification. Durham, N.C. 1949. pp.lxiii.389. [974.]

EDWIN WOLF, American song sheets, slip ballads and poetical broadsides 1850–1870. A catalogue of the collection of the Library company. Philadelphia 1963. pp.vii.205. [2916.]*

[ALBERT ALOYSIUS BIEBER], The Albert A. Bieber collection of american plays, poetry and songsters. New York 1963. pp.[v].103. [708.]

Yugoslavia

JOSIP MILAKOVIĆ, Bibliografja hrvatske i srpske narodne pjesme. Sarajevu 1919. pp.304.

Drama and stage. [*see also* **Music** *and* **Opera.**]

1. *Manuscripts*

[RICHARD BATKA], Aus der musik- und theater-welt. Beschreibendes verzeichnis der autographen-sammlung Fritz Donebauer. Prag 1894. pp. lxxx.151. [1200.]

2. *General*

[AMBROISE LALOÜETTE], Histoire de la comédie et de l'opéra, où l'on prouve qu'on ne peut y aller sans pécher. 1697. pp.viii.120.12. [500.]

ANTOINE FRANÇOIS DELANDINE, Bibliothèque de

Lyon. Catalogue des livres qu'elle renferme dans la section du théâtre. [*c*.1820]. pp.[viii].589. [7500.]

— — [another issue]. Bibliographie dramatique, ou tablettes alphabétiques du théâtre des diverses nations. [*c*.1820]. pp.[viii].590. [7500.]

P. L. JACOB [*pseud.* PAUL LACROIX], Bibliothèque dramatique de monsieur [Martineau] de Soleinne. 1843–1845. pp.[iii].xvi.322+44+[iii].393+xi.368 +56+xi.961[*sic,* 228]+vii.260+vi.68. [7500.]

— — Table générale... par m. [J.] Goizet. 1845. pp.iv.144.

— — Bibliothèque dramatique de Pont de Vesle, augmentée et complétée par les soins du bibliophile Jacob [Paul Lacroix]. Catalogue rédigé d'après le plan du catalogue Soleinne et destiné à servir de complément à ce catalogue. 1846. pp. viii.279. [5000.]

— — Table ... Par [Jacques] Charles Brunet. Publiée par Henri [James Nathaniel Charles, baron] de Rothschild. 1914. pp.[iv].491.

— — Essai d'une bibliographie générale du théâtre, ou Catalogue raisonné de la bibliothèque d'un amateur, complétant le catalogue Soleinne. [By Joseph de Filippi]. 1861. pp.[v].vii.224. [1950.] *200 copies printed.*

CATALOGUE de la bibliothèque théâtrale de

m. Joseph de Filippi. 1861. pp.[ii].vi.184+[iv].
114. [3500.]

HISTORICAL fiction, novels, plays, poems. Public
library: Boston 1871. pp.9. [1000.]

— A chronological index to historical fiction,
including prose fiction, plays and poems. Second
... edition. 1875. pp.iv.32. [2500.]

CATALOGUE of the dramas and dramatic poems
contained in the Public library of Cincinnati.
Cincinnati 1879. pp.192. [7500.]

КАТАЛОГЪ изданій театральной библіотеки
С. Ѳ. Разсохина за ... (1875-1900). [Moscow
1900] pp.vi.98. [1750.]

[VIKTOR VIKTOROVICH PROTOPOPOV], Биб-
ліотека В. В. Протопопова ... Театръ.
С.-Петербургъ 1912. pp.[ii].151. [2161.]

A CATALOGUE of the Allen A. Brown collection
of books relating to the stage. Public library:
Boston 1919. pp.viii.952. [10,000.]

[JOSEPH GREGOR], Katalog der ausstellung
'Komödie' im Prunksaale der Nationalbibliothek.
Bundestheaterverwaltung [*and*] Nationalbiblio-
thek: Wien 1922. pp.121. [200.]

FRANCIS K[EESE] W[YNKOOP] DRURY, Viewpoint

in modern drama. An arrangement of plays according to their essential interest. American library association: Viewpoint series: Chicago 1925. pp.119. [800.]

LUIS PARIS, Catálogo provisional. Museo-archival teatral: Madrid 1932. pp.viii.207. [1750.]

A CATALOGUE of the Division of drama library. University of Washington: Seattle [1934]. pp. [vi].69. [3000.]
— Supplement. [1934]. ff.[i].20. [300.]*

JOHN H[ENRY] OTTEMILLER, Index to plays in collections . . . published between 1900 and 1942. New York 1943. pp.130. [3844.]
—— Fourth edition. Washington 1964. pp. 370. [15,000.]

[JOAQUÍN MONTANER], La colección teatral de don Arturo Sedó [y Guichard]. Barcelona 1951. pp.353. [2000.]

A[LFRED] H[ORACE] WHARRIER, Worthwhile one-act plays. A list of . . . plays, british, continental and american. Revised edition. British drama League: 1952. pp.[46]. [370.]

VEDY o umeni. Divadlo. Bibliografické zprávy Štátnej vedeckej knižnice v Košiciach. [Košice] 1953 &c.

Drama & Stage

3. Works on the drama and stage

ADOLPH BÜCHTING, Bibliotheca theatralis oder verzeichniss aller in bezug auf das theater in . . . 1847–1866 im deutschen buchhandel erschienenen bücher und zeitschriften. Nordhausen 1867. pp.48. [500.]

JAMES HARRY PENCE, The magazine and the drama. An index. Dunlap society: [Publications (new ser., no.2):] New York 1896. pp.xvi.190. [4000.]

LIST of books chiefly on the drama and literary criticism. Columbia university: Publications (no.1): New York 1897. pp.64. [2250.]

CLARA NORTON [and others], Modern drama and opera. A reading list [Reading lists] on the works of [various authors]. Useful reference series (nos.4, 13): Boston 1911–1915. pp.93+[iv].255. [4000.]

PAUL ALFRED MERBACH, Bibliographie für theatergeschichte, 1905–1910. Gesellschaft für theatergeschichte [: Schriften (vol.xxi)]: Berlin 1913. pp. [v].264. [5500.]

LIST of references on the technic of the drama. Library of Congress: Washington 1915. ff.2. [21.]*

LIST of references on the theatre and show business, its management and finance. Library of Congress: Washington 1915. ff.3. [41.]*

LIST of references on endowed theatres: national and municipal. Library of Congress: Washington 1916. ff.5. [68.]*

BRIEF list of references on the drama. Library of Congress: Washington 1918. ff.2. [17.]*

WILLIAM BURT GAMBLE, The development of scenic art and stage scenery. A list of references in the New York public library. New York 1920. pp.[iii].128. [2471.]

[PAUL HUF and J. W. F. WERUMEUS BUNING], Catalogus der boekerij. Stedelijk museum: Theater tentoonstelling: Amsterdam 1922. pp.3–44. [450.]

THEATERGESCHICHTE, bearbeitet von Friedrich Michael. Musikwissenschaft, bearbeitet von Rudolf Schwartz. Jahresberichte des Literarischen zentralblattes über die wichtigsten wissenschaftlichen neuerscheinungen des gesamten deutschen sprachgebietes (1924, vol.xiii): Leipzig 1925. pp. 99. [Drama: 300.]

THE DRAMA and the theatre. A selected list of books and articles prepared by students of the

St. Louis library school. Public library: St. Louis 1929. pp.15. [300.]

[AUGUSTE RONDEL], Catalogue analytique sommaire de la collection théâtrale Rondel. . . . Suivi d'un guide pratique à travers la bibliographie théâtrale. Bibliothèque de l'Arsenal: 1932. pp.x. 52. [350.]
the Catalogue *merely sets out the classification.*

FREDERIC ARDEN PAWLEY, Theatre architecture. A brief bibliography. National theatre conference: New York [1932]. pp.32. [250.]

ROSAMOND GILDER, A theatre library. National theatre conference: New York 1932. pp.xv.74. [100.]

BLANCH M[ERRITT] BAKER, Dramatic bibliography. An annotated list of books on the history and criticism of the drama and stage and on the allied arts of the theatre. New York 1933. pp.xvi. 320. [4000.]
— — [another edition]. Theatre and allied arts. A guide to books dealing with the history, criticism, and technic of the drama and theatre and related arts and crafts. 1952. pp.xiv.536. [6000.]
limited to works in english.

LOUISE DAMERON, Bibliography of stage settings.

Enoch Pratt free library: Baltimore, Md. 1936. ff.[i].48. [80.]*

SAMUEL SELDEN, *ed.* Research in drama and the theatre in the universities and colleges of the United States, 1937–1942. A bibliography: American educational theatre association: Meadville, Pa. [1944]. pp.[iii].48. [750.]*

LIST of selected books on theatre and drama. Corporation public libraries: Glasgow 1950. pp. 12. [125.]

READERS' guide to stagecraft and the theatre. Library association: County libraries section: [Readers' guide (new series, no.15): 1952]. pp.30. [350.]

FRANZ HADAMOWSKY and HEINZ KINDERMANN, Europäische theaterausstellung. Katalog. Biblosschriften (vol.11): Wien &c. [1955]. pp.367. [4000.]

GISELA SCHWANBECK, Bibliographie der deutschsprachigen hochschulschriften zur theaterwissenschaft von 1885 bis 1952. Gesellschaft für theatergeschichte: Schriften (vol.58): Berlin 1956. pp. xiv.566. [3309.]*

S. YANCEY BELKNAP, Guide to the performing arts, 1961. New York 1962. pp.451. [12,000.]*

Drama & Stage

WILLIAM W. MELNITZ, Theatre arts publications in the United States, 1947–1952. American educational theatre association: Monograph (no.1): [Dubuque 1959]. pp.xiii.91. [4063.]*

PAT M. RYAN, History of the modern theatre: selective bibliography. Tucson [1960]. ff.28. [700.]*

HANS JÜRGEN ROJEK, Bibliographie der deutschsprachigen hochschulschriften zur theaterwissenschaft von 1953 bis 1960. Gesellschaft für theatergeschichte: Schriften (vol.61): Berlin 1962. pp. xvi.170. [558.]*

OSCAR G[ROSS] BROCKETT, SAMUEL L. BECKER and DONALD C. BRYANT, A bibliographical guide to research in speech and dramatic art. Chicago [1963]. pp.118.

A. E. SANTANIELLO, Theatre books in print. New York 1963. pp.iii–xiii.266.[vi]. [2000.]*

4. Countries &c.

America, latin

J[OSÉ] LUIS TRENTI ROCAMORA, El repertorio de la dramática colonial hispano americana. Buenos Aires 1950. pp.3–111. [100.]

M[ADELEINE] HORN-MONVAL, Répertoire bibliographique des traductions et adaptations françaises
du théâtre étranger, du xve siècle à nos jours.
Tome IV. 1: Théâtre espagnol. 2: Théâtre de
l'Amérique latine. 3: Théâtre portugais. 1961. pp.
127. [1153.]

Austria

OTTO RUB, Das Burgtheater. Statistischer Rückblick auf die Tätigkeit . . . vom 8. April 1776 bis
1. Januar 1913. Wien 1913. pp.iii–xvi.308. [2405.]

KATALOGE der theatersammlung der Nationalbibliothek in Wien. Wien.

    i. Friedrich Arnold Mayer, Felix Trojan and
       Franz Hadamowsky, Katalog der 'alten
       bibliothek' des theaters an der Wien. 1928.
       pp.167. [4000.]

    iii. F. Hadamowsky, Das theater in der
       Wiener Leopoldstadt 1781–1860. 1934. pp.
       416. [4000.]

    iv. B. Niederle, Der nachlass Josef Kainz.
       1942. pp.xx.94.

vol.ii is a catalogue of drawings.

OTTO ERICH DEUSCH, Das Freihaustheater auf
der Wieden, 1787–1801. . . . Zweite, verbesserte
auflage. Wien &c. [1937]. pp.[ii].48. [500.]

    previously published in the Mitteilungen des

Vereines für geschichte der stadt Wien (*1937*), *xvi.30–73*.

KATALOG der ausstellung wiener theater im prunksaale der Österreichischen nationalbibliothek. Gesellschaft der freunde der Österreichischen nationalbibliothek: Wien 1951. pp.111. [1000.]

Basque

G[EORGES] HÉRELLE, Les pastorales basques. Notice, catalogue des manuscrits & questionnaire. Bayonne 1903. pp.[iii].87. [200.]
250 copies printed.

G[EORGES] HÉRELLE, État des manuscrits de pastorales basques conservés actuellement . . . dans des dépôts publics. 1906. pp.7. [113.]

GEORGES HÉRELLE, Répertoire du théâtre basque. Catalogue sommaire de toutes les 'pastorales' connues à ce jour. 1922. pp.53. [119.]

G[EORGES] HÉRELLE, Études sur le théâtre basque. Le répertoire du théâtre tragique. 1928. pp.148. [100.]

Belgium

A[LEXANDRE] DUPONT, Guide dramatique belge. Liége 1870. pp.x.162. [1000.]

—— [on cover: 2ème édition]. Répertoire dra-

matique belge. 1884–1885. pp.xviii.227 + 224.
[1250.]

FRÉDÉRIC FABER, Documents authentiques et
inédits tirés des Archives générales du royaume
et bibliographie concernant le théâtre français en
Belgique depuis son origine jusqu'à 1830 [de 1830
à nos jours]. Bruxelles 1880. pp.[v].355+[iii].319.
[6000.]

FRANCIS LAUTERS, Les revues bruxelloises de fin
d'année. Bibliographie anecdotique. Bruxelles
1936. pp.39. [150.]

Bulgaria

БИБЛИОГРАФСКИ указател в помощ на
театралните самодейни колективи. [Бъл-
гарски библиографски институт:] София
1952. pp.32. [350.]*

Catalan

[SALVADOR SANPERE Y MIGUEL and G. ROCA Y
SANPERE], Katalog der Ausstellung des königreiches Spanien. Internationale ausstellung für
musik- und theaterwesen: Wien 1892. pp.95.
[1000.]
consists largely of a list of catalan plays.

JOAN GIVANEL I MAS, Materials per a la biblio-

grafía del teatre català. (Traduccions). Barcelona
1935. pp.3–58. [250.]
limited to translations into catalan.

Chile

NICOLÁS ANRIQUE [Y] R[EYES], Ensayo de una
bibliografía dramática chileña. Santiago de Chile
1899. pp.[ii].184. [449.]

WALTER RELA, Contribución a la bibliografía del
teatro chileno 1804–1960. Facultad de humanida-
des y ciencias: Departamento de literature ibero-
americana: Montevideo 1960. pp.52. [1000.]

JULIO DURÁN CERDA, Repertorio del teatro chileno. Bibliografía. Instituto de literatura chileno:
Publicaciones (ser. C, no.1): Santiago de Chile
1962. pp.247. [1710.]

China

LIST of references on the chinese drama and
theatre. Library of Congress: Washington 1923.
ff.6. [72.]*

Croatia, see also Serbia

JOSIP BADALIĆ, Bibliografija hrvatske dramske i
kazališne književnosti. Hrvatska bibliografija:
Zagreb 1948. pp.xvi.318. [3212.]

Drama & Stage

Cuba

JOSÉ LUÍS PERRIER, Bibliografía dramática cubana, incluye a Puerto Rico y Santo Domingo. New York 1926. pp.vi.115. [1000.]

JOSÉ RIVERO MUÑIZ, Bibliografía del teatro cubano. Biblioteca nacional: Habana 1957. pp.120. [898.]

Czechoslovakia

J. J. STANKOVSKÝ, Divadelní slovník. Příspěvek k české bibliografii vůbec a k historii českého divadla zvlášť. Praze 1876. pp.148. [2500.]

NÁRODNÍ divadlo ke svému padesátému výročí. Praze 1932. pp.63. [2000.]
includes the season of 1932–1933.

MARION MOORE COLEMAN, Czech drama and theatre. Articles, monographs, translations available in english. A tentative bibliography compiled for the American association of teachers of slavonic and east european languages. Columbia university: New York 1946. pp.5. [50.]*

LITERATURA o divadle a divadelní hry. Soupis knižních publikací, vydaných v letech 1945–1955. Universitní knihovny: Olomouc 1957. pp.255. [2130.]

[VLADIMIR ŠRÁMEK], Hry k 40. výročí velké říjnové revoluce. [Prague 1957]. pp.104. [200.]*

Denmark

TH[OMAS] OVERSKOU, Fortegnelse over alle dramatiske arbeider som siden det Kongeliske theaters aabning, 18de december 1748. Kjøbenhavn 1838. pp.xiv.128. [1250.]

— — [another edition]. Haandbog for yndere og dyrkere of dansk dramatisk litteratur og kunst, indeholdene de Kongelige theaters repertoire ... fra ... 1748. 1865. pp.[ix].199. [1494.]

ARTHUR AUMONT and EDGAR COLLIN, Det Danske nationaltheater, 1748–1889. En statistik fremstelling. København 1896–1899. pp.[vi].113+[iv].76+[iii].56+[iii].516+[iii].514. [1879.]

DAN FOG, The Royal danish ballet 1760–1958 and Auguste Bournonville. A chronological catalogue of the ballets ... performed at the royal theatres of Copenhagen and a catalogue of Bournonville's works. Copenhagen 1961. pp.[ii].79. [571.]

Dominica

VETILIO ALFAU DURÁN, Hojas sueltas. Contribucuón a la bibliografía dominicana. Ciudad Trujillo 1956. pp.[ii].xxxvii. [195.]

Drama & Stage

Finland

VILHO RUOTSALAINEN, Suomenkielinen teatteri-kirjallisuus 1879–1953. Suomen teatterijarjestöjen keskuliiton julkaisuja (no.7): Helsinki 1954. pp.40. [1000.]

France

i. *Bibliography*

AUGUSTE RONDEL, La bibliographie dramatique et les collections de théâtre. Lille 1913. pp.32. [100.]

500 copies printed.

ii. *Manuscripts*

[EMMANUEL] HENRI [PARENT] DE CURZON, État sommaire des pièces et documents concernant le théâtre et la musique, conservés aux Archives nationales. 1899. pp.28. [large number.]

iii. *General*

[MAUPOINT], Bibliothèque des théâtres, contenant le catalogue alphabétique des pièces dramatiques, opéra, parodies, & opéra comiques; & le tems de leurs représentations. 1733. pp.[iii].369 [*sic*, 371].[iii]. [1500.]

there is another issue, with a different imprint; a copy in the Bibliothèque nationale contains ms. notes by Thomas Simon Gueullette and Riccoboni.

[PIERRE FRANÇOIS GODART] DE BEAUCHAMPS, Recherches sur les théâtres de France, depuis l'année onze cens soixante & un, jusques à présent. 1735. pp.[xxiv].508+[iv].544+[iv].523. [3500.]

[FRANÇOIS and CLAUDE PARFAICT], Histoire du théâtre françois, depuis son origine jusqu'à présent, avec la vie des plus célèbres poëtes dramatiques, un catalogue exact de leurs piéces, & des notes. 1734–1749. pp.xxiv.486.[v] + xviii.568.[v] + [ii]. xv.16.584 + [ii].12.xii.552 + [ii].xii.492 + [ii]. xvi.431 + [ii].vi.455 + [ii].xvi.430 + [ii].424.40 + [ii].viii.456 + [ii].x.504 + [ii].iv.564 + [ii].xvi. 456+[ii].vii.574+[ii].viii.496. [3000.]

the first volume was reprinted Amsterdam 1735 and Paris 1745.

[CHARLES DE FIEUX] DE MOUHY, Tablettes dramatiques, contenant l'abrégé de l'histoire du théâtre françois . . . un dictionnaire des pièces, et l'abrégé de l'histoire des auteurs & des acteurs. 1752. pp. xxiii.244.88. [2000.]

—— Supplément.
    1752–1753. pp.8. [25.]
    1753–1754. pp.9–16. [25.]
    1754–1755. pp.17–24. [25.]
    1755–1756. pp.25–32. [25.]

1756–1757. pp.33–40. [25.]
1757–1758. pp.41–48. [25.]

[CHARLES DE FIEUX] DE MOUHY, Le répertoire de toutes les pièces restées au théâtre françois, avec la date, le nombre des représentations, & les noms des auteurs & des acteurs vivans. 1753. pp.[v].vi. [iv].148. [300.]

[ANTOINE DE LÉRIS], Dictionnaire portatif des théâtres, contenant l'origine des différens théâtres de Paris; le nom de toutes les piéces qui y ont été représentées depuis leur établissement, & des piéces jouées en province, ou qui ont simplement paru par la voie de l'impression depuis plus de trois siècles; . . . avec une chronologie des piéces qui ont paru depuis vingt-cinq ans. 1754. pp.xlviii.560. [2000.]

— — Deuxième édition. Dictionnaire portatif historique et littéraire des théâtres. 1763. pp. xxxiv.730[*sic*, 738]. [3500.]

[DU GÉRARD], Tables alphabétiques & chronologiques des pièces représentées sur l'ancien théâtre italien depuis son établissement jusqu'en 1697 qu'il a été fermé. 1750. pp.[ii].xiv.116. [vii]. [64.]

[FRANÇOIS and CLAUDE PARFAICT and QUENTIN

GODIN D'ALGUERBE], Dictionnaire des théâtres de
Paris. 1756. pp.xvi.508+[iii].667+[iii].519+[iii].
566+[iii].592+[iii].338+[ii].339–757. [7500.]
reprinted in 1767.

[LOUIS FRANÇOIS CLAUDE MARIN *and others*],
Bibliothèque du théâtre françois, depuis son origine, contenant un extrait de tous les ouvrages
composés pour ce théâtre. Dresde 1768. pp.[iii].
xx.576+[iii].584+[iii].504. [3500.]
*also attributed, wrongly, to Louis César de La
Baume Le Blanc, duke de La Vallière.*

[JEAN MARIE BERNARD CLÉMENT and JOSEPH DE
LA PORTE], Anecdotes dramatiques; contenant . . .
toutes les pièces de théâtre . . . qui ont été jouées
à Paris ou en province . . . depuis l'origine des
spectacles en France. 1775. pp.[vii].iv.590.[iv]+
[iii].580+[iii].576. [6000.]

[BABAULT, A. P. F. MÉNÉGAULT *and others*],
Annales dramatiques, ou dictionnaire général des
théâtres, contenant . . . l'analyse de tous les ouvrages dramatiques; tragédie, comédie, drame, opéra,
opéra-comique, vaudeville, etc., représentés sur
les théâtres de Paris, depuis Jodelle jusqu'à ce jour;
la date de leur représentation, le nom de leurs
auteurs, avec des anecdotes théâtrales. . . . Par une
société de gens de lettres.

i. A–B. 1808. pp.498. [500.]
ii. B–C[oriolan]. 1809. pp.[iii].iii.496. [500.]
iii. C[orisande]–D–E. 1809. pp.[iii].476. [500.]
iv. F–G–H. 1809. pp.[iii].480. [500.]
v. H–I–J–K–L. 1810. pp.[iii].414. [500.]
vi. M. 1810. pp.[iii].446. [500.]
vii. N O P. 1811. pp.[iii].2.536. [500.]
viii. Q R S. 1811. pp.[iii].428. [500.]
ix. T U V X Y Z. 1812. pp.[vi].428. [500.]
*the Bibliothèque nationale copy contains ms. notes
by Guillaume François Marion Dumersan.*
— 2ᵉ édition. Tome I. 1819. pp.lx.448. [500.]

[GABRIEL ANTOINE JOSEPH HÉCART], Recherches historiques, bibliographiques . . . sur le théâtre de Valenciennes. Par G. A. J. H★★★. 1816. pp.x.184. [150.]

J. B. COLSON, Répertoire du théâtre français, ou détails essentiels sur 360 tragédies et comédies. Bordeaux [1819]. pp.xvi.240 + viii.280 + 352. [360.]

[JOSEPH OCTAVE DELEPIERRE], Description bibliographique et analyse d'un livre unique qui se trouve au Musée britannique. Par Tridace-Nafé-Théobrome, gentilhomme breton. Meschacébé 1849. pp.viii.171. [64.]
the volume in question is C.20 e 13, which contains a

collection of french farces and moralities, printed 1542–1548; 100 copies privately printed; one of the copies in the British museum contains ms. additions by the author.

L[OUIS EDMOND HENRI] MAGGIOLO, Inventaire chronologique et sommaire des pièces représentées en Lorraine sur le théâtre de la Compagnie de Jésus de 1582 à 1736. Quatrième mémoire pour servir à l'histoire de l'université de Pont-à-Mousson. 1866. pp.20. [15.]

J. GOIZET and A. BURTAL, Dictionnaire universel du théâtre en France et du théâtre français à l'étranger. [1867]. pp.637+64+122. [7500.]
A–Deux avares only of the list by titles and A only of the list by authors; no more published.

ÉMILE PICOT, La sottie en France. Fragment d'un répertoire historique et bibliographique de l'ancien théâtre français. Nogent-le-Rotrou 1878. pp. 3–96. [100.]

HIPPOLYTE MINIER, Le théâtre à Bordeaux. Étude historique . . . suivie de la nomenclature des auteurs dramatiques bordelais et de leurs ouvrages, établie en collaboration avec Jules Delpit. Bordeaux 1883. pp.106. [1000.]

L[OUIS] PETIT DE JULLEVILLE, Histoire du théâtre en France. Répertoire du théâtre comique en France au moyen-âge. 1886. pp.vii.411. [1600.]

COUNT GUSTAVE DE HAUTECLOCQUE, Les représentations dramatiques et les exercices littéraires dans les collèges de l'Artois avant 1789. Abbeville 1888. pp.131. [300.]
100 copies printed.

L[OUIS] HENRY LECOMTE, Napoléon et l'empire racontés par le théâtre, 1797–1899. 1900. pp.[v]. vi.541. [600.]

HENRI SCHOEN, Le théâtre alsacien. Bibliographie complète du théâtre alsacien. Strasbourg 1903. pp.330.xli.

L[OUIS] HENRY LECOMTE, Histoire des théâtres [de Paris], 1402–1904.
    Notice préliminaire. 1905. pp.[iii].60.
    Le Panorama dramatique, 1821–1823. 1900. pp.85. [68.]
        a new edition forms part of the Jeux gymniques *volume below.*
    La Renaissance, 1838– . . . 1904. 1905. pp.[iii]. 151. [300.]
    Le Théâtre historique, 1847– . . . 1891. 1906. pp.[iii].167. [65.]

Le Théâtre national, le Théâtre de l'égalité, 1793–1794. 1907. pp.[iii].160. [128.]

Les Nouveautés, 1827–... 1906. 1907. pp.[iii].213. [443.]

Les Jeux gymniques, 1810–1812. Le Panorama dramatique, 1821–1823. 1908. pp.[iii].153. [145.]

> *the second part is a new edition of the volume set out above, 1900.*

Les Variétés amusantes, 1778–... 1815. 1908. pp.[ii].263. [638.]

Les Folies-nouvelles, 1854– ... 1880. 1909. pp.[iii].168. [165.]

Le Théâtre de la cité, 1792–1807. 1910. pp.[iii].300. [438.]

Les Fantaisies-parisiennes — L'Athénée — Le théâtre Scribe — L'Athénée-comique, 1865–1911. 1911. pp.[iii].228. [343.]

150–200 copies printed; the dates in the general title appear only in the Notice; *no more published.*

A. JOANNIDÈS, La Comédie-française de 1680 à 1900. Dictionnaire général des pièces et des auteurs. 1901. pp.[v].xxiii.136.[cclxxiv]. [2250.]

— — La Comédie-française de 1680 à 1920. Tableau des représentations par auteurs et par pièces. 1921. pp.[v].iv.143. [2500.]

250 copies printed.

LOUIS BETHLÉEM, Les pièces de théâtre. . . . Analyse critique des principaux ouvrages représentés dans les théâtres de Paris et de province. 1910. pp.viii.320. [3000.]

—— Les pièces de théâtre. Manuel pratique à l'usage des honnêtes gens. . . . Troisième édition. 1935. pp.iii–viii.509. [4000.]

SELECT list of references on the modern french drama and theatre. Library of Congress: Washington 1911. ff.11. [140.]*

HAROLD WILLIAM SCHOENBERGER, American adaptations of french plays on the New York and Philadelphia stages from 1790 to 1833. A thesis . . . of the university of Pennsylvania. Philadelphia 1924. pp.99. [60.]

JEAN BONNEROT, Bibliographie théâtrale. Vingt-cinq ans de littérature française (fascicule 7): [1925]. pp.193–224. [1750.]

LUIGI FERRARI, Le traduzioni italiane del teatro tragico francese nei secoli XVIIᵉ e XVIIIᵉ. Saggio bibliografico. Bibliothèque de la Revue de littérature comparée (vol.xiii): 1925. pp.iii–xiii.311. [600.]

JOACHIM ROLLAND, Le théâtre comique en

France avant le xve siècle. (Essai bibliographique). 1926. pp.135. [1100.]

—— [Nouvelle édition]. 1930. pp.138. [1100.]

JOACHIM ROLLAND, Les origines latines du théâtre comique en France. (Essai bibliographique). 1927. pp.5–218. [750.]

FRANCIS J[AMES] CARMODY, Le répertoire de l'Opéra-comique en vaudevilles de 1708 à 1764. University of California: Publications in modern philology (vol.xvi, no.4): Berkeley 1933. pp.[v]. 373–438. [900.]

PIERRE MÉLÈSE, Répertoire analytique des documents contemporains d'information et de critique concernant le théâtre à Paris sous Louis XIV, 1659–1715. Société des historiens du théâtre: Bibliothèque (vol.vii): 1934. pp.239. [4000.]

PIERRE CORNEILLE et le théâtre de son temps. Exposition organisée pour la célébration du troisième centenaire du *Cid*. Bibliothèque nationale: 1936. pp.41. [293.]

THOMAS SIMON GUEULLETTE, Notes et souvenirs sur le Théâtre-italien au xviiie siècle. Publiés par J.-E. Gueullette. Bibliothèque de la Société des historiens du théâtre (vol.xiii): 1938. pp.217. [750.]

WILLARD AUSTIN KINNE, Revivals and importations of french comedies in England, 1749–1800. New York 1939. pp.xv.310. [500.]

HAMILTON MASON, French theatre in New York. A list of plays, 1899–1939. New York 1940. pp. ix.442. [1443.]

SEYMOUR TRAVERS, Catalogue of nineteenth century french theatrical parodies. A compilation of the parodies between 1789 and 1914 of which any record was found. Submitted in ... Columbia university. New York 1941. pp.133. [1225.]

G. SAGEHOMME, Répertoire alphabétique de 13.000 auteurs . . . qualifiés quant à leur valeur morale. 6e édition revue ... par E. Dupuis. 1944. pp.608. [46,000.]

JOACHIM ROLLAND, Essai paléographique et bibliographique sur le théâtre profane en France avant le xve siècle. 1945.
this is in effect a new edition of the two books entered above under 1926–1927.

CLARENCE D[IETZ] BRENNER, A bibliographical list of plays in the french language 1700–1789. Berkeley, Cal. 1947. pp.v.229. [11,662.]*

CLARENCE D[IETZ] BRENNER, Dramatizations of french short stories in the eighteenth century, with special reference to the "contes" of La Fontaine, Marmontel, and Voltaire. University of California. Publications in modern philology (vol.xxxiii, no.1): Berkeley &c. 1947. pp.[iii].33. [209.]

CHARLES BEAUMONT WICKS [iii: and JEROME W. SCHWEITZER], The parisian stage. Alphabetical indexes of plays and authors. University of Alabama: Studies (nos.6, 8): University.
    i. 1800–1815. 1950. pp.[ix[.89. [3018.]
    ii. 1816–1830. 1953. pp.[xii].107. [3069.]
    iii. 1831–1850. 1961. pp.288. [8014.]

INFORMATIONS bibliographiques et documentation sur le théâtre, à l'intention des bibliothèques publiques. Services des bibliothèques de France et de la lecture publique: 1951. pp.27. [400.]

ARCH SANDERS LACEFIELD and MARY PICKFORD HINKLE, Short title list of a collection of french plays in the Margaret I. King library. University of Kentucky: Margaret I. King library: Occasional contributions (no.20): Lexington 1951. ff.177. [2041.]*

CATALOGUE des ouvrages de théâtre pouvant être prêtés directement aux usagers. Bibliothèque centrale de prêt du département des Deux-Sèvres: Niort 1952. pp.58. [2500.]*

CLAUDE PORTANT, Que jouerons-nous? Répertoire analytique de pièces de théâtre. Iᵉ série:
Hommes et jeunes gens. 1954. pp.191. [400.]

CATALOGUE des pièces de théâtre. Bibliothèque
centrale de prêt de Loir-et-Cher: Blois 1955. ff.28.
[750.]*

PETIT répertoire d'art dramatique à l'usage des
associations théâtrales d'amateurs du Maroc.
Direction de l'instruction publique: Service de la
jeunesse et des sports du Maroc: [Rabat] 1955.
pp.[i].28. [300.]*

JEAN BERGEAUD, Je choisis. . . mon théâtre.
Encyclopédie du théâtre contemporain. Collection je choisis: [1956]. pp.712. [5000.]

[JACQUELINE LEINER], Catalogue de l'exposition:
Le théâtre en France au Moyen-Age. Institut
d'études françaises: [Sarrebruck 1958]. pp.ix.36.
[100.]*

M[ADELEINE] HORN-MONVAL, Répertoire bibliographique des traductions et adaptations françaises
du théâtre étranger du xvᵉ siècle à nos jours.
Centre national de la recherche scientifique.

    i. Théâtre grec antique. 1958. pp.viii.123.
      [2388.]
    ii. 1. Théâtre latin antique. 2. Théâtre latin

médiéval et moderne. 1959. pp.115. [1957.]

iii. 1. Théâtre italien. 2. Opéras italiens (livrets). 1960. pp.180. [2152.]

iv. 1. Théâtre espagnol. 2. Théâtre de l'Amérique latine. 3. Théâtre portugais. 1961. pp.127. [1153.]

v.

vi. Théâtre allemand.

vii. Théâtre flamand, hollandais et scandinave.

viii. Théâtre slave, théâtre du proche- et extrême-orient. Divers.

CATALOGUE 1959. Bibliothèque théâtrale, partitions pour chorales. Ligue de l'enseignement: Fédération départementale des œuvres laïques de la Vienne: Poitiers [1959]. pp.52. [500.]

Germany

i. *Periodicals*

WILHELM HILL, Die deutschen theaterzeitschriften des achtzehnten jahrhunderts. Forschungen zur neueren literaturgeschichte (vol.xlix): Weimar 1915. pp.[viii].154. [133.]

ii. *General*

JOHANN CHRISTOPH GOTTSCHED, Nöthiger vor-rath zur geschichte der deutschen dramatischen dichtkunst, oder verzeichniss aller deutschen trauer- lust- und sing-spiele, die im druck erschienen, von 1450 bis zur hälfte des jetzigen jahrhunderts. Leipzig 1757. pp.[xxxvi].336.[xii]. [1500.]

—— Herrn Gottfried Christian Freieslebens... Kleine nachlese, zu . . . herrn . . . Gottscheds nöthigem vorrathe. 1760. pp.78. [200.]

—— Des nöthigen vorraths . . . zweyter theil. . . . Als ein anhang ist hrn. rath Freyeslebens nachlese. 1765. pp.[xvi].303. [500.]

T[HEODOR] C[HRISTIAN] F[RIEDRICH] ENSLIN, Bibliothek der schönen wissenschaften oder verzeichniss der vorzüglichsten . . . in Deutschland erschienenen romane, gedichte, schauspiele. Berlin 1815. pp.[iii].104. [3000.]

—— Zweite auflage . . . herausgegeben von Wilhelm Engelmann. Leipzig 1837. pp.x.506. [15,000.]

——— [Supplement]. Zweiter band . . . bis zur mitte des jahres 1845. 1846. pp.vi.374. [10,000.]

CHRISTIAN GOTTLOB KAYSER, Deutsche bücherkunde oder alphabetisches verzeichniss der von 1750 bis ende 1823 erschienenen bücher. . . . Anhang, enthaltend romane und theater. Leipzig 1827. pp.[iv].244. [drama: 5500.]

L[UDWIG] FERNBACH, Der wohl unterrichtete theaterfreund . . . enthaltend ein verzeichniss von sämmtlichen, seit 1740 . . . erschienenen, deutschen dramatischen schriften. Berlin 1830. pp.vi.366.[iv]. [10,000.]

— — Zweiter band . . . von 1830 bis ende 1839. 1840. pp.[iv].217. [6000.]

— — Dritter band . . . von 1840 bis ende 1849. 1850. pp.[iv].118. [2000.]

— — [another edition]. Der theaterfreund . . . enthaltend die dramatischen erscheinungen des buchhandels bis zum Jahre 1848. 1860. pp.[vi]. 630. [18,000.]

— — — Vierter band . . . von 1849 bis 1859. 1860. pp.71. [1000.]

CHRISTIAN GOTTLOB KAYSER, Index locupletissimus librorum qui inde ab anno MDCCL usque ad annum MDCCCXXXII in Germania et in terris confinibus prodierunt. . . . Schauspiele. Leipzig 1836. pp.[ii].114. [8000.]

LUDWIG WOLLRABE, Chronologie sämmtlicher hamburger bühnen . . . 1230 bis 1846. Hamburg 1847. pp.viii.328. [500.]

LEOPOLD LASSAR, Verzeichniss von sämmtlichen, während des jahres 1852 im buchhandel erschienenen deutschen dramatischen schriften. Berlin 1853. pp.32. [200.]

ADOLPH BÜCHTING, Catalog der in den jahren 1850–1859 in deutscher sprache erschienenen theaterstücke im original und uebersetzung. Nordhausen 1860. pp.iv.70. [750.]

—— 1860–1864. 1865. pp.56. [600.]

C. SCHÄFER and C. HARTMANN, Die königlichen theater in Berlin. Statistischer rückblick . . . von 5. December 1786 bis 31. December 1885. Berlin 1886. pp.[vii].304. [2900.]

—— [Supplement]. Georg Droescher, Die vormals königliche, jetzt preussischen staatstheater zu Berlin. Statistischer rückblick . . . 1. Januar 1886 bis 31. Dezember 1935. 1936. pp.149. [1259.]

C[ARL] A[UGUST] H[UGO] BURKHARDT, Das repertoire des weimarischen theaters unter Goethes leitung, 1791–1817. Theatergeschichtliche forschungen (vol.i): Hamburg &c. 1891. pp.xl.152. [648.]

KARL BIESENDAHL, Deutsches theaterjahrbuch. Ein bibliographisches handbuch der dramatischen literatur der gegenwart. Berlin 1892. pp.x.510.

KARL GLOSSY, Fach-katalog der abtheilung für deutsches drama und theater. Internationale ausstellung für musik und theaterwesen: Wien 1892. pp.xvi.550. [500.]

KONRAD GRETHLEIN, Allgemeiner deutscher theaterkatalog. Ein verzeichnis der im druck und handel befindlichen bühnenstücke und dramatischen erzeugnisse. Münster i. W. 1894. pp.[iv]. coll.808. [15,000.]

P[AUL] BAHLMANN, Jesuiten-dramen der niederrheinischen ordensprovinz. Centralblatt für bibliothekswesen (beiheft 15): Leipzig 1896. pp.iv. 351. [502.]

FRIEDRICH WALTER, Archiv und bibliothek des Grossh. hof- und nationaltheaters in Mannheim. Leipzig 1899. pp.[iii].486+[iii].442. [5000.]

ROBERT F. ARNOLD, Bibliographie der deutschen bühnen seit 1830. Wien 1908. pp.24. [400.]
— — Zweite . . . auflage. Strassburg 1909. pp. 57. [500.]

ADOLF BARTELS, Chronik des weimarischen Hoftheaters, 1817–1907. Weimar 1908. pp.xxxvi. 376. [1500.]

VERZEICHNIS der im verlage von Felix Bloch erben . . . erschienenen bühnenwerke. Berlin 1920. pp.292. [3712.]

MAXIMILIAN J[OSEF] RUDWIN, A historical and bibliographical survey of the german religious drama. University of Pittsburgh: Studies in language and literature: Pittsburgh 1924. pp.xxiii. 286. [4500.]

[FRIEDRICH ERNST SCHULZ], Schauspiel-mentor. Titel- und autoren-verzeichnis. Berlin [1926]. pp.48. [4000.]

—— [another edition]. Die weltdramatik. 1928. pp.302. [10,000.]

——— [supplement]. Bühnenwerke, 1929–30. 1931. pp.112.

——— Nachtrag.

   i. 1932. pp.16.

   ii. 1933. pp.16.

   iii. 1934. pp.16.

   iv. 1935. pp.16.

JOHANNES HÜBNER, Bibliographie des schlesischen musik- und theaterwesens. Historische kommission für Schlesien: Schlesische bibliographie (vol.vi, no.2): Breslau 1934. pp.xv.280. [drama: 621.]

JOSEPH PINATEL, Répertoire des drames bourgeois en Allemagne au XVIIIe siècle. Lyon 1938. pp.219. [3000.]

[MARIANNE SCHMIDT and   FENIMORE],

Fifty years of german drama. A bibliography of modern german drama, 1880–1930, based on the [Alfred] Loewenberg collection in the Johns Hopkins university library. Baltimore 1941. pp. ix.111. [3000.]

ALFRED JULIUS SCHMIDT, Allemão-portuguez, portuguez-allemão. Pequena lista da peças de theatro. Rio de Janeiro 1941. pp.102. [1240.]
lists of plays available in german and portuguese, but not necessarily originally written in those languages.

FRIEDRICH ERNST SCHULZ, Dramenlexikon. Ein wegweiser zu . . . urheberrechtlich geschützten bühnenwerken. Köln.
—— [another edition]. Dramenlexikon. Ein wegweiser zu . . . urheberrechtlich geschützten bühnenwerken der jahre 1945–1957. . . . Neu herausgegeben von Wilhelm Allgayer. Köln &c. [1958]. pp.594. [10,000.]

WILHELM KOSCH, Deutsches theater-lexikon. Biographisches und bibliographisches handbuch. Klagenfurt 1951– . pp.[vi].864+[v].865–1728 +
in progress.

CLAUDE HILL and RALPH LEY, The drama of german expressionism. A german-english bibliography. University of North Carolina: Studies in the germanic languages and literatures (no.28): Chapel Hill [1960]. pp.xii.211. [4011.]

DAS LAIENSPIEL in der ost- und mitteldeutschen kulturarbeit. Schriftenreihe zur förderung der ostdeutschen kulturarbeit (no.3): Kiel 1961. pp.31. [60.]

IRMTRUD PETERS, Theater, rundfunk und musik in Bremen. Eine bibliographie. Herausgegeben von Rolf Engelsing. Bremische bibliographie (vol.2): Bremen 1963. pp.65. [540.]

Great Britain

i. *Periodicals*

FELIX SPEER, The periodical press of London, theatrical and literary (excluding the daily newspaper), 1800–1830. Useful reference series (no. 60): Boston 1937. pp.58. [300.]

ii. *General*

LIST of plays wholly or partially the property of Thomas Hailes Lacy. 1864. pp.11. [400.]
issued for the Dramatic authors' society.

[JOHN GENEST], Some account of the english stage, from the restoration in 1660 to 1830. Bath 1932.

i. [1660–1690]. pp.[iv].cxl.500. [600.]
ii. [1691–1719]. pp.[iii].660. [750.]
iii. [1719–1742]. pp.[iii].656. [750.]
iv. [1741–1762]. pp.[iii].664. [750.]
v. [1762–1777]. pp.[iii].632. [750.]
vi. [1777–1790]. pp.[iii].607. [750.]
vii. [1790–1806]. pp.[iii].719. [750.]
viii. [1895–1819]. pp.[iii].704. [750.]
ix. [1818–1830. Old plays]. pp.[iii].600. [750.]
x. [Old plays in continuation. Plays printed,
   but not acted. Corrections and additions.
   Irish stage]. pp.[iii].551.viii. [600.]

*a supplement, continuing the lists from 1830 to
the closing years of the century, appears in Clement
Scott,* The drama of yesterday and to-day (*1899*),
ii.479–558.

CATALOGUE of dramatic pieces, the property of
the members of the Dramatic authors' society.
[1865]. pp.41. [1600.]

[WENTWORTH HOGG], Guide to selecting plays;
or, managers' companion. [1881]. pp.78. [1500.]
—— [another edition]. [1939]. pp.xvi.388.
[2250.]
   there are numerous intermediate editions.

THE DRAMA & poetry. Public libraries: Class

list of books in the reference library (no.6): Nottingham 1885. pp.50. [drama: 300.]

J[OHN] POTTER BRISCOE, Author-list of fiction, poetry, and the drama. Public lending library: Nottingham 1894. pp.viii.71. [9000.]

KATHARINE LEE BATES and LYDIA BOKER GODFREY, English drama. A working basis. Wellesley college: Boston [printed] 1896. pp.151. [4500.]
privately printed.

CATALOGUE of the [George] Becks collection of prompt books in the New York public library. [New York 1906]. pp.49. [1250.]

REGINALD CLARENCE [*pseud.* H. J. ELDRIDGE], 'The stage' cyclopædia. A bibliography of plays. An alphabetical list of plays . . . of which any record can be found since the commencement of the english stage. 1909. pp.504. [30,000.]
the number of play listed is incorrectly given on the titlepage as 'nearly 50,000'.

MATERIALS for the study of the english drama (excluding Shakespeare). A selected list of books in the Newberry library. Newberry library: Publications (no.1): Chicago 1912. pp.vii.90. [1250.]

DEBORAH B. MARTIN and SYBIL SCHUETTE, Plays

and books on the drama in the Kellogg public library. Green Bay, Wis. 1916. pp.9. [300.]

W[ILLIAM] DAVENPORT ADAMS, A dictionary of the drama. A guide to the plays, playwrights, players, and playhouses of the United Kingdom and America from the earliest times to the present. ... Vol.i. A–G. 1924. pp.viii.627. [10,000.]
no more published.

DRAMA loan service. Indiana university: Extension division: Bulletin (vol.xii, no.4): [Bloomington] 1926. pp.140. [1300.]

PLAYS. A guide to the works in the library of the National operatic and dramatic association. 1929. pp.153. [1593.]
— Supplement. [1933]. pp.24. [750.]

E. M. AUDREY HAULTAIN, Standard british drama from the fourteenth century to the nineteenth century, excluding the works of Shakespeare, also those of living authors. [National book council:] Bibliography (no.110): 1929. pp.[4]. [150.]

VIOLET KENT, The player's library and bibliography of the theatre. British drama league library: 1930. pp.xvi.401. [6500.]
[—] — [another edition]. The player's library: the catalogue of the library of the British drama

league. [By Margaret Burnham]. 1950. pp.iii–xvi. 1115. [30,000.]

LOAN play library service. Announcement of current plays, declamations, drama literature. University of Arizona: Record (vol.xxvi &c.): Tucson.

> 1932–1933. . . . (vol.xxvi, no.1). pp.54. [1500.]
>
> 1933–1934. . . . (vol.xxvii, no.1). pp.78. [1500.]
>
> 1937–1938. . . . (vol.xxxi, no.1). pp.99. [2000.]

MARJORIE JARVIS, HESTER THOMPSON and MARIE TREMAINE, Presentable plays . . . and how to produce them. Being a catalogue of the Provincial dramatic library of Ontario. [Toronto] 1933. pp. viii.64. [800.]

PLAYS and their production. Lancashire county library: [*s.l.*] 1936. pp.100. [1650.]

BERNARD SOBEL, *ed.* The theatre handbook and digest of plays. New York 1940. pp.xvi.21–908. [5000.]

reprinted in 1943 as a so-called second edition.

[J. BELL], Catalogue of play sets. Public libraries: Nottingham 1946. pp.79. [750.]

LOAN library play-list. University of Kansas: Bulletin (vol.49, no.15): Topeka 1948. pp.108. [5000.]

supplements are issued about every two years.

PLAYS for play reading and drama groups. Free public libraries: [Sheffield].
— Play catalogue. Third . . . edition. [1959]. pp.ii.101. [1250.]*

INDEX of plays available in the Bristol public libraries. Bristol 1950. pp.[iii].204. [7000.]*

IFAN KYRLE FLETCHER, British theatre, 1530–1900. An exhibition of books, prints, drawings, manuscripts and playbills. National book league: 1950. pp.72. [400.]

PLAYS for reading & production. Nottingham-shire county library: [Nottingham] 1951. pp.[ii]. 98. [2000.]

— [another edition]. 1953. pp.[iv].112. [2500.]
— — Supplement. 1958. pp.[23]. 400.]*

PLAY index. New York.
  1949–1952. Edited by Dorothy Herbert West and Dorothy Margaret Peake.
  1953–1960. Edited by Estelle A. Fidell and D. M. Peake. 1963. pp.404. [4592.]

A GUIDE to the play collection. Public libraries: Bristol 1955. pp.52. [600.]

PLAY reviews. National union of towns-wimen's guilds. 1955 &c.*
in progress.

SETS of plays for reading and production. Northamptonshire county library: [Northampton] 1957. pp.41. [867.]

DRAMA catalogue. Essex county library: Chelmsford 1958. pp.172. [5500.]

REPERTORY plays. Sets available for loan from the Central lending library. Second edition. [Manchester] 1958. pp.108. [2200.]

LIST of plays in english for adults and children. Natal provincial library service: Pietermaritzburg 1958. pp.[iv].86. [1250.]*

PLAYS and their plots. [1960]. pp.166. [750.]

A CATALOGUE of the play collection. Public libraries: Bristol 1960. pp.[iv].48. [500.]*

CATALOGUE of an exhibition "William Shakespeare to Christopher Fry". Shakespeare birthplace trust: [Stratford-upon-Avon 1963]. ff.17. [93.]*

GAIL PLUMMER, Dramatists' guide to selection of plays and musicals. Dubuque [1963]. pp.144.

Drama & Stage

iii. *Early drama*

[RICHARD ROGERS and WILLIAM LEY], An exact
and perfect catalogue [*sic*] of all playes that are
printed. [1656]. pp.[6]. [500.]

*issued with T. G[offe], The careless shepherdess
1656; reprinted by sir W. W. Greg, A list of masques
(1902), pp.xlvii–cxx.*

[EDWARD ARCHER], An exact and perfect catalogue of all the plaies that were ever printed;
together with all the authors names and what are
comedies, histories, interludes, masks, pastorals,
Tragedies. pp.   [600.]

*issued with Massinger, Middleton and Rowley,
The old law, 1656; reprinted by sir W. W. Greg, A
list of masques (1902), pp.xlvii–cxx.*

[FRANCIS KIRKMAN], A true, perfect, and exact
catalogue of all the comedies, tragedies, tragi-
comedies, pastorals, masques and interludes, that
were ever yet printed and published, till this
present year 1661. 1661. pp.16. [690.]

*issued with Tom Tyler and his wife, an excellent
old play, 1661; the whole was reprinted in the same
year, and reproduced in facsimile in 1912 as one of the
Tudor facsimile texts; the play list was reprinted by
sir W. W. Greg, A list of masques (1902), pp.xlvii–
cxx.*

[—] — till this present year 1671. [1671]. pp.16. [806.]

issued with [Pierre] Corneille, Nicomede, 1671; reprinted by sir W. W. Greg, A list of masques (1902), pp.xlvii–cxx.

[NICHOLAS COX], An exact catalogue of all the comedies, tragedies, tragi-comedies, opera's, masks, pastorals and interludes that were ever yet printed and published, till this present year 1680. Oxon. 1680. pp.[ii].16. [900.]

GERARD LANGBAINE, Momus triumphans: or the plagiaries of the english stage; expos'd in a catalogue of all the comedies, tragi-comedies, masques, tragedies, opera's, pastorals, interludes, &c. both ancient and modern, that were ever yet printed in England.... With an account of the various originals, as well english, french, and italian, as greek and latine; from whence most of them have stole their plots. 1688. pp.[xvi].32.[viii]. [1000.]

GERARD LANGBAINE, An account of the english dramatick poets. Or, some observations . . . on the lives and writings, of all those that have publish'd either comedies, tragedies, tragi-comedies, pastorals, masques, interludes, farces, or opera's in the english tongue. Oxford 1691. pp.[xvi].556. [xxxi]. [1000.]

—— [another edition]. The lives and characters of the english dramatick poets . . . improv'd
and continued down to this time, by a careful
hand [Charles Gildon]. 1698. pp.[xvi].182.[xvi].
[1200.]

reissued in the same year with a different imprint;
the British museum has several copies of each issue
containing voluminous notes and additions in ms. &.;
reissued again in 1699.

[WILLIAM MEARS], A true and exact catalogue of
all the plays that were ever yet printed in the
english tongue; . . . continued down to October,
1713. 1713. pp.16. [1500.]

reissued in 1715 with the following prefixed:

[—] — Continuation of the following catalogue of plays to October, 1715. To which is
prefix'd a catalogue of plays, printed in 12mo.
[1715]. pp.2. [130.]

[JOHN DOWNES], Roscius anglicanus, or an
historical review of the stage: after it had been
suppres'd by means of the late unhappy civil war,
begun in 1641, till the time of king Charles the IIˢ.
restoration in May 1660. . . . With the names of the
most taking plays; and modern poets . . . from
1660, to 1706. 1708. pp.[iv].52. [200.]

—— [another edition]. With additions, by . . .

Thomas Davies. [Edited by Francis Godolphin Waldron]. 1789. pp.70.[ii].26. [200.]

reprinted in The literary museum, *1792.*

— A fac-simile reprint. . . . With an historical preface by Joseph Knight. 1886. pp.xxxv.[iv].52. *135 copies printed.*

— [another edition]. Edited by Montague Summers. [1928]. pp.xviii.286.

[GILES JACOB], The poetical register: or, the lives and character of the english dramatick poets. With an acount of their writings. 1719. pp.[iii].vii.[xii]. 433[*sic*, 334].[xxii]. [1500.]

one of the British museum copies contains numerous ms. notes by Joseph Haslewood, and newspaper cuttings.

[—] — The poetical register: or, the lives and characters of all the english poets [&c.]. 1723. pp.[iii].vii.[xii].444[*si*, 344].[xx] + xxvi.[vii].328. [viii]. [Plays: 1550.]

the original issue of the second volume is entered below under Poetry: Great Britain; reissued in 1724.

[WILLIAM MEARS], A compleat catalogue of all the plays that were ever yet printed in the english language. 1719. pp.96. [1400.]

[—] — The second edition. Continued to this present year. 1726. pp.104. [1500.]

this is a reissue (the last page reprinted) of the first edition, with the addition of an 'appendix'.

[W. FEALES], A true and exact catalogue of all the plays and other dramatick pieces, that were ever yet printed in the english tongue, . . . continu'd down to April 1732. 1732. pp.36. [1750.]
issued with Ben Jonson, The three celebrated plays, 1732; the dates of most of the plays in the catalogue are supplied in ms. in a copy in the British museum.

THOMAS WHINCOP, Scanderbeg: or, love and liberty. A tragedy. . . . To which are added a list of all the dramatic authors, with some account of their lives; and of all the dramatic pieces ever published in the english language, to the year 1747. 1747. pp.[xii].viii.xx.320.[xxx]. [2000.]
one of the British museum copies contains numerous ms. additions by Joseph Haslewood, and newspaper cuttings.

W[ILLIAM] R[UFUS] CHETWOOD, The british theatre. Containing the lives of the english dramatic poets; with an account of all their plays. Dublin 1750. pp.[ii].xvi.[vi].200.[xxviii]. [2000.]
reissued London 1752.

THEATRICAL records: or, an account of english

dramatic authors, and their works. 1756. pp.135. [xxxii]. [2000.]

this is substantially a reprint from Colley Cibber's Apology[4] *(1756), ii.169–303.*

[DAVID ERSKINE BAKER], The companion to the play-house: or, an historical account of all the dramatic writers (and their works) that have appeared in Great Britain and Ireland, from the commencement of our theatrical exhibitions. 1764. pp.xlii.[336]+[380]. [5000.]

— — Biographia dramatica, or a companion to the playhouse. A new edition, carefully corrected, greatly enlarged, and continued . . . to 1782 [by Isaac Reed]. 1782. pp.lii.496+[iii].442. [6000.]

one of the British museum copies contains numerous additions in ms.; see also, below, the 1801 edition of Egerton's Theatrical remembrancer, *1788.*

— — Brought down to the end of November 1811, with very considerable additions and improvements throughout, by Stephen Jones. 1812. pp.lxxvi.384 + [ii].385–790 + [ii].404 + [ii]. 478. [8000.]

J[OHN] BROWNSMITH, The dramatic time-piece: or perpetual monitor. Being a calculation of the length of time every act takes in the performing, in all the acting plays at the Theatres-royal of

Drury-lane, Covent-garden, and Hay-market. 1767. pp.[iv].75.[iv]. [150.]

THE PLAYHOUSE pocket-companion, or theatrical vade-mecum: containing, I. A catalogue of all the dramatic authors who have written for the english stage, with a list of their works. . . . II. A catalogue of anonymous pieces. III. An index of plays and authors. 1779. pp.[iv].13–179. [2750.]

E[WARD] C[APELL], Notitia dramatica; or, tables of ancient plays, (from their beginning to the restoration of Charles the second) so many as have been printed, with their several editions. [1780]. pp.[64]. [1000.]

this is a reprint from the author's [Notes and various readings to Shakespeare]. Volume the third. The school of Shakespeare [*1779–1780*].

[JOHN EGERTON], Egerton's Theatrical remembrancer, containing a complete list of all the dramatic performances in the english language; their several editions. . . . Together with an account of those which . . . are unpublished, and a catalogue of such latin plays as have been written by english authors, from the earliest productions of the english drama to the end of the year MDCC-LXXXVII. 1788. pp.viii.354. [3500.]

— — Barker's Continuation of Egerton's Theatrical remembrancer, Baker's Biographia dramatica, &c. . . . to 1801. . . . By Walley Chamberlain Oulton. [1801]. pp.[iv].336. [4000.]

James Barker was the publisher.

— — Barker's complete list of plays . . . to 1803. To which is added a continuation to the Theatrical remembrancer. [By W. C. Oulton]. [1804]. pp. [iv].350. [4500.]

the text is a reissue of the 1801 edition, with a supplementary appendix.

— — The drama recorded; or, Barker's list of plays . . . to 1814. [By W. C. Oulton]. pp.[iv].212. [7000.]

a copy in the British museum contains a few additions in ms.

A NEW theatrical dictionary. Containing an account of all the dramatic pieces that have appeared from the commencement of theatrical exhibitions to the present time. 1792. pp.[viii]. 400. [3500.]

[WALLEY CHAMBERLAIN OULTON], The history of the theatres of London: containing an annual register of all the new and revived tragedies, comedies, operas, farces, pantomimes, &c., that have been performed at the theatres-royal, in

London, from the year 1771 to 1795. 1796. pp.vi.
196+vi.117[*si*, 217]. [1250.]

— — Continuation . . . from the year 1795 to
1817. 1817. pp.iv.384+[ii].360+266. [2000.]

THE THESPIAN dictionary: or, dramatic biography of the eighteenth century. 1802. pp.[284].
[1500.]

— — Second edition. 1805. pp.[398]. [2500.]

THOMAS GILLILAND, The dramatic mirror: containing the list of the stage, from the earliest
period to the present time; including a biographical and critical account of all the dramatic
writers, from 1660. 1808. pp.xii.630[*sic*, 624] +
[ii].625–1048. [1500.]

CATALOGUE of early english poetry and other
miscellaneous works, illustrating the british
drama, collected by Edmond Malone, esq., and
now preserved in the Bodleian library. Oxford
1836. pp.viii.52. [2000.]

JAMES O[RCHARD] HALLIWELL [–PHILLIPPS], A
dictionary of old english plays, existing either in
print or in manuscript, from the earliest times to
the close of the seventeenth century. Including also
notices of latin plays written by english authors.
1860. pp.viii.296. [2750.]

Drama & Stage

FREDERICK GARD FLEAY, A chronicle history of
the London stage, 1559–1642. 1890. pp.x.424.
[1750.]
*460 copies printed, most of which were destroyed by
fire; photographically reproduced, New York 1909.*

FREDERICK GARD FLEAY, A biographical chronicle of the english drama, 1559–1642. 1891. pp.
[vii].387+[v].406. [1750.]

W[ILLIAM] CAREW HAZLITT, A manual for the
collector and amateur of old english plays. Edited
from the material formed by Kirkman, Langbaine,
Downes, Oldys, and Halliwell-Phillipps, with
extensive additions and corrections. 1892. pp.[ii].
viii.284. [2500.]
250 copies printed.

A SHORT hand-list of english plays, masques, and
pageants from the time of queen Elizabeth to the
restoration. Grolier club: 1893. pp.67.
privately printed.

[SIR] WALTER WILSON GREG, A list of english
plays written before 1643 and printed before 1700.
Bibliographical society: 1900. pp.iii–xi.158.
[1250.]
— — [supplement]. A list of masques, pageants,
&c. 1902. pp.iii–xi.35.[ii].cxxxi. [125.]

DRAMATIC folios of the seventeenth century exhibited at the Grolier club. New York 1903. pp.27. [36.]

JEANETTE MARKS, English pastoral drama from the restoration to the date of the publication of the 'Lyrical ballads' (1660–1798). 1908. pp.xiii.228. [250.]

includes some italian and spanish pastorals.

ALLARDYCE NICOLL, A history of restoration drama, 1660–1700. Cambridge 1923. pp.vii.398. [450.]

—— Third edition. 1940. pp.ix.412. [450.]

ALLARDYCE NICOLL, A history of early eighteenth century drama, 1700–1750. Cambridge 1925. pp.xii.432. [1500.]

ALLARDYCE NICOLL, A history of late eighteenth century drama, 1750–1800. Cambridge 1927. pp. x.387. [2750.]

ISAK [G. A.] COLLIJN, The Hamilton collection of english plays in the Royal library, Stockholm. Uppsala 1927. pp.23. [103.]

A HANDLIST of english plays and masques printed before 1750 in the library of Worcester college, Oxford. Oxford 1929. pp.27. [900.]

— Plays added up to March, 1948. [1948]. pp.[8]. [225.]

ALLARDYCE NICOLL, A history of early nineteenth century drama, 1800–1850. Cambridge 1930. pp.x.234.xviii+[v].235–558. [8500.]
a supplement by R. Crompton Rhodes appears in The Library (*1936*), *4th ser., xvi.91–112, 210–231.*

W. P. BARRETT, Chart of plays, 1584 to 1623. Shakespeare association: Cambridge 1934. pp.40. [400.]

MONTAGUE SUMMERS, A bibliography of the restoration drama. [1935]. pp.143. [1500.]
250 copies printed.

DOUGALD MAC MILLAN, Drury Lane calendar, 1747–1776. . . . Published in co-operation with the Huntington library. Oxford 1938. pp.xxxiv. 364. [300.]

DOUGALD MAC MILLAN, Catalogue of the Larpent plays. Huntington library: Lists (no.4): San Marino 1939. pp.xv.442. [2502.]

WILLARD AUSTIN KINNE, Revivals and importations of french comedies in England, 1749–1800. New York 1939. pp.xv.310. [500.]

[SIR] W[ALTER] W[ILSON] GREG, A bibliography of the english printed drama to the restoration.

Bibliographical society: Illustrated monographs (no.xxiv): 1939– . pp.xxxv.492+xxxv.493–1008+ .

ALFRED HARBAGE, Annals of english drama 975–1700. An analytical record of all plays, extant or lost. Philadelphia 1940. pp.viii.264. [1500.]

a supplement by Alfred Howard Carter appears in Modern philology (*Chicago 1942*), *pp.201–212.*

HENRY W. WELLS, A chronological list of extant plays produced in or about London, 1581–1642. New York 1940. pp.[ii].17. [450.]

[GERARD EADES BENTLEY], A rough check-list of the university of Chicago libraries holdings in seventeenth century editions of plays in english. [Chicago 1942]. ff.[i].26. [500.]

reproduced from typewriting.

GERTRUDE L. WOODWARD and JAMES G[ILMER] MCMANAWAY, A check list of english plays, 1641–1700. Newberry library: Chicago 1945. pp.[ix]. 155. [1350.]

— — A supplement . . . by Fredson Bowers. University of Virginia: Bibliographical society: Charlottesville 1949. ff.22. [75.]*

ALLARDYCE NICOLL, A history of late nineteenth century drama, 1850–1900. Volume II.

[Hand-list of plays produced between 1850 and 1900]. Cambridge 1946. pp.[v].229–772. [17,500.]

G. WILLIAM BERGQUIST, Three centuries of english and american plays: a checklist. England: 1500–1800, United States: 1714–1830. New York &c. 1963. pp.xii.281. [5500.]*

ALFRED HARBAGE, Annals of english drama, 975–1700. . . . Revised by S. Schoenbaum. [1964]. pp.xvii.321.

iv. *Modern drama*

HENRY EASTMAN LOWER and GEORGE HERON MILNE, The dramatic books and plays (in english) published during 1913 [&c.]. Boston.

    1913. pp.37. [500.]
    1914. pp.44. [600.]
    1915. pp.62. [800.]
    1916. pp.42. [600.]

no more published; issued as a supplement to F. W. Faxon, The dramatic index.

FLORENCE E[LIZABETH] FOSHAY, Twentieth century dramas. Public library: Library school: New York 1915. pp.12. [400.]

MODERN english drama. Public libraries: Subject lists (no.3): Newport [Mon.] 1925. pp.4. [150.]

INA TEN EYCK FIRKINS, Index to plays, 1800–

1926. New York 1927. pp.[ix].307. [7872.]

—— Supplement. 1935. pp.ix.140. [3284.]

PLAYS of today; 100 of the best modern dramas. A reading list for students. Brown university: [Providence, R.I. 1927]. pp.36. [100.]

MODERN drama, 1900–1938. A select list of plays published since 1900, and of works on dramatic theory and other related subjects. Library association: County libraries section: 1939. pp.v. 77. [2600.]

— 1939–1945. 1946. pp.iv.44. [1225.]

DOROTHY H[ERBERT] WEST and DOROTHY M[ARGARET] PEAKE, Play index, 1949–1952. New York 1953. pp.239. [2616.]

POSTWAR drama. Surrey county library: Book list (no.18): [Esher 1959]. pp.[iii].24. [225.]*

v. *Special types and subjects*

ELIZABETH A[PTHORP] MCFADDEN and LILIAN E. DAVIS, A selected list of plays for amateurs and students of dramatic expression. Cincinnati 1907. pp.96. [500.]

reissued London 1908.

A GUIDE and index to plays, festivals and masques for use in school, clubs and neighborhood centers. New York &c. 1913. pp.[iii].44. [200.]

SELECT list of references on children's drama and theatre. Library of Congress: Washington 1913. ff.5. [57.]*

JOHN MANTEL CLAPP, Plays for amateurs. Drama league of America: Chicago 1915. pp.48. [197.]
— — [another edition]. Arranged by Winifred Ward. 1922. pp.32. [300.]

SAMUEL KAPLAN, Actable one-act plays. Public library: Chicago 1916. pp.15. [150.]

DRAMATIZED tales. Novels, short stories, poems, legends, and fairy tales, together with their dramatizations. A select list. Public library: Brooklyn 1917. pp.23. [250.]

GERTRUDE E[LIZABETH] JOHNSON, Choosing a play. Suggestions and bibliography for the director of amateur dramatics. New York [1918]. pp. [ii].41. [500.]
— — Revised. 1920. pp.xi.177. [500.]

E[LSIE] V[ENNER] ANDREWS, Dramatization in the grades. Reference list of fables, fairy tales, stories, and historical events which have been dramatized. Useful reference series (no.22): Boston 1919. pp.v.32. [650.]

also issued as Michigan state normal college, Library bulletin (no.4).

FRANK SHAY, The plays and books of the little theatre. New York 1919. pp.72. [900.]

— — [another edition]. One thousand and one plays for the little theatre. Cincinnati [1923]. pp.91.

DANIEL C[ARL] HASKELL, Foreign plays in english. A list of translations in the New York public library. New York 1920. pp.[iii].86. [1750.]

MICHAEL J. CONROY, One act plays in English, 1900–1920. Public library: Brief reading lists (no.14): Boston 1920. pp.[iii].40. [450.]

FREDERICK [HENRY] KOCH and NETTINA STRO-BACH, Plays for schools and little theatres. University of North Carolina: Extension bulletin (vol.ix, no.8): Chapel Hill 1921. pp.88. [700.]

— — A new descriptive list. By F. H. Koch, Betty Smith, Robert Finch. . . . (vol.xvi, no.4): 1937. pp.vii.111. [1000.]

BRITISH and american longer plays, 1900–1923. Public library: Brief reading lists (no.26): Boston 1923. pp.[ii].66. [800.]

S[AMUEL] MARION TUCKER, Plays for amateurs. A selected list. Second edition. New York 1923. pp.34. [350.]

CECILIA M[ARY] YOUNG, A catalogue and review of plays for amateurs. Chicago 1923. pp.152. [2500.]
— — [another edition]. 1924. pp.190. [3000.]

SARA TRAINOR FLOYD, One hundred plays for out-door theatres. A selected list. New York 1924. pp.[x].19.

HANNAH LOGASA and WINIFRED VER NOOY, An index to one-act plays. Useful reference series (no.30): Boston 1924. pp.327. [4250.]
— — Supplement 1924–1931.... (no.46): 1932. pp.[iv].432. [6000.]
— — Second supplement 1932–1940. . . . (no. 68): 1941. pp.[iv].556. [8000.]
— — Third supplement 1941–1948.... (no.78): 1950. pp.318. [3000.]

FRANK SHAY, A guide to longer plays. New York &c. 1925. pp.[vii].131. [1250.]

LIST of pageants and plays for children, for young people, for adults. National council for prevention of war: Education department: Washington [c.1928]. ff.6.7.7. [122.]*

MARJORIE SELIGMAN and LOUISE M[ICHELBACHER] FRANKENSTEIN, Plays for junior and senior high school. New York 1931. pp.89. [400.]
— — Second . . . edition. 1932. pp.47. [750.]

EDWARD D[AVIDSON] COLEMAN, The Bible in english drama. An annotated list of plays, including translations from other languages. Public library: New York 1931. pp.iv.212. [3250.]
— — [supplement]. The Jew in english drama. [Edited by Daniel Carl Haskell]. 1943. pp.xx.237.

AEOLA L. HYATT, Index to children's plays. Third edition. American library association: Chicago 1931. pp.ix.214. [2500.]

A LIST of plays for village players. British drama league: 1934. pp.[ii].34. [600.]

A LIST of plays for boys and men. British drama league: [1934]. pp.[iv].259–348. [225.]

A LIST of plays for girls and women. British drama league: [1934]. pp.[iv].179–263. [225.]

MILTON [MYERS] SMITH, Guide to play selection. A descriptive index of full-length and short plays for production by schools, colleges and little theaters. National council of teachers of english: New York &c. 1934. pp.ix.174. [1000.]

HILAH PAUL MIER, An index to holiday plays for schools. New York 1936. pp.[vii].59. [1200.]

HAROLD A[DAM] EHRENSPERGER, A dramatic calendar for churches. International council of religious education: Chicago [1937]. pp.63. [1000.]

FLORENCE S[ELMA] HELLMAN, The radio drama. A bibliographical list. Library of Congress: Washington] 1937. ff.12. [133.]*

THE GUIDE to plays for amateurs. (Revised edition). [1938]. pp.3-153. [750.]

JEAN CARTER [OGDEN], Annotated list of labor plays. Affiliated schools for workers: Labor education service: New York [1938]. ff.[ii].18. 19.[200.]*
— — Revised by J. C. Ogden and Nancy Faulkner. [1945]. ff.[iii].20. [75.]*

NORMA OLIN IRELAND and DAVID E. IRELAND, An index to monologs and dialogs. Useful reference series (no.65): Boston 1939. pp.xxiii.127. [4000.]

PLAYS for adults (two or more acts) for school and community use. University of Florida: General extension division record (vol.xxi, no.5): Gainesville 1939. pp.48. [900.]

SUBJECT index to children's plays. American

library association: Chicago 1940. pp.xx.279.
[7500.]

CATALOGUE of plays for children, plays for
theatre and puppetry. Association of the Junior
leagues of America: New York [1942]. ff.[ii].72.
[500.]*

PLAY library service for school and community.
University of South Carolina: Extension division:
Bulletin (new ser., no.xvi): Columbia 1942. pp.65.
[2000.]

DRAMA loan service. Loan library play-list . . .
for the director and teacher. University of Kansas:
Bulletin (vol.44, no.23): Topeka 1943. pp.79.
[4000.]

RELIGIOUS drama. Compiled by the Religious
drama society. National book council: Book list
(no.201): 1944. pp.[4]. [150.]

BERNARD J. STARKOFF, 250 selected plays of
jewish interest. An index. Union of american
hebrew congregations: Cincinnati [1945]. ff.xi.133
[*sic*, 135]. [250.]

RUTH GIBBONS THOMSON, Index to full length
plays, 1926 to 1944. Useful reference series (no.71):
Boston 1946. pp.ix.306. [1500.]

ENGLISH theatre guild's catalogue [of plays for amateur dramatic societies]. [1948]. pp.[vii].23. [100.]

JOAN M[ARY] COLLINS, Books and material for school and youth drama. Theatre in education series: 1950. pp.112. [1500.]

CATALOGUE of religious plays. Recommended by the Committee on religious drama appointed by the conference of the Methodist church. [1951]. pp.16. [153.]

JESSIE POWELL and KATHLEEN BAINBRIDGE-BELL, A catalogue of selected plays. Religious drama society: Library: 1951. pp.77. [750.]

PLAYS and entertainments for schools, clubs, churches, and other community groups. University of Minnesota: Bulletin (vol.liv., no.46): Minneapolis 1951. pp.109. [4700.]

A. H. WHARRIER, Worthwhile one-act plays. [Revised edition]. British drama league: [1952]. pp.[52]. [370.]

WILLIS KNAPP JONES, Latin America through drama in english. Pan american union: Bibliographical monographs (no.i): Washington 1950. ff. [iii].12. [125.]*

an earlier edition appeared in Hispania (*May 1945*).

J. C. TREWIN, Verse drama since 1800. National book league: Reader's guides (2nd ser., no.8): Cambridge 1956. pp.27. [100.]

SPOTLIGHT. Part one — one-act play. East riding county library: Beverley 1960. pp.55. [3500.]

MATHEW O'MAHONY, Progress guide to anglo-irish plays. Dublin [1960]. pp.xx.184. [500.]

A CATALOGUE of short plays for schools, clubs, churches, and other community groups. University of Minnesota: Drama advisory service: Minneapolis 1962. pp.73. [2000.]*

ROBERT ALFRED O'BRIEN, Spanish plays in english translation. An annotated bibliography. American educational theatre association: New York 1963. pp.70.

vi. *Works on the drama and stage*

[JAMES ORCHARD HALLIWELL-PHILLIPPS], A list of works illustrative of the life and writings of Shakespeare, the history of Stratford-on-Avon, and the rise and progress of the early english drama, printed for ... J. O. Halliwell. 1867. pp.71. [82.]

[J. O. HALLIWELL-PHILLIPPS], A brief hand-list of the selected parcels in the shakespearian and dramatic collections of J. O. Halliwell-Phillipps. 1876. pp.32. [450.]

[J. O. HALLIWELL-PHILLIPPS], An inventory of a selected portion of manuscripts and printed books, chiefly relating to Shakespeare and the old english drama, in the library of J. O. Halliwell-Phillipps. Brighton 1883. ff.8. [67.]

25 copies printed.

[J. O. HALLIWELL-PHILLIPPS], A hand-list of sixty folio volumes, containing collections made by J. O. Halliwell-Phillipps, from 1864 to 1887, on the life of Shakespeare, and the history of the english stage. Brighton 1887. pp.7. [60.]

ROBERT W[ILLIAM] LOWE, A bibliographical account of english theatrical literature from the earliest times to the present day. 1888. pp.xii.384. [3000.]

500 copies printed.

THE DRAMATIC index. . . . Covering articles and illustrations concerning the stage and its players in the periodicals of American and England; with a record of books on the drama and of texts of plays. Boston.

1909. Edited by Frederick Winthrop Faxon. pp.241–468. [4000.]
1910. pp.260. [5000.]
1911. pp.250. [5000.]

1912. pp.322. [6000.]

1913. pp.329.37. [6500.]

1914. pp.298.44. [6000.]

1915. pp.326.62. [7000.]

1916. pp.297.42. [6000.]

1917. pp.236. [4500.]

1918. pp.196. [4000.]

1919. pp.223. [4500.]

1920. pp.289. [5500.]

1921. pp.237.85. [5500.]

1922. pp.264.80. [6000.]

1923. pp.232.64. [5500.]

1924. pp.254.93. [6000.]

1925. pp.250.76. [6000.]

1926. pp.269.70. [6000.]

1927. pp.264.65. [6000.]

1928. pp.281.74. [6500.]

1929. pp.254.60. [6000.]

1930. pp.286.70. [6500.]

1931. pp.284.68. [6500.]

1932. pp.264.63. [6000.]

1933. pp.320.64. [7000.]

1934. pp.286.72. [6500.]

1935. pp.333.92. [7500.]

1936. Edited by Mary E[stella] Bates. pp.324. 83. [7000.]

1937. pp.296.86. [6500.]

1938. pp.295.77. [6500.]

1939. pp.332.134. [7500.]

1940. pp.293.119. [6500.]

1941. Edited by M. E. Bates and Anne C. Sutherland. pp.268.102. [6000.]

1942. pp.234.78. [5500.]

1943. pp.243.75. [5500.]

1944. Edited by A. C. Sutherland. pp.251.70. [5500.]

1945. pp.244.51. [5500.]

1946. pp.293.71. [6500.]

1947. Edited by A. C. Sutherland and Beulah C. Rathburn. pp.375.81. [8000.]

1948. [1950]. pp.336.93. [7000.]

1949. Edited by A. C. Sutherland and John F. Shea. [1952]. pp.392.89. [8000.]

issued as part II of the Annual magazine subject-index.

ALLARDYCE NICOLL, What to read on english drama. Public libraries: Leeds 1930. pp.30. [200.]

HISTORY of British drama. A selected list of books compiled by the British drama league. Fifth edition. National book council: Book list (no.56): 1935. pp.[4]. [60.]

COMMUNITY drama. A selected list of books compiled by the British drama league. Fourth edition. [National book council]: Book list (no.

31): 1936. pp.[2]. [60.]
— Fifth edition. 1942. pp.[4]. [100.]

NATIONAL theatre. House of commons: Library: Bibliography (no.57): [1948]. pp.7. [41.]*

ENGLISH dramatic criticism, 1910–1930: a brief list of references. Library of Congress: Washington 1949. ff.5. [33.]*

REGISTER of playbills, programmes and theatre cuttings. British museum: Department of printed books: [1950]. ff.54. [2000.]*

ALFRED LOEWENBERG, The theatre of the British Isles excluding London. A bibliography. Society for theatre research: 1950. pp.ix.75. [2000.]

LIBRARY catalogue. Society for theatre research: [1953]. pp.[iv].37. [400.]*

ALEC CLUNES, British theatre history. National book league: Reader's guides (2nd ser., no.iii): Cambridge 1955. pp.27. [100.]

Greece

PAUL GEISSLER, Chronologie der altattischen komödie. Philologische untersuchungen (no. xxx): Berlin 1925. pp.[v].86. [100.]

M[ADELEINE] HORN-MONVAL, Répertoire bibliographique des traductions et adaptations françaises du théâtre étranger du xvᵉ siècle à nos jours. Tome I. Théâtre grec antique. 1958. pp.viii.123. [2388.]

Hungary

LAJOS BARTA, A magyar színműirodalom könyvjegyzéke. Budapest 1899. pp.44. [1000.]

GÉZA STAUD, Bibliographia theatralis hungarica. Magyar színészeti bibliografía. Magyar színháztudományi és színpadművészeti társaság: Budapest 1938. pp.352. [1560.]

EMRO JOSEPH GERGELY, Hungarian drama in New York. American adaptations 1908–1940. Philadelphia 1947. pp.[ix].197. [53.]

KÁROLY SAKÁTS, A magyar szinikritika 1945–től 1949–ig. Fővárosi lapok, adattár. Szinháztörténeti füzetek (no.38): Budapest 1960. pp.170. [376.]*

India

MONTGOMERY SCHUYLER, A bibliography of the sanskrit drama. Columbia university: Indo-iranian series (vol.iii): New York 1906. pp.xi.105. [750.]

Ireland

S. C. HUGHES, The pre-victorian drama in Dublin. Dublin 1904. pp.[iii].ix.179. [250.]

KATHARINE LEE BATES, The new irish drama. Drama league of America: [*s.l.* 1911]. pp.16. [75.]

JAMES J. O'NEILL, A bibliographical account of irish theatrical literature. . . . Part I. — General theatrical history, players, and theatrical periodicals. Bibliographical society of Ireland (vol.i, no.6): Dublin 1920. pp.[iv].61–88. [200.]
no more published.

IRISH plays: [Compiled by Play department, National service bureau]. Works progress administration: Federal theatre project (National service bureau, publication no.47–L): New York 1938. ff.[ii].xiii.110. [100.]

MATHEW O'MAHONY, Progress guide to anglo-irish plays. Dublin [1960]. pp.xx.184. [500.]

Italy

LEONE ALLACCI, Drammatvrgia. Roma 1666. pp.[xxiv].816. [2250.]
—— Accresciuta e continuata [by Giovanni Cedoni and Giovanni degli Agostini. Edited by Girolamo Zanetti]. Venezia 1755. pp.[viii].coll. 1016. [6000.]
a copy in the British museum contains additions in ms.; an index of composers, by Joseph de Filippi, appears in La chronique musicale *(1874), vi.31.*

[DU GÉRARD], Tables alphabétique & chronologique des pièces représentées sur l'ancien théâtre
italien, depuis son établissement jusqu'en 1697
qu'il a été fermé. 1750. pp.xiv.119.

[JACOPO MORELLI], Catalogo di commedie italiane. Venezia 1776. pp.vi.179.28. [1000.]
*a catalogue of the collection formed by Tommaso
Giuseppe Farsetti.*

VISCOUNT [PAUL] COLOMB DE BATINES, Bibliografia delle antiche rappresentazioni italiane sacre
e profane stampate nei secoli XV e XVI. Firenze
1852. pp.92. [1250.]
*150 copies printed; a supplement by Enrico Narducci
appears in* Il bibliofilo (*Firenze 1881*), ii.73–74,
87–88.

LODOVICO SETTIMO SILVESTRI, Effemeridi sto-
rico - critico - statistico - biografico - artistico -
bibliografiche teatrali o serie cronologica di tutte
le rappresentazioni dei teatri di Milano da 1547 a
tutt' oggi. Milano 1874.

GIOVANNI MARTINAZZI, Accademia de' Filo-
drammatica di Milano (già Teatro patriottico).
Milano 1879. pp.[iii].180. [750.]

GIOVANNI and CARLO SALVIOLI, Bibliografia
universale del teatro drammatico italiano, con

particolare riguardo alla storia della musica italiana.... Volume primo. Venezia [1894–] 1903. pp.ix.coll.936.56. [10,000.]

A–Czarina only; no more published; a supplement by Mario Menghini appears in the Rivista delle bibliotheche *(1896), vi.64–77.*

CATALOGO delle produzioni teatrali ... tutelate dalla società. Società italiana degli autori: Milano 1896. pp.[iv].335. [4000.]

has numerous blank pages.

—— Aggiunte. [1896]. single leaf. [11.]

—— Aggiunte ... (num.2). [1897]. ff.[6]. [100.]

[DIOMEDE BONAMICI], Bibliografia delle cronistorie dei teatri d'Italia. Livorno 1896. pp.22. [100.]

100 copies printed.

—— Seconda edizione. 1905. pp.29. [150.]

150 copies printed; a supplement by Guido Bustico appears in the Rivista musicale italiana *(1919). xxvi.*

LUIGI RASI, I comici italiani. Biografia, bibliografia, iconografia. Firenze [1894–] 1897–1905. pp.viii.1068+[vi].786. [2500.]

SELECT list of references on italian drama, chiefly modern. Library of Congress: Washington 1911. ff.8. [86.]*

[LUIGI RASI], Catalogo generale della raccolta drammatica italiana di Luigi Rasi. Firenze 1912. pp.360.

C. MICLASCEFSKY [KONSTANTIN MIKLASHEVSKY], Опыть библіографи. . . . Saggio di bibliografia della Commedia all'improviso. [Петербургъ 1917]. pp.xiv. [342.]
also issued as a supplement to the author's La commedia dell'arte, *1914–1917*.

CESARE LEVI, Il teatro. Guide bibliografiche: Roma 1921. pp.[ii].87. [400.]
limited to the contemporary theatre.

LUIGI FERRARI, Le traduzioni italiane del teatro tragico francese nei secoli XVIIᵉ e XVIIIᵉ Saggio bibliografico. Revue de littérature comparée: Bibliothèque (vol.xiii): 1925. pp.iii–xxiii.311. [600.]

NARDO LEONELLI, Attore tragici, attore comici. Enciclopedia biografica e bibliografica "italiana" (9th ser.): Milano [1940–1944]. pp.477+3–491. [5000.]

SANDRO PIANTANIDA, LAMBERTO DIOTALLEVI and GIANCARLO LIVRAGHI, Autori italiani del seicento. Catalogo bibliografico. IV. Il teatro. Milano 1951. pp.xiii.309. [431.]

Drama & Stage

UMBERTO MANFERRARI, Dizionario universale delle opere melodrammatiche. Biblioteca bibliographica italica (vols.4, 8, 10): Firenze 1954–1957. pp.3–412+3–410+3–442. [20,000.]

M[ADELEINE] HORN-MONVAL, Répertoire bibliographique des traductions et adaptations françaises du théâtre étranger du xve à nos jours. Tome III. 1. Théâtre italien. 2. Opéras italiens (livrets). Centre national de la recherche scientifique: 1960. pp.180. [2175.]

BEATRICE CORRIGAN, Catalogue of italian plays, 1500–1700, in the library of the university of Toronto. Toronto 1961. pp.xviii.134. [500.]*

Japan

LIST of references on japanese pantomimes. Library of Congress: Washington 1915. ff.2. [13.]*

SHIO SAKANISHI, MARION H[ELEN] HADDINGTON and P[ERCIVAL] D[ENSMORE] PERKINS, A list of translations of japanese drama into english, french, and german. American council of learned societies: Washington 1935. pp.viii.89. [550.]*

RENÉ SIEFFERT, Bibliographie du théâtre japonais. Maison franco-japonaise: Bulletin (no.iii): Tōkyō 1954. pp.[iii].154. [700.]

Drama & Stage

Jews

A. S. FREIDUS, List of dramas in the New York public library relating to the Jews, and of dramas in hebrew, judeo-spanish, and judeo-german, together with essays on the jewish stage. New York 1907. pp.34. [457.]

Latin

P[AUL] BAHLMANN, Die lateinischen dramen vom Wimphelings Stylpho bis zur mitte des sechzehnten jahrhunderts, 1480–1550. Münster 1893. pp.114. [1000.]

M[ADELEINE] HORN-MONVAL, Répertoire bibliographique des traductions et adaptations françaises du théâtre étranger, du XVᵉ siècle à nos jours. Tome II. 1: Théâtre latin antique. 2: Théâtre latin médiéval et moderne. 1959. pp.115. [1957.]

Mexico

FRANCISCO MONTERDE [GARCÍA ICAZBALCETA], Bibliografía del teatro en México. Monografías bibliográficas mexicanas (no.28): México 1933. pp.lxxx.652. [3000.]

RUTH S. LAMB, Bibliografía del teatro mexicano del siglo XX. Colección studium (no.33): México 1962. pp.144. [3500.]

Drama & Stage

Netherlands

[JOHANNES HILMAN], Alphabetisch overzicht der tooneelstukken in de bibliotheek van Joh⁵ Hilman [vols.(ii)–iii: Ons tooneel]. Amsterdam [Leiden] 1878–1881. pp.[vii].355+ + .
privately printed.

TH[OMAS] J[AMES] I. ARNOLD, Nederlandsch tooneel. Met supplement bewerkt door Louis D[avid] Petit. Maatschappij der nederlandsche letterkunde te Leiden: Bibliotheek: Catalogus (vol.ii, part 3): Leiden 1887. pp.cclxxix. [4000.]

[F. Z. MEHLER and M. B. MENDES DA COSTA], Tooneel-catalogus. Nederland. Universiteit: Bibliotheek: Amsterdam 1895. pp.vii.coll.ccxvi. [2000.]

GERD AAGE GILLHOFF, The Royal dutch theatre [Koninklijke nederduitsche schouwburg] at The Hague, 1804–1876. The Hague 1938. pp.iii–xi.205. [1000.]

LIEN KESLER-VAN TWISK, Jeugdtooneel. Een poging tot samenstelling van . . . tooneelstukken . . . voor kinderen, jongeren en jeugdige volwassenen. Tweede druk. Arnhem 1940. pp.107.

Drama & Stage

Norway

CARL JUST, Litteratur om norsk teater. Små-skrifter for bokvenner (no.81): Oslo 1953. pp.32. [100.]

400 copies printed.

Oriental

LIST of works in the New York public library relating to the oriental drama. [New York 1906]. pp.6. [175.]

Persia

ETTORE ROSSI and ALESSIO BOMBACI, Elenco di drammi religiosi persiani (fondo mss. vaticani Cerulli). Biblioteca apostolica vaticana: Studi e testi (no.209): Città del Vaticano 1961. pp.[ii]. lx.416. [1200.]

Philippines

W[ENCESLAS] E[MILIO] RETANA, Noticias histó-rico-bibliográficas de el teatro en Filipinas desde sus origenes hasta 1898. Madrid 1909. pp.184. [100.]

Poland

i. Periodicals

STEFAN STRAUS, Bibliografia tytułów czasopism teatralnych. Państwowy instytut sztuki: Washington 1953. pp.156. [389.]

Drama & Stage

ii. *General*

K[AROL] ESTREICHER, Repertoar sceny polskiej od roku 1750 do 1871. Pisarze i tłumacze sceniézni. Kraków 1871. pp.76. [7500.]

LUDWIK BERNACKI, Teatr, dramat i muzyka za Stanisława Augusta. Zakład narodowa imienia Ossolińskich: Lwów 1925. pp.xv.475 + 444. [1000.]

KATALOG wystawy zbiorów teatralnych i muzycznych. Bibljoteka narodowa: Katalogi wystaw (vol.iii): Warszawa 1934. pp.[viii].155. [drama: 624.]

JAN LORENTOWICZ, Teatr polski w Warszawie, 1913–1938. Warszawa 1938. pp.lxxvi.107. [361.]

MARION MOORE COLEMAN, Polish drama and theatre. Articles, monographs, translations available in english. A tentative bibliography compiled for the Association of teachers of slavonic and east european languages. Columbia university: New York 1946. pp.6. [60.]*

PIOTR CRZEGORCZYK, Teatr ochotniczy i tańce polskie. Bibliografia informacyjna. Warszawa 1948. pp.64. [306.]

MARIA KRYSTINA MACIEJEWSKA and ANNA
POLAKOWSKA, Czasopisma teatralne dziesięcio-
lecia, 1944–1953. Bibliografia zawartósci. Materiały do dziejów teatru w Polsce (vol.iii): Wrocław
1956. pp.xvi.659. [20,000.]

STEFAN STRAUS, Bibliografia żródel do historii
teatru w Polsce. Drucki zwarte i ulotne. Polska
akademia nauk: Instytut badań literackich:
Wrocław 1957. pp.xi.495. [2980.]

WANDA RENIKOWA, Historia teatru w Polsce.
Bibliografia prac o polskim teatrze ogłoszonych
drukiem w latach 1945–1959. Warszawa 1960.
pp.84. [213.]*

Portugal, see also *Spain*

ALFRED JULIUS SCHMIDT, Allemão-portuguez,
portuguez-allemão. Pequena lista da peças de
theatro. Rio de Janeiro 1941. pp.102. [1240.]
*lists of plays available in german and portuguese, but
not necessarily originally written in those languages.*

Russia

драмматической словарь, или показанія
по алфавиту всѣхъ россійскихъ театраль-
ныхъ сочиненій и переводовъ. Москвѣ 1787.
pp.166. [350.]

*a type-facsimile was published St Petersburg 1880
[on cover: 1881].*

PIMEN ARAPOV, Лѣтопись русскаго театра.
С.-Петербургъ 1861. pp.[iv].iii.387. [1000.]

M[IKHAIL] N[IKOLAIEVICH] LONGINOV, Рус-
скій театръ въ Петербургѣ и Москвѣ (1749–
1774). Сборникъ отдѣленія русскаго языка
и словесности Императорской академіи
наукъ (vol.xi, no.1): Санктпетербургъ 1873.
pp.[ii]. 38. [500.]
also issued as vol.xxiii, no.2 of the Academy's
Записки.

[A. I. VOLF], Хроника петербургскихъ
театровъ съ конца 1826 до начала 1855 года.
Часть II. Статистике драматической. С.-Пе-
тербургъ 1877. pp.iv.214.lvi. [1750.]

N[IKOLAI] M[IKHAILOVICH] LISOVSKY, Обозрѣніе литературы по театру и музыкѣ за
1889–1891 гг. С.-Петербургъ 1893. pp.62. [334.]
25 copies printed.

V. P. POGOZHEV, Столѣтіе организацій
императорскихъ московскихъ театровъ...
выпускъ первый. Книга II.... Послѣдова-
тельный, по днямъ, репертуаръ... съ 1806 г.
по 1825 г. включительно. С.-Петербургъ
1908. pp.[iii].v.304. [2500.]

каталогъ изданій журнала Театръ и искусство съ указаніемъ. [St Petersburg] 1914. pp.159. [1500.]

covers the period 1897–1914.

— 1-й дополнительный. [1915]. pp.10. [175.]

v[SEVOLOD NIKOLAEVICH] VSEVOLODSKY, Библіографическій и хронологическій указатель матеріаловъ по исторіи театра въ Россіи въ XVII и XVIII в.в. Народный комиссаріатъ по просвѣщенію: Театральный отдѣлъ: Сборникъ историко-театральной секціи (vol.i, no.8): Петроградъ 1918. pp.71. [2000.]

A SHORT list of references on the russian theater. Library of Congress: Washington 1923. ff.2. [22.]*

N[IKOLAI] A[LEKSANDROVICH] RAVICH, *ed.* Репертуарный указатель ГРК [Главный комитет по контролю над репертуаром]. Москва 1929. pp.197.

H. W. L. DANA, Handbook on soviet drama. . . . Lists of theatres, plays, operas, ballets, films and books and articles about them. American russian institute for cultural relations with the Soviet Union: New York 1938. pp.158. [2500.]

VEN[IAMIN EVGENEVICH] VISHNEVSKY, Театральная периодика... библиографический

указатель. Всероссийское театральное об-
щество: Москва 1941.

    i. 1774–1917. pp.128. [384.]
    ii. 1917–1940. pp.148. [542.]
limited to russian periodicals.

RUSSIA. A check list preliminary to a basic
bibliography of materials in the russian language.
Part VIII. Theatre and music [prior to 1918].
Library of Congress: Reference department:
Washington 1944. ff.[i].23. [398.]*

AMREI ETTLINGER and JOAN M. GLADSTONE,
Russian literature, theatre and art. A bibliography
of works in english published 1900–1945. [1947].
pp.96.

ДРАМАТИЧЕСКИЙ театр. Государственная
публичная библиотека имени М. Е. Салты-
кова–Щедрина: [Leningrad 1961]. pp.16. [50.]

Scotland

RALSTON INGLIS, The dramatic writers of Scotland. Glasgow 1868. pp.[ii].156. [600.]

JAMES CAMERON, A bibliography of scottish
theatrical literature. Edinburgh bibliographical
society: Papers (session 1891–1892, no.iv): Edinburgh 1892. pp.8. [175.]
    — — Supplement ... (session 1894–1895, no.ii):
1895. pp.2. [30.]

Drama & Stage

Serbia

VLADAN JOVANOVIĆ, Библиографија српско-хрватске драмске књижевности. Српска краљевска академија: Споменик (vol.xlv: Други разред, 38): Београд 1907. pp.[iii].127. [1550.]

Spain

i. Plays

CATÁLOGO de comedias de los mejores ingenios de España. Madrid 1681. pp.40. [600.]

a catalogue of the Primera [&c.] parte de comedias escogidas, *1652 &c.*

VICENTE GARCÍA DE LA HUERTA, Theatro hespañol. . . . Catálogo alphabetico de las comedias, tragedias, autos, zarzuelas, entremeses y otras obras correspondientes al theatro hespañol. Madrid 1785. pp.256. [5000.]

a copy in the British museum contains voluminous additions in ms. by Ludwig Tieck.

CAYETANO ALBERTO DE LA BARRERA Y LEIRADO, Catálogo bibliográfico y biográfico del teatro antiguo español, desde sus orígenes hasta mediados del siglo XVIII. Madrid 1860. pp.xiii.727. [10,000.]

one of the British museum copies contains ms. notes by J. R. Chorley.

[A. PAZ Y MÉLIA], Catálogo de las piezas de teatro que se conservan en el Departamento de manuscritos de la Biblioteca nacional. Madrid 1899. pp.724. [4307.]

—— Segunda edición. [By Julián Paz]. 1934–1935. pp.[ix].701+viii.721. [10,323.]

only the first volume is of the second edition; the second volume, containing the modern plays, is a new work.

EMILIO COTARELO Y MORI, Teatro español anterior a Lope de Vega. Catálogo de obras dramáticas impresas pero no conocidas hasta el presente. Madrid 1902. pp.46. [176.]

ALFRED MOREL-FATIO and LÉO ROUANET, Le théâtre espagnol. Société des études historiques: Bibliothèque de bibliographies critiques [no.7]: [1910]. pp.47. [500.]

SELECT list of references on modern spanish and portuguese drama and theatre. Library of Congress: Washington 1911. ff.4. [35.]

LEANDRO FERNANDEZ DE MORATÍN, Orígenes del teatro español. Paris [1914]. pp.[iii].500. [1000.]

contains a detailed catalogue of plays before Lope de Vega and a short-title list of plays published down to 1825; previously published, without the latter list, as the introduction to vol.x of the Tesoro de teatro español (*Paris 1838*).

SPANISCHES theater. Eine von der Preussischen staatsbibliothek erworbene sammlung von theaterstücken in spanischer sprache. Preussische staatsbibliothek: Berliner titeldrucke (1927, sonderband): Berlin 1928. pp.[v].1058. [10,000.]

TEATRO español. Catálogo abreviado de una colección dramática española hasta fines del siglo XIX y de obras relativas al teatro español. Madrid 1930. pp.[ii].164. [1846.]

EDUARDO JULIÁ [MARTÍNEZ], Aportaciones bibliográficas. Comedias raras existentes en la Biblioteca provincial de Toledo: Madrid 1932. pp.48. [225.]

EMILIO COTARELO Y MORI, Catálogo descriptivo de la gran colección de comedias escogidas. Madrid 1932. pp.269. [575.]

ADA M. COE, Catálogo bibliográfico y crítico de las comedias anunciadas en los periódicos de Madrid desde 1661 hasta 1819. Johns Hopkins studies in romance literatures and languages (extra vol.ix): Baltimore 1935. pp.xii.270. [1500.]

A COLLECTION of spanish dramatic works presented to the Library of Congress by the Hispanic society of America. [New York] 1938.*

PAUL PATRICK ROGERS, The spanish drama collection in the Oberlin college library. A descriptive catalogue. Oberlin 1940. pp.iii–ix.469. [7530.]

LAURETTA M. BELLAMY and ANNA CAROL KLEMME, A list of the plays in García Rico y cía.'s Colección de comedias españoles de los siglos XIX y XX. University of Colorado: Libraries: Boulder 1956. ff.140. [3749.]*

J. A. MOLINARO, J. H. PARKER and EVELYN RUGG, A bibliography of comedias sueltas in the university of Toronto library. [Toronto] 1959. pp.ix.149. [723.]*

the collection was that of Milton Alexander Buchanan, presented by him to the library.

CARTELERA teatral madrileña. Por el Seminario de bibliografía hispánica de la Facultad de filosofía y letras de Madrid: Cuadernos bibliográficos (no.iii &c.): Madrid.

 i. 1830–1839. 1961. pp.95. [994.]
in progress.

ROBERT ALFRED O'BRIEN, Spanish plays in english translation. An annotated bibliography. American educational theatre association: New York 1963. pp.70.

ii. *Works on the drama and stage*

EMILIO COTARELO Y MORI, Bibliografía de las controversias sobre la licitud del teatro en España. Madrid 1904. pp.745. [223.]

ANTONIO RESTORI, Saggi di bibliografia teatrale spagnuola. Biblioteca dell' 'Archivum romanicum' (ser.i, vol.viii): Genève 1927. pp.[iii].121. [250.]

Sweden

REPERTOAR för Stockholms theatrar. År 1861. Stockholm 1862. pp.56. [400.]

G[USTAV] E[DVARD] KLEMMING, Sveriges dramatiska litteratur till och med 1875. Bibliografi. Stockholm 1863–1879. pp.[vi].652. [4000.]
also issued as nos.40, 55, 71, 72 of the Samlingar *of the Svenska fornskrift-sällskapet.*

F. A. DAHLGREN, Förteckning öfver svenska skådespel uppförda på Stockholms theatrar, 1737–1863. Stockholm 1866. pp.xv.688. [2763.]

AKSEL G[USTAV] S[ALOMON] JOSEPHSON, Bidrag till en förteckning över Sveriges dramaturgiska litteratur. Uppsala 1891. pp.15. [200.]

Switzerland

EMIL [OTTOKAR] WELLER, Das alte volks-theater

der Schweiz. Frauenfeld 1863. pp.[iv].289. [100.]

FRITZ WEISS, Das Basler stadttheater, 1834–1934.
Theaterverein: Basel [1934]. pp.384. [2500.]

[ENZO ERTINI and RUDOLF JOHO], Schweizerische
bühnenwerke in deutscher sprache. Berufstheater.
Elgg 1955. pp.xi.214. [750.]

Ukraine

V. KULYK, Український радянський дра-
матичний театр. Анотований покажчик лі-
тератури. Державна наукова бібліотека
ім. А. М. Горького: Майстри мистецтва
України (vol.ii): Харків 1957. pp.92. [250.]

United States

JAMES REES, The dramatic authors of America.
Philadelphia 1845. pp.144. [250.]

INDEX to american poetry and plays in the collection of C[aleb] Fiske Harris. Providence 1874.
pp.[iv].171. [5000.]
*privately printed; the collection is now in the library
of Brown university.*

ROBERT F. RODEN, Later american plays, 1831–
1900. Dunlap society: New York 1900. pp.[vii].
132.[iv]. [600.]
265 copies printed.

OSCAR WEGELIN, Early american plays, 1714–1830. Being a compilation of the titles of plays by american authors published and performed in America previous to 1830. . . . Edited . . . by J. Malone. Dunlap society: New York 1900. pp. xxvi.113. [250.]

265 copies printed.

— — Second edition. Early american plays, 1714–1830. A compilation of the titles of plays and dramatic poems written by authors born in or residing in north America previous to 1830. New York 1905. pp.94. [300.]

200 copies printed.

DANIEL C[ARL] HASKELL, A list of american dramas in the New York public library. New York 1916. pp.63. [1500.]

DRAMATIC compositions copyrighted in the United States 1870 to 1916. [Edited by Henry Spaulding Parsons]. Library of Congress: Copyright office: Washington 1918. pp.[ii].v.1662+[ii].1663–3547. [60,000.]

LIST of references on the american drama. Library of Congress: Washington 1918. ff.8. [81.]*

J. BENTLEY MULFORD, Dramas and plays. An index to dramatic compositions published (in english) in the United States during 1921. Boston 1922. pp.85. [750.]

issued as a supplement to The dramatic index.

HAROLD WILLIAM SCHOENBERGER, American adaptations of french plays on the New York and Philadelphia stages from 1790 to 1833. A thesis ... of the university of Pennsylvania. Philadelphia 1924. pp.99. [60.]

IRENE FISSE, Recent plays by american authors. Public library: St. Louis 1925. pp.[ii].9. [300.]

CATALOGUE of copyright entries. Part I, group 3. Dramatic compositions and motion pictures. Library of Congress: Copyright office: Washington.

    i. 1928. pp.iii.527. [drama: 4332.]
    ii. 1929. pp.iii.572. [5017.]
    iii. 1930. pp.iii.642. [5816.]
    iv. 1931. pp.iii.601. [5993.]
    v. 1932. pp.iii.555. [6480.]
    vi. 1933. pp.iii.535. [6199.]
    vii. 1934. pp.iii.567. [6223.]
    viii. 1935. pp.iii.575. [6478.]
    ix. 1936. pp.iii.598. [6984.]
    x. 1937. pp.iii.622. [7745.]
    xi. 1938. pp.iii.487. [7060.]
    xii. 1939. pp.iii.328. [6682.]

xiii. 1940. pp.iii.299. [5511.]
xiv. 1941. pp.iii.299. [5188.]
xv. 1942. pp.iii.235. [4299.]
xvi. 1943. pp.[iii].205. [3705.]
xvii. 1944. pp.[iii].230. [5419.]
xviii. 1945. pp.[iii].263. [5020.]
xix. 1946. pp.[iii].387. [5848.]
[*continued as:*]

Catalogue of copyright entries. Third series. Parts 3–4. Dramas and works prepared for oral delivery.

i. 1947. pp.iv.126+iv.127–230. [5523.]
ii. 1948. pp.v.124+v.125–211. [6924.]
iii. 1949. pp.vi.98+vi.99–186. [6053.]
iv. 1950. pp.vi.90+vi.91–167. [5067.]
v. 1951. pp.vii.88+vii.89–170. [4569.]
vi. 1952. pp.vii.96+vii.97–189. [4834.]
vii. 1953. pp.viii.91+viii.93–172. [4167.]*
viii. 1954. pp.ix.88+ix.89–173. [4306.]*
ix. 1955. pp.ix.94+ix.95–177. [4125.]*
x. 1956. pp.ix.97+ix.99–179. [3020.]*
xi. 1957. pp.ix.76+ix.77–141. [2853.]*
xii. 1958. pp.ix.71+ix.73–136. [2647.]*
xiii. 1959. pp.ix.66+ix.67–105. [3429.]*
xiv. 1960. pp.ix.63+ix.64–121. [3522.]*
xv. 1961. pp.ix.74+ix.75–142. [3999.]*
xvi. 1962. pp.ix.66+ix.67–134. [3825.]*

in progress; issues for earlier years form part of the main text of part 1 of the Catalogue.

REESE D. JAMES, Old Drury of Philadelphia . . . 1800–1835. Philadelphia 1932. pp.xv.694. [1250.]

THOMAS CLARK POLLOCK, The Philadelphia theatre in the eighteenth century. Philadelphia 1933. pp.xviii.445. [500.]

FRANK PIERCE HILL, American plays printed 1714–1830. Stanford university: 1934. pp.xii.152. [347.]

ARTHUR HERMAN WILSON, A history of the Philadelphia theatre 1835 to 1855. Philadelphia 1935. pp.xi.724. [2500.]

JOSEPH GAER, *ed.* The theatre of the gold rush decade in San Francisco. California literary research: Monograph (no.5): [*s.l.* 1935]. ff.99. [1250.]*

EDGAR J[OSEPH] HINKEL, *ed.* Bibliography of California fiction, poetry, drama. Volume three. Drama. Alameda county library: Oakland, Cal. 1938. ff.[ii].306. [750.]

HAMILTON MASON, French theatre in New York. A list of plays, 1899–1939. New York 1940. pp.ix. 442. [1443.]

ROBERT L. SHERMAN, Drama cyclopedia. A bibliography of plays and players . . . giving a complete list of, substantially, every play produced in America by a professional company, from the first recorded in 1750, down to 1940. Chicago [1944]. pp.[ii].iii.612. [11,000.]

privately reproduced from typewriting.

ADA P. BOOTH, Early american drama. A guide to an exhibition. William L. Clements library: Bulletin (no.50): Ann Arbor 1947. [50.]

JOSEPH A[BRAHAM] WEINGARTEN, Modern american playwrights, 1918–1945. A bibliography. New York 1946–1947. pp.72+56. [3500.]

EMRO JOSEPH GERGELY, Hungarian drama in New York. American adaptations 1908–1940. Philadelphia 1947. pp.[ix].197. [53.]

ALBERT VON CHORBA, Check list of american drama published in the english colonies of north America and the United States through 1865 in the possession of the library, university of Pennsylvania. Philadelphia 1951. ff.x.92. [592.]*

COMPLETE catalogue of plays. Dramatists play service: New York.

    1960–1961. pp.144. [500.]
    1961–1962. pp.158. [600.]
in progress.

[ALBERT ALOYSIUS BIEBER], The Albert A. Bieber collection of american plays, poetry and songsters. New York 1963. pp.[v].103. [708.]

Wales

E[WARD] R[HYS] HARRIES, Y ddrama Gymraeg. Llyfrgell sir Fflint: yr Wyddgrug 1950. pp.36. [600.]

5. Medieval drama

FRANCIS H[OVEY] STODDARD, References for students of miracle plays and mysteries. University of California: Library bulletin (no.8): Berkeley 1887. pp.68. [750.]

P[AUL] BAHLMANN, Die erneuerer des antiken dramas und ihre ersten dramatischen versuche, 1314–1478. Eine bibliographische darstellung der anfänge der modernen dramendichtung. Münster 1896. pp.60. [30.]

LOUIS DUVAL, Curiosités bibliographiques relatives au drame chrétien. Evreux [printed] 1911. pp.16. [15.]

CARL J[OSEPH] STRATMAN, Bibliography of medieval drama. Berkeley &c. 1954. pp.x.423. [3800.]*

RUDOLF GLUTZ, Miracles de nostre dame par personnages. Kritische bibliographie und neue studien zu text, entstehungszeit und herkunft. Deutsche akademie der wissenschaften zu Berlin: Institut für romanische sprachwissenschaft: Veröffentlichungen (no.9): Berlin 1954. pp.239. [250.]

M[ADELEINE] HORN-MONVAL, Répertoire bibliographique des traductions et adaptations françaises du théâtre étranger du XVe siècle à nos jours. Tome II. 1. Théâtre latin antique. 2. Théâtre latin médiéval et moderne. Centre national de la recherche scientifique: 1959. pp.115. [2000.]

ALFREDO CIONI, Bibliografia delle sacre rappresentazioni. Biblioteca bibliografica italiana (vol. 22): Firenze 1961. pp.3–358. [1500.]

6. *Miscellaneous*

A PARTIAL list of war plays in the Library of Congress: Washington 1921. ff.4. [51.]★

SELECT list of references on the social influence of the drama and theatre. Library of Congress: Washington 1911. ff.3. [27.]★

SELECT list of references on municipal theatres Library of Congress: Washington 1911. ff.2. [17.]*

BRIEF list of references on sacred and religious drama. Library of Congress: Washington 1921. ff.3. [22.]*

LIST of references on the little theatre. Library of Congress: Washington 1922. ff.5. [70.]*

JOZEF BOON, Het lijden Christi en paschen in de dramatiek. "Opbouwen": Brugge &c. [1944]. pp.16. [50.]

THEATRES. Public library of South Australia: Research service: [Adelaide] 1956. ff.6. [88.]*

BIBLIOGRAPHIE internationale, théâtre et jeunesse. Institut international du théâtre. Bruxelles.
 i.
 ii. [By] Jean Guimaud. [?1957]. pp.96. [500.]

RECENT publications on theatre architecture. University of Pittsburgh: Department of speech [and theatre arts]: Pittsburgh.*
 [1]. 1960. [By Ned A. Bowman]. ff.3. [18.]
 [2]–4. 1961. ff.3.3.6. [89.]
 5–7. 1962. Compiled by Ned A. Bowman
  and Glorianne Engel. ff.4.5.9. [119.]
 8–10. 1963. pp.5. .ff.9. [138.]
 in progress.

[ANDRÉ VEINSTEIN and CÉCILE GITEAU], Gordon Craig et le renouvellement du théâtre. Bibliothèque nationale: 1962. pp.101. [200.]
an exhibition catalogue.

Special Subjects

Accordion.

J. H. LÖBEL, Führer durch die akkordeonliteratur. Schriftenreihe zur akkordeonistischen musikwissenschaft (vol.iv): Berlin 1939. pp.108. [2500.]

Acting.

A SELECTED bibliography and critical comment on the art, theory and technique of acting. American educational theatre association: Committee on research: [Ann Arbor 1948]. pp.32. [290.]

Albinoni, Tomaso.

REMO GIAZOTTO, Tomaso Albinoni. . . . (1671–1750). Con il catalogo tematico delle musiche per strumenti. Storia della musica (2nd ser., vol.2): Milano 1945. pp.363. [35.]

Albrechtsberger, Johann Georg.

ANDREAS WEISSENBÄCK, Thematisches verzeichnis der kirchenkompositionen von Johann Georg Albrechtsberger. [Stift Klosterneuburg: Jahrbuch (vol.vi): Wien &c. 1914]. pp.[vi].160. [279.]

Alfieri, Pietro.

CATALOGO delle opere di musica sacra publicate da monsig. Pietro Alfieri Romano. [Rome 1863]. pp.8. [75.]

André, Johann.

HAUPT-KATALOG des musikaliens-verlags von Johann André. Offenbach 1900. pp.[ii].xv. 569.18. [25,000.]

Artaria & co.

ALEXANDER WEINMANN, Vollständiges verlags-verzeichnis Artaria & comp. Beiträge zur geschichte des alt-wiener musikverlages (2nd ser., vol.2): Wien 1952. pp.179. [3176.]*

Bach, family of.

VERZEICHNISS des musikalischen nachlasses des verstorbenen capellmeisters Carl Philipp Emanuel Bach. Hamburg 1790. pp.[ii].142. [1000.]

reprinted in the Bach-jahrbuch (*1938–1948*), *xxxv–xxxvii.*

SYLVIA W. KENNEY [*and others*], Catalog of the Emilie and Karl Riemenschneider memorial Bach library. Baldwin-Wallace college: New York 1960. pp.xvii.295. [2537.]

Bach, Carl Philipp Emanuel.

ALFRED WOTQUENNE, Thematisches verzeichnis der werke von Carl Philipp Emanuel Bach. Leipzig &c. 1905. pp.[iii].112. [272.]

Bach, Johann Christian.

CHARLES SANFORD TERRY, John Christian Bach. 1929. pp.xvi.374. [500.]
consists in large part of a thematic catalogue.

Bach, Johann Sebastian.

ALFRED DÖRFFEL, Thematisches verzeichniss der instrumentalwerke von Joh. Seb. Bach. Leipzig [1867]. pp.89. [1000.

— — [Zweite auflage]. [1882]. pp.92. [1000.]

CARL TAMME, Thematisches verzeichniss der vocalwerke von Joh. Seb. Bach. Leipzig [*c*.1890]. pp.xvi.155. [1736.]

OSKAR FLEISCHER, Führer durch die Bach-ausstellung im festsaale des berliner Rathauses. Berlin [1901]. pp.46. [97.]

AUS ZWEI jahrhunderten deutscher musik. Ausstellung zur Deutschen Bach-Händel-Schützfeier. Preussische staatsbibliothek: Berlin 1935. pp.52. [Bach: 145.]

COMMEMORATIVE exhibition of the two hundred and fiftieth anniversary of the births of George Frederick Handel... and Johann Sebastian Bach. Fitzwilliam museum: [Cambridge] 1935. pp.[8]. [41.]

GEORG KINSKY, Die originalausgaben der werke Johann Sebastian Bachs. Ein beitrag zur musikbibliographie. Wien &c. 1937. pp.3–134. [12.]

MAY DE FOREST PAYNE, Melodic index to the works of Johann Sebastian Bach. New York [1938]. pp.xvii.101. [3500.]

IRMGARD ENGELS, J. S. Bach in der hausmusik. Werkverzeichnis und praktische hinweise. Leipzig [1942]. pp.8.

[GUSTAV ADOLF TRUMPFF and ALFRED DÜRR], Johann Sebastian Bach documenta. Heraus-

gegeben . . . von Wilhelm Martin Luther. Nie-
dersächsische staats- und universitätsbibliothek:
Kassel &c. [1950]. pp.[iii].148. [400.]

*catalogue of an exhibition organized during the
Bachfest, Göttingen 1950.*

WOLFGANG SCHMIEDER, Thematisch-systemati-
sches verzeichnis der musikalischen werke von
Johann Sebastian Bach. Leipzig 1950. pp.xxiii.
747. [1269.]

PAUL KAST, Die Bach-handschriften der Berliner staatsbibliothek. Tübinger Bach-studien
(no.2/3): Trossingen 1958. pp.x.150. [1900.]

Bagpipe.

GILBERT ASKEW, A bibliography of the bagpipe.
Northumbrian pipers' society: Newcastle-upon-
Tyne 1932. pp.27. [100.]

Beethoven, Ludwig van.

[FRIEDRICH HOFMEISTER], Thematisches verzeichniss der compositionen für instrumentalmusik welche von den berühmtesten tonsetzern
unsersers [*sic*] zeitalters erschienen sind. . . . . 1ˢ heft.
Louis van Beethoven. Leipzig 1819. pp.[vi].25.
[102.]

CATALOGUE des œuvres de Louis van Beethoven
qui se trouvent chez Artaria & compag: à Vienne......
Revidirt von Louis v. Beethoven. [Completed by
Anton Graeffer]. Vienne [*c*.1830]. pp.6. [200.]

THEMATISCHES verzeichnis sämtlicher im druck
erschienenen werke Ludwig van Beethoven.
Leipzig 1851. pp.vii.167. [500.]
— Zweite vermährte auflage. Zusammenge-
stellt [or rather, edited] ... von [Martin] G[ustav]
Nottebohm. 1868. pp.vii.220. [1000.]
— — — (Anastatischer druck der 2. auflage).
. . . Nebst bibliographie von Emerich Kastner.
Leipzig 1913. pp.vii.230.vi.46. [2000.]

*the bibliography by Kastner was also published
separately; see below.*

WILHELM DE [VON] LENZ, Beethoven et ses trois
styles. Analyse des sonates de piano, suivies de
l'essai d'un catalogue critique, chronologique et
anecdotique de l'œuvre de Beethoven. St.-Péters-
bourg 1852. pp.xi.292+[v].276. [500.]
— — [another edition]. Paris 1855. pp.[iii].212
+[iii].193. [500.]
— — Édition nouvelle, avec ... une bibliographie des ouvrages relatifs à Beethoven, par M. D.
Calvocoressi. Paris 1909. pp.ix.503. [700.]

WILH[ELM] VON LENZ, Beethoven. Eine kunst-
studie. 3[–5] Theil. Kritischer katalog sämtlicher
werke Ludw. von Beethovens mit analyse der-
selben. Hamburg 1860. pp.x.1274.

ALEXANDER W[HEELOCK] THAYER, Chronologisches verzeichniss der werke Ludwig van
Beethoven's. Berlin 1865. pp.viii.208. [298.]

OTTO MÜHLBRECHT, Beethoven und seine werke.
Eine biographisch-bibliographische skizze. Leipzig 1866. pp.vii.120. [500.]

ERNST CHALLIER, Tabellarische uebersicht sämmtlicher clavier-sonaten von L. v. Beethoven in allen
jetzt noch vorhandenen ausgaben. Berlin 1887.
pp.16. [1500.]

[ERICH PRIEGER and F. A. SCHMIDT], Katalog der
mit der Beethoven-feier zu Bonn . . . verbundenen
ausstellung von handschriften, briefen, bildnissen,
reliquien Ludwig van Beethoven's. Bonn 1890.
pp.75. [300.]
— — Nachtrag. [1890]. pp.[4]. [7.]

GUIDO ADLER, Verzeichniss der musikalischen
autographe von Ludwig van Beethoven . . . im
besitze von A[ugust] Artaria. Wien 1890. pp.22.
[96.]

F. A. SCHMIDT and P. E. SONNENBURG, Führer durch das Beethoven-haus zu Bonn. Bonn [*c*.1895]. pp.xvi.56. [389.]

— — Nachtrag. [*c*.1895]. pp.9. [50.]

EMERICH KASTNER, Bibliotheca beethoveniana. Versuch einer Beethoven-bibliographie, enthaltend alle vom jahre 1827 bis 1913 erschienenen werke über den grossen tondichter, nebst hinzufügung einiger aufsätze in zeitschriften etc. Leipzig 1913. pp.vi.46. [1000.]

— — 2. Auflage . . . von Theodor Frimmel. 1925. pp.vi.84. [1500.]

FÜHRER durch die Beethoven-ausstellung der stadt Wien. Wien 1920. pp.vii.88. [519.]

FÜHRER durch die Beethoven-zentenarausstellung der stadt Wien, "Beethoven und die wiener kultur seiner zeit". Wien 1927. pp.xi.248. [800.]

M[IKHAIL] P[AVLOVICH] ALEKSEEV and Y[AKOV] Z[INOVEVICH] BERMAN, Бетховен. Материалы для библиографического указателя русской литературы о нем. Публичная библиотека: Труды: Одесса 1927. pp.35. [335.]

[RICHARD G. APPEL], Beethoven, 1770–1827. A selected bibliography prepared in connection with

the Beethoven centenary festival. Public library:
Boston [1927]. ff.15. [200.]

LUDWIG VAN BEETHOVEN. Fővárosi könyvtár:
Aktuális kérdések irodalma (no.37): [Budapest
1927]. pp.4. [60.]

JOSEPH SCHMIDT-GÖRG, Katalog der handschriften des Beethoven-hauses und Beethoven-archivs
Bonn. Kataloge des Beethoven-hauses und Beethoven-archivs (vol.i): Bonn 1935. pp.76. [138.]

MAX UNGER, Eine schweizer Beethovensamm-
lung. Schriften der Corona (vol.xxiv): Zürich
[1939]. pp.[vii].239. [550.]

ANTONIO BRUERS, Beethoven. Catalogo storico-
critico di tutte le opere. Roma 1940.
— — Quarta edizione. 1951. pp.681. [350.]

DONALD WALES MACARDLE, A check list of the
chamber music of Beethoven. [1945.]
includes an index to certain references in Cobbett's
Cyclopedic survey of chamber music.

DONALD WALES MACARDLE, Beethoven abstracts.
[New Rochelle, N.Y. 1947–   ].*

GIOVANNI BIAMONTI, Catalogo cronologico di
tutte le musiche di Beethoven. Roma.

i. 1781–1800. [1951]. pp.[xiv].391. [203.]
in progress?

[HARRY GOLDSCHMIDT], Ludwig van Beethoven
und seine zeit. Illustrierter führer durch die deutsche Beethoven-ausstellung. Staatliche kommission für kunstangelegenheiten: [Leipzig] 1952.
pp.3–80. [300.]

PAUL [ADOLF] HIRSCH and C[ECIL] B[ERNARD]
OLDMAN, Contemporary english editions of Beethoven. [1953]. pp.35. [400.]

SONDERAUSSTELLUNG aus der Beethoven-samm-
lung H[ans] C[onrad] Bodmer-Zürich. Beetho-
venhaus: Bonn 1953. pp.19. [60.]

GEORG KINSKY, Das werk Beethovens. Thema-
tisch-bibliographisches verzeichnis seiner sämtlichen vollendeten kompositionen.... Abgeschlossen
und herausgegeben von Hans Halm. München &c.
[1955]. pp.xxiii.808. [5000.]

GIOVANNI BIAMONTI, Schema di un catalogo
generale cronologico delle musiche di Beethoven,
1781–1827. Roma [1954]. pp.186.

WILLY HESS, Verzeichnis der nicht in der ge-
samtausgabe veröffentlichten werke Ludwig van
Beethovens. Wiesbaden 1957. pp.116. [401.]

N. L. FISHMAN, Автографы Л. Бетховена в хранилищах СССР. Справочник. Государственный центральный музей музыкальной культуры имени М. И. Глинки: Москва 1959. pp.13. [41.]

Bell, William Henry.

L. E. TAYLOR, Catalog of the music manuscripts of William Henry Bell, 1873–1946. University of Cape Town: Library: Cape Town 1948. ff.11. [100.]*

Berlioz, Louis Hector.

CECIL HOPKINSON, A bibliography of the musical and literary works of Hector Berlioz, 1803–1869. Edinburgh bibliographical society: Edinburgh 1951. pp.xix.205. [500.]

A[NDRÉ] ESPIAU DE LA MAËSTRE, Catalogue des manuscrits et documents de H. Berlioz conservés à Vienne. Université de Paris: Institut français [Vienna]: 1953. pp.8. [40.]*

[RICHARD P. S. MACNUTT], Hector Berlioz. Exhibition. Institut français d'Écosse: [Edinburgh] 1963. pp.[iv].41. [127.]*

Bizet, Georges Alexandre César Léopold.

[JEAN CORDEY *and others*], Georges Bizet (1838–1875). Exposition pour commémorer le centenaire de sa naissance . . . au Théâtre national de l'opéra. [1938]. pp.[iii].iv.46. [200.]

Bournonville, Antoine Auguste.

DAN FOG, The Royal danish ballet 1760–1958 and Auguste Bournonville. A chronological catalogue of the ballets . . . performed at the royal theatres of Copenhagen and a catalogue of Bournonville's works. Copenhagen 1961. pp.[ii].79. [571.]

Brahms, Johannes.

THEMATISCHES verzeichniss der bisher im druck erschienenen werke von Johannes Brahms. Berlin [1887].
— [second edition]. Thematisches verzeichniss sämmtlicher im druck [&c.]. 1897.
— Neue ausgabe. [Edited by Otto Keller]. 1902. pp.[iii].175. [1000.]
— Neue vermehrte ausgabe. 1904.
— Fünfte . . . ausgabe. 1910. pp.[iv].180. [1000.]

VOLLSTÄNDIGES verzeichniss sämmtlicher werke

und sämmtlicher arrangements der werke von Johannes Brahms. Berlin [1897]. pp.32. [900.]

VERZEICHNISS der compositionen von Johannes Brahms nebst ihren bearbeitungen aus dem verlage von J. Rieter-Biedermann. Leipzig 1898. pp.16. [200.]
— [another edition]. 1908. pp.16. [200.]

KATALOG einer kleinen Brahms-ausstellung aus anlass der enthüllung des Brahms-denkmals von A. Hildebrand. Meiningen 1899. pp.16. [100.]

A COMPLETE catalogue of Johannes Brahms' works, original and arrangements. 1906. pp.iv.68. [750.]

VOLLSTÄNDIGES verzeichnis aller im druck erschienenen werke von Johannes Brahms nebst systematischem verzeichnis und register aller textanfänge. Berlin &c. 1908. pp.42. [1000.]

MAX BURKHARDT, Johannes Brahms. Ein führer durch seine werke. Berlin [1912]. pp.44. [200.]

EDWIN EVANS, Historical, descriptive & analytical account of the entire works of Johannes Brahms, treated in the order of their opus number. 1912-[1936]. pp.xix.599+viii.304+xiii.351+xv.327. [1000.]

the title varies; the collective title, as above, appears only in the first and last volumes.

BRAHMS, werkverzeichnis. Leipzig [1927]. pp. 52. [800.]

JOHANNES BRAHMS. Verzeichnis seiner werke. Leipzig [1928]. pp.xxiii.50. [1000.]

ALFRED VON EHRMANN, Johannes Brahms. Thematisches verzeichnis seiner werke. Leipzig 1933. pp.vi.164. [1000.]

H. KRAUS, K. GEIRINGER and V. LUITHLEN, J. Brahms zentenar-ausstellung der Gesellschaft der musikfreunde in Wien. Beschreibendes verzeichnis. [Wien 1937]. pp.121. [200.]*

LAJOS KOCH, Brahms-bibliográfia. Fővarosi könyvtar: Budapest 1943. pp.81. [1000.]

Breitkopf & Härtel.

VERZEICHNIS des musikalien-verlages von Breitkopf & Härtel. . . . Vollständig bis ende 1902. Leipzig [1903]. pp.xxv.1200.36. [30,000.]
— Nachtrag . . . 1903 bis anfang 1915. 1918. pp.40. [7500.]

Britten, Edward Benjamin.

BENJAMIN BRITTEN. A complete catalogue of his works. 1963. pp.47. [300.]

Bruch, Max Christian Friedrich.

VOLLSTÄNDIGES verzeichnis sämtlicher im druck erschienener werke u. sämtlicher bearbeitungen der werke von Max Bruch. Berlin &c. [1908]. pp.[ii].28. [500.]

Bruckner, Anton.

VERZEICHNIS sämmtlicher im druck erschienenen werke von Anton Bruckner. Wien [1898]. pp.7. [50.]

Busch, Wilhelm.

ALBERT VANSELOW, Die erstdrucke und erstausgaben der werke von Wilhelm Busch. Leipzig 1913. pp.x.104. [130.]

Busoni, Ferruccio.

BREITKOPF & HÄRTEL, Ferruccio Busoni werkverzeichnis. Auf grund der aufzeichnungen Busonis zusammengestellt. Leipzig [1924]. pp.62. [400.]

Byrd, William.

LIST of the music of William Byrd...obtainable in modern editions. Drawn up by the Byrd tercentenary committee. [1923]. pp.11. [300.]

Chaikovsky, Petr Ilich.

B. JURGENSON, Catalogue thématique des œuvres de P. Tschaikowsky. Moscou [1897].
— — [another edition]. New York [*c.*1945].

[и. ф. кунин], Петр Ильич Чайковский. Краткий рекомендательный указатель. Публичная библиотека: Москва 1953. pp.47. [250.]

[B. V. DOBROKHOTOV and V. A. KISELEV], Автографы П. И. Чайковского в фондах... Музея музыкальной культуры им. М. И. Глинки: [Москва] 1956. pp.79. [412.]

Chamber music.

AN ACCOUNT of printed musick, for violins, hautboys, flutes, and other instruments, by several masters. [London *c.*1725]. pp.24. [350.]

CONSTANTIN ALBRECHT, Thematisches verzeichnis der streich- und clavier-trios, quartette und quintette von Haydn, Mozart, Beethoven, Schubert, Mendelssohn-Bartholdy, und Schumann. Leipzig &c. 1890.

WILHELM ALTMANN, Kammermusik-literatur. Verzeichnis von seit 1841 erschienenen kammermusikwerken. Leipzig 1910. pp.viii.134. [5000.]
— — Sechste . . . auflage. 1945. pp.xii.400. [20,000.]

JOHN F. RUSSELL, List of chamber music in the Henry Watson music library. Public libraries: Music lists (no.2): Manchester 1913. pp.vi.143. [3000.]

A COMPLETE handbook and guide to chamber music. J. & W. Chester's lending library: [1922]. pp.36. [1750.]

JOHN D. HAYWARD, Chamber music for amateurs. Notes from a library. 'The Strad', library (no.xxii): 1923. pp.[vii].84. [200.]

[GUSTAV GROSCHWITZ], Violoncello-musik und kammermusik werke. Vollständiges verzeichniss mit ausführlichen angaben. Leipzig [c.1930]. pp. viii.218. [2000.]

WILHELM ALTMANN, Handbuch für streichquartettspieler. Ein führer durch die literatur des streichquartetts. Max Hesses handbücher (vols.

lxxxvi, lxxxvii, xcii, xciv): Berlin 1928–1931.
pp.340+354+373+244. [2000.]
not limited to quartets.

WILHELM ALTMANN, Handbuch für klaviertrio-
spieler. Wegweiser durch die trios für klavier,
violine und violoncell. Wolfenbüttel 1934. pp.
237. [1000.]

SANFORD M[ARION] HELM, Catalog of chamber
music for wind instruments. National association
of college wind and percussion instrument instructors: Publication (no.1): Ann Arbor, Mich.
1952. pp.85.

FRANZ A. STEIN, Verzeichnis der kammermusikwerke von 1650 bis zur gegenwart. Dalp-taschen-
bücher (vol.360): Bern &c. [1962]. pp.107. [1500.]

JOHANNES FRIEDRICH RICHTER, Kammermusik-
katalog. Verzeichnis der von 1944 bis 1958 veröffentlichten werke für kammermusik. Leipzig
1960. pp.320. [6000.]

Chancerel, Léon.

BIBLIOGRAPHIE du centre dramatique dirigé par
Léon Chancerel. Histoire, doctrine, technique et
répertoire, 1932–1945. [1945]. pp.48. [80.]

Chaplin, Charles Spencer.

GLAUCO VIAZZI, Chaplin e la critica. Antologia di saggi, bibliografia ragionata, iconografia e filmografia. Biblioteca della spettacolo (no.3): Bari 1955. pp.[iv].557. [1041.]

Charades.

LIST of collections of charades. Library of Congress: Washington 1906. ff.6. [45.]*

Chávez, Carlos.

CARLOS CHÁVEZ. Catalog of his works. Pan american union: Music division: Music series (no.10): Washington 1944. pp.xxxii.16. [150.]
500 copies printed; not limited to his own works.

Cherubini, Maria Luigi Carlo Zenobio Salvatore.

[M. L. C. Z. S. CHERUBINI], Notice des manuscrits autographes de la musique composée par feu M.-L.-C.-Z.-S. Cherubini 1843. pp.[iv].36. [400.]

EDWARD BELLASIS, A chronological catalogue of Cherubini's works. Birmingham [printed] 1904. pp.xxxii. [442.]

FRANÇOIS LESURE and CLAUDIO SARTORI, Tentativo di un catalogo della produzione di Luigi Cherubini. Firenze [1961]. pp.135–187. [200.]

Chopin, Fryderyk Franciszek.

THEMATISCHES verzeichniss der im druck erschienenen compositionen von Friedrich Chopin. Leipzig 1852.
— Neue . . . ausgabe. 1888. pp.[vi].86. [2500.]

THEMATISCHES verzeichniss der in Deutschland im druck erschienenen instrumental-compositionen von Friedrich Chopin. Leipzig [1871.]

FRÉDÉRIC CHOPIN, Exposition de tableaux, gravures, manuscrits, souvenirs (1810–1849) organisée par la Bibliothèque polonaise. Paris [1932]. pp.97. [300.]

BRONISŁAV EDWARD SYDOW, Bibliografia F. F. Chopina. Towarzystwo naukowe warszawskie: Warszawa 1949. pp.xxvii.586. [8738.]

[ÉLISABETH LEBEAU], Frédéric Chopin. Exposition du centenaire. Bibliothèque nationale: 1949. pp.84. [234.]

MAURICE J[OHN] E[DWIN] BROWN, Chopin. An index of his works in chronological order. 1960. pp.xiii.200. [168.]

Special Subjects

[KRYSTYNA KOBYLANSKA, *ed.*], Exposition Frédéric Chopin. Opéra: Bibliothèque: 1960. ff.[vi]. [60.]

A[LFRED ERDMANN] W[ERNER] BÖHME, Friedrich Chopin als motiv in der deutschsprachigen schöngeistigen literatur (bühnenwerke, romane, novelle und lyrik). Eine . . . erste zusammenstellung. [Niederdollendorf] 1960. ff.39.iii. [29.]*

[ULF ABEL], Frédéric Chopin. Kungl. bibliotek: Utställningskatalog (no.21): [Stockholm 1960]. pp.7. [20.]

KAROL MUSTOŁ, Chopiniana w bibliotece Państwowej wyisnej szkoły muzycznej. Katowicek 1961. pp.37. [388.]

Cimarosa, Domenico.

[BARON ANGELO DE EISNER-ESSENHOF and JOSEF MANTUANO], Katalog der ausstellung anlässlich der centenarfeier Domenico Cimarosa's. Wien 1901. pp.169. [400.]

Clementi, Muzio.

ERNST CHALLIER, Sonaten-tabelle. Eine nach tonarten geordnete aufstellung sämmtlicher clavier sonaten von Clementi, Haydn, Mozart in allen ausgaben. 3ᵗᵉ ...auflage. Giessen 1890. pp.14. [Clementi: 300.]

RICCARDO ALLORTO, Le sonate per pianoforte di Muzio Clementi. Studio critico e catalogo tematico. Historiæ musicæ cultores: Biblioteca (vol. xii): Firenze 1959. pp.151. [125.]

Cleopatra.

GEORG HERMANN MOELLER, Die auffassung der Kleopatra in der tragödienliteratur der romanischen und germanischen nationen. Ulm 1888. pp.[iii].94. [30.]

GEORG HERMANN MÖLLER, Beiträge zur dramatischen Cleopatra-literatur. Schweinfurt 1907. pp.39. [127.]

THEODORE [DEODATUS NATHANIEL] BESTERMAN, A bibliography of Cleopatra. 1926. pp.8. [189.]
the British museum pressmarks are added in ms. to one of the copies in that library.

Couperin, François.

MAURICE CAUCHIE, Thematic index of the works of François Couperin. Monaco [1949]. pp.133. [506.]

Special Subjects

Curschmann, Karl Friedrich.

VERZEICHNISS sämmtlicher lieder und gesänge von Fr. Curschmann, Fr. Gumbert, Fr. Kücken, W. Taubert. Zürich 1876. pp.[ii].54. [2250.]

Czerny, Carl.

VERZEICHNISS (thematisches) der werke von C. Czerny. Wien [c.1825].

Dance.

SELECT list of references on indian music and dances. Library of Congress: Washington 1911. ff.4. [31.]*

LIST of references on dancing, with special reference to classic, greek, and interpretation dancing. Library of Congress: Washington 1917. ff.3. [28.]*

CYRIL W[ILLIAM] BEAUMONT, A bibliography of dancing. 1929. pp.xi.228. [500.]
limited to works in the British museum; a facsimile was published New York [1963].

GUIDE to dance periodicals. An analytical index of articles. Asheville [iv, viii–   ]: New York; v–vii: Gainesville].*

Special Subjects

i. 1931–1935. Compiled by S. Yancey Bel-
    knap. 1959. pp.[iv].124. [2500.]
ii. 1936–1940. 1950. pp.[iv].68. [4000.]
iii. 1941–1945. 1948. pp.68. [4000.]
iv. 1946–1950. [1951]. pp.[iv].177. [4000.]
v. 1951–1952. 1955. pp.vi.130. [4000.]
vi. 1953–1954. 1956. pp.vi.165. [5000.]
vii. 1955–1956. 1958. pp.[v].180. [5500.]
viii. 1957–1958. 1960. pp.[446]. [5500.]
in progress.

AN INDEX to folk dances and singing games.
Compiled by she staff of the Music department,
Minneapolis public library. American library
association: Chicago 1936. pp.xiv.202. [500.]

PAUL DAVID MAGRIEL, A bibliography of dancing
. . . and related subjects. New York 1936. pp.229.
[5000.]

— — Third cumulated supplement, 1936–1939.
1940. pp.80. [1500.]

BERNARD C. EVANS, Ballet and dancing. National
book council: Book list (no.173): 1940. pp.[2].
[50.]

WILIARD HALL, Bibliography of social dancing.
Hastings-on-Hudson, N. Y. 1940. ff.[ii].105.
[1500.]*

ARNOLD L[IONEL] HASKELL, Ballet. National book league: Reader's guide: 1947. pp.12. [50.]
the bibliography proper is by William Arthur Munford.

READERS' guide to ballet. Library association: County libraries section: [Readers' guide (new series, no.1): 1948]. pp.16. [200.]

IFAN KYRLE FLETCHER, Bibliographical descriptions of forty rare books relating to the art of dancing, in the collection of P[hilip] J[ohn] S[ampey] Richardson. 1954. pp.20. [40.]

IVOR [FORBES] GUEST, Ballet. An exhibition of books, mss, playbills, prints &c. illustrating the development of the art from its origins until modern times. National book league: [1957]. pp.70. [319.]

V. BEDNÁŘOVÁ and R. TRAUTMANN, Tanec. Seznam tanečni literatury v universitní knihovně. Universita: Knihovna: Výběrový seznam (no.18): Brně 1957. pp.44. [150.]*

LIETUVIŲ liaudies šokių ir žaidimų autorinis sąrašas. Respublikiniai liaudies kūrybos namai: Vilnius 1957. pp.18. [100.]

VIRGINIA MOOMAW, *ed.* Dance research. Reference materials. American association for health, physical education and recreation: National section on dance: [Washington 1958]. pp.[v].54. [800.]*

MARIAN EAMES, When all the world was dancing. Rare and curious books from the Cia Fornaroli collection. Public library: New York 1958. pp.16. [20.]

BIBLIOGRAFIA zagadnień sztuki tanecznej. Centralna poradnia amatorskiego ruchu artystycznego: Warszawa.*

    1945–1955. 1959. pp.122. [761.]
    1956–1957. Opracowała Irena Ostrowska. 1960. pp.115. [803.]

JARMILA HOROVÁ-GLOSOVÁ and MIRKO PŘÍHODA, Tanec. Soupis knih o tanci. Městská lidová knihovna: Knihovna Bodřicha Smetany: Bibliografie: Praha 1960. ff.[ii].55. [500.]*

Debussy, Claude Achille.

CATALOGUE de l'œuvre de Claude Debussy. 1962. pp.134. [300.]

EXPOSIÇÃO comemorativa do centenário de Claude Debussy. Fundação Calouste Gulbenkian: Lisboa [1962]. pp.3–75. [328.]

[FRANÇOIS LESURE], Claude Debussy. Bibliothèque nationale: 1962. pp.73. [300.]
an exhibition catalogue.

HOMMAGE à Debussy. Musée du Palais Gran-
velle: Besançon 1962. pp.[4]. [26.]
an exhibition catalogue.

Donizetti, Domenico Gaetano Maria.

CHARLES MALHERBE, Centenaire de Gaetano
Donizetti. Catalogue bibliographique de la section
française à l'exposition de Bergame. 1897. pp.[iii].
xiv.215. [551.]

DONIZETTI (DOMENICO GAETANO MARIA), [British
museum: Music catalogue:] [*n.d.*]. ff.102. [1500.]

Dvořák, Antonín Leopold.

OTAKAR ŠOUREK, Dvořák's werke. Skladby
Dvořákovy. Ein vollständiges verzeichnis in chro-
nologischer, thematischer und systematischer anordnung. Berlin [1917]. pp.[ii].xxxix.121. [300.]

JARMIL BURGHAUSER, Antonín Dvořák. The-
matický katalog. Bibliografie. Praha 1960. pp.736.
[1500.]

Eitner, Robert.

VERZEICHNIS der im druck erschienenen musik-
historischen arbeiten von Robert Eitner. Leipzig
1893. pp.8. [35.]

Elgar, sir Edward.

LOUISE B. M. DYER, Music by british composers.
A series of complete catalogues. No.2. Sir
Edward Elgar. [1931]. pp.20. [250.]

Fauré, Gabriel.

RAOUL THAUZIÈS, Essai sur Gabriel Faure et ses
derniers ouvrages. Albi [1946]. pp.47. [100.]

VITTORIA RICCARDI, Bibliografia delle opere di
Gabriel Faure. Bari 1952. pp.12. [120.]

[FRANÇOIS LESURE], Gabriel Fauré. Bibliothèque
nationale: 1963. pp.16. [100.]
an exhibition catalogue.

Fesca, Friedrich Ernst.

THEMATISCHES verzeichnis der compositionen
von F. Fesca, mit tempobezeichnung nach Mälzl's
metronome. Leipzig [c.1815]. single leaf.

Fesch, Willem de.

FR. VAN DEN BREMT, Willem de Fesch (1687–
1757?), Nederlands componist en virtuoos. Ko-
ninklijke belgische academie: Klasse der schone
kunsten: Verhandelingen: Verzameling in-8°
(vol.v, no.4): Brussel 1949. pp.vi.349. [300.]

Flute.

CATALOGO dei soli, duetti, trii e concerti per il
flauto . . . che si trovano in manuscritto nella
officina musica di Breitkopf in Lipsia. [Leipsic]
1763. pp.34. [600.]

CATALOGUE thématique de tous les œuvres pour
la flûte traversière composés par F. A. Hoffmeister.
Vienne 1800.

LIST of works relating to the flute in the library
of Dayton C. Miller. Cleveland, Ohio, 1922.
pp.20. [300.]
privately printed.

H[ENRY] MACAULAY FITZGIBBON, Guide to the
best flute music of all kinds. 1922.
— — A supplemental guide. Greystones 1926.
ff.[ii].iii.37. [300.]
privately printed.

DAYTON C. MILLER, The Dayton C. Miller collections relating to the flute. II. Catalogue of books and literary material. Cleveland 1935. pp.120. [1200.]

privately printed; collection I consists of instruments; both collections now form part of the Library of Congress.

HUGO ALKER, Blockflöten-bibliographie, aufführungspraxis — literatur — spielgut. Biblosschriften (vol.27): Wien 1960. pp.[ii].96. [800.]*
—— Ergänzungen und nachträge.... (vol.28): 1961. pp.[ii].111. [600.]

Forberg, Robert.

VERZEICHNIS des musikalien-verlags von Rob. Forberg. Leipzig 1894. pp.lxxii.416. [7500.]
— Erster nachtrag. [1900]. pp.[ii].82. [1500.]

Foster, Stephen Collins.

WALTER R. WHITTLESEY and O[SCAR] G[EORGE] THEODORE] SONNECK, Catalogue of first editions of Stephen C. Foster (1826–1864). Library of Congress: Washington 1915. pp.78. [200.]

JOHN TASKER HOWARD, The literature on Stephen Foster. [*s.l.* 1944]. pp.8. [10.]

JAMES J. FULD, A pictorial bibliography of the first editions of Stephen C. Foster. Musical americana: Philadelphia 1957. pp.[v].27. [204.]

Garnier, Charles.

[ÉLISABETH LEBEAU *and others*], Charles Garnier et l'Opéra. Exposition. Bibliothèque de l'Opéra: 1961. pp.40. [145.]

Gelinek, Josef.

VERZEICHNISS (thematisches) von Gelinek's erschienenen variationen. Wien [*c.*1815].

THEMATISCHES verzeichniss der variationen des abbé Gelinek für das pianoforte. Offenbach [*c.*1820]. [100.]

Giuliani.

VERZEICHNISS (thematisches) von Giuliani's gedruckten werke. Wien [*c.*1815].

Glazunov, Aleksandr Konstantinovich.

ALEXANDRE GLAZOUNOV. Catalogue complet des œuvres. Leipzig 1935. pp.35. [700.]

Glinka, Mikhail Ivanovich.

K. ALBRECHT, Thematic list of romances, songs and operas of M. I. Glinka. Moscow 1891.

A. S. LYAPUNOVA, Рукописи М. И. Глинки. Каталог. Библиотека им. М. Е. Салтыкова-Щедрина: Ленинград 1950. pp.100. [317.]

[T. V. POLOVA], Михаил Иванович Глинка. Краткий рекомендательный указатель. Библиотека СССР имени В. И. Ленина: Москва 1953. pp.48. [100.]

A. S. LYAPUNOVA, Каталог-справочник произведений М. И. Глинки издания 1917–1954 гг. Ленинград 1958. pp.248. [1750.]

Gluck, Christoph Willibald von.

ALFRED WOTQUENNE, Catalogue thématique des œuvres de Chr. W. von Gluck. Leipzig 1904. pp. xi.249. [80.]

— — Thematisches verzeichnis der werke von Chr. W. v. Gluck. . . . Deutsche übersetzung von Josef Liebeskind. Leipzig &c. 1904. pp.iii–xiii. 250. [80.]

— — — Ergänzungen und nachträge . . . von J. Liebeskind. 1911. pp.vi.20. [13.]

further corrections and additions, by M. A. Arend, appear in Die musik *(1913), xlix.288–289.*

STEPHANW ORTSMANN, Die deutsche Gluck-literatur. Nürnberg 1914. pp.ix.121. [500.]

CECIL HOPKINSON, A bibliography of the works of C. W. von Gluck. 1959. pp.xv.79. [150.]
300 copies privately printed; interleaved.

Gramophone.

PATENTS for inventions. Fifty years subject index, 1861–1910. Class 40 (ii). Phonographs, gramophones, and like sound transmitting and reproducing instruments. Patent office: 1915. pp.8. [800.]

LIST of references on the phonograph (talking machines). Library of Congress: Washington 1915. ff.9. [133.]*
— Additional references. 1918. ff.2. [19.]*

ABRIDGMENTS of specifications. Class 40 (ii). Phonographs, gramophones, and like sound transmitting and reproducing instruments. Patent office.
1909–1915. pp.x.196. [600.]
1916–1920. pp.ix.138. [400.]
1921–1925. pp.xiii.305. [1000.]

1926–1930. pp.xix.459. [1250.]
no more published.

GRAMOPHONES and records. A selected list of books, now in print, compiled by the The gramophone. Second edition. National book council: Book list (no.124): 1935. pp.[2]. [30.]

THE GRAMOPHONE: pre-war technical books and articles, with a selection of later date. Science library: Bibliographical series (no.363): 1938. ff.5. [95.]*

Grieg, Edvard Hagerup.

EDVARD GRIEG. Verzeichnis seiner werke. Leipzig [1910]. pp.72. [1000.]

[SIGURD GUNDERSEN and SVERRE JORDAN], Edvard Grieg. Manuskripter og minner. Utstilling i Bergens kunstforening. . . . Katalog (med tillegg: Fortegnelse over ikke utstillte manuskripter i Bergens off. bibliotek og i universitetsbiblioteket i Oslo). Bergen [1953]. pp.27. [150.]

EDVARD GRIEG . . . utstilling. Offentlige bibliotek: [Bergen 1962]. pp.55. [168.]

Händel, Georg Friedrich.

CATALOGUE of a Handel collection formed by

Newman Flower. Sevenoaks [1921]. pp.32. [400.]
privately printed.

WILLIAM BARCLAY SQUIRE, The Handel manuscripts. British museum: Catalogue of the King's
music library (part i): 1927. pp.xi.143. [4000.]

[EMIL] KURT TAUT, Verzeichnis des schrifttums
über Georg Friedrich Händel. Händel-jahrbuch
(vol.vi = Veröffentlichungen der Händel-gesell-
schaft, no.9): Leipzig 1933. pp.viii.153. [3000.]
—— [another edition]. Konrad Sasse, Händel
bibliographie. [1963]. pp.356. [4750.]*

AUS ZWEI jahrhunderten deutscher musik. Aus-
stellung zur deutschen Bach-Händel-Schütz-feier.
Preussische staatsbibliothek: Berlin 1935. pp.52.
[Händel: 29.]

KATALOG der Händel-ausstellung im städtischen
Moritzburg-museum. [Halle 1935]. pp.[12]. [175.]
a duplicated supplementary leaf was issued.

COMMEMORATIVE exhibition of the two hundred
and fiftieth anniversary of the births of George
Frederick Handel . . . and Johann Sebastian Bach.
Fitzwilliam museum: [Cambridge] 1935. pp.[8].
[41.]

[WILLIAM CHARLES SMITH], George Frideric Handel, 1685–1759. Catalogue of an exhibition National library of Scotland: Edinburgh 1948 pp.20.

[ALEXANDER HYATT KING], Handel's Messiah. Catalogue of an exhibition. British museum: 1951. pp.16. [23.]

VICTOR SCHOELCHER, An alphabetical index of songs in french, german, italian, latin & spanish composed by mr. Handel. With an appendix of further titles of unpublished and additional songs. [Edited by Frederick James Simkin Hall]. Walmer 1953. ff.iii.53. [1500.]*

[ALEXANDER HYATT KING], Henry Purcell, 1659(?)–1695, George Frideric Handel, 1685–1759. Catalogue of a commemorative exhibition. British museum: 1959. pp.47. [Handel: 180.]

QUELLENWERKE zur Händelforschung. Katalog. Musikbibliothek der stadt: Leipzig 1959. pp.[iv]. 29. [150.]*

V. G. ALEKSEEVA and A. M. PERELMAN, Георг Фридрих Гэндель .... Каталог выставки к 200-летию со дня смерти. Государственный центральный музей музыкальной культуры имени М. И. Глинки: Москва 1959. pp.13. [62.]

WILLIAM C[HARLES] SMITH and CHARLES HUM-
PHRIES, Handel. A descriptive catalogue of the
early editions. 1960. pp.xxiii.366. [1700.]

Harp.

CATALOGO dei soli, duetti, trii, terzetti, qvartetti
e concerti per il cembalo e l'harpo, che si trovano
in manuscritto nella officina musica di Breitkopf
in Lipsia. [Leipsic] 1763. pp.24. [400.]

Harpsichord.

CATALOGO dei soli, duetti, trii, terzetti, qvartetti
e concerti per il cembalo e l'harpo, che si trovano
in manuscritto nella officina musica di Breitkopf
in Lipsia [Leipsic] 1763. pp.24. [400.]

Harwood, Basil.

MUSICAL compositions by Basil Harwood.
[1951]. pp.23. [100.]

Hassler, Hans Leo von.

ROBERT EITNER, Chronologisches verzeichniss
der gedruckten werke von Hans Leo von Hassler
und Orlandus de Lassus. Monatshefte für musik-

geschichte (vols.v–vi, beilage): Berlin 1894.
pp.[iii].cxl. [Hassler: 300.]

Haydn, Franz Josef *and* Johann Michael.

[CONSTANT WURZBACH VON TANNENBERG],
Joseph Haydn und sein bruder Michael. Zwei bio-
bibliographische künstler-skizzen. Wien 1861. pp.
48. [500.]

ERNST CHALLIER, Sonaten-tabelle. Eine nach
tonarten alphabetisch geordnete aufstellung
sämmtlicher clavier sonaten von Clementi,
Haydn, Mozart in allen ausgaben. 3te . . . auflage.
Giessen 1890. pp.14. [Haydn: 400.]

[LAJOS KOCH], Joseph Haydn. Fővárosi nyil-
vános könyvtár: Budapest 1932. pp.78. [1000.]

HEDWIG KRAUS and KARL GEIRINGER, Führer
durch die Josef Haydn kollektion im museum der
Gesellschaft der musikfreunde in Wien. 2. Aufl.
[Wien 1932]. pp.56. [125.]*

[HERMANN REUTHER and ALFRED OREL], Katalog
der Haydn-gedächtnisausstellung. Wien [1932].
pp.40. [700.]

[ENDRE CSATKAI], Joseph Haydn. Katalog der
gedächtnisausstellung in Eisenstadt, 1932, zur feier
der 200jährigen wiederkehr seines geburtsjahres.

[Eisenstadt 1932]. pp.18. [200.]
a catalogue of the Sándor Wolf collection.

JOS. HAYDN werkverzeichnis. Leipzig [*c.*1935].

DREI Haydn kataloge in faksimile . . . herausgegeben von Jens Peter Larsen. Kopenhagen 1941.
pp.[iv].141. [300.]

CECIL HOPKINSON and C[ECIL] B[ERNARD] OLD-
MAN, Haydn's settings of scottish songs in the
collections of Napier and Whyte. Edinburgh
1954. pp.[ii].87–120. [221.]
20 copies privately printed.

ANTHONY VAN HOBOKEN, Joseph Haydn. The-
matisch-bibliographisches werkverzeichnis. Mainz
1957 &c.
in progress.

[LEOPOLD NOWAK], Joseph Haydn. Ausstellung
zum 150. todestag. Nationalbibliothek. Biblos-
schriften (vol.24): Wien 1959. pp.87. [107.]

E. N. RUDAKOVA and A. M. PERELMAN,
Иосиф Гайдн.... Каталог выставки к 150-
летию со дня смерти. Государственный центральный музей музыкальной культуры
имени М. И. Глинки: Москва 1959. pp.19. [71.]

Special Subjects

Heller, Stephen.

CATALOG der im druck erschienenen compositionen von Stephen Heller. Leipzig 1868. pp.12.
[135.]

Hindemith, Paul.

ELISABETH WESTPHAL, Paul Hindemith. Eine
bibliographie des in- und auslandes seit 1922 über
ihn und sein werk. Bibliothekar-lehrinstitut des
landes Nordrhein-Westfalen: Bibliographische
hefte (no.2): Köln 1957. pp.48. [518.]*

Hoffmeister, Franz Anton.

CATALOGUE thématique de toutes les œuvres
pour la flûte traversière composés par F. A. Hoffmeister. Vienne 1800.

Holst, Gustav.

LOUISE B. M. DYER, Music by british composers.
Series of complete catalogues (no.1): Gustav
Holst. [1931]. pp.12. [150.]

Jazz.

ALAN P. MERRIAM and ROBERT J. BENFORD, A
bibliography of jazz. American folklore society:

Publications: Bibliographical series (vol.iv): Philadelphia 1954. pp.xv.145. [3437.]

ROBERT GEORGE REISNER, The literature of jazz. A selective bibliography. Second edition. Public library: New York 1959. pp.63. [1750.]

Kiesewetter, Raphael Georg.

CATALOG der sammlung alter musik des . . . Raphael Georg Kiesewetter. [Vienna] 1847. pp. xxviii.96. [1000.]

Kistner & Siegel.

WALTER LOTT, Musik aus vier jahrhunderten, 1400–1800. Leipzig [1932]. pp.[ii].60. [450.]

Kreisler, Fritz.

FRITZ KREISLER. Vollständiges verzeichnis seiner werke. Mainz [*c*.1935.]

Lanner, Josef Franz Karl.

ALEXANDER WEINMANN, Verzeichnis der im druck erschienenen werke von Joseph Lanner, sowie listen der plattennummern der original-ausgaben für alle besetzungen. Beiträge zur geschichte des Alt-Wiener musikverlages (1st ser., no.1): Wien [1948]. pp.32. [250.]

Lassus, Orlandus de.

ROBERT EITNER, Chronologisches verzeichniss der gedruckten werke von Hans Leo von Hassler und Orlandus de Lassus. Monatshefte für musik-geschichte (vols.v–vi, beilage): Berlin 1874. pp. [iii].cxl. [Lassus: 1500.]

Laub, Thomas.

POVL HAMBURGER, Bibliografisk fortegnelse over Thomas Laubs litterære og musikalske arbejder. København 1932. pp.46. [575.]

Lejeune, Claude.

ERNEST BOUTON, Esquisse biographique et bibliographique sur Claude Lejeune . . . sur-nommé le Phénix des musiciens. Valenciennes [printed] [1845]. pp.[ii].vi.39.[xi]. [25.]

Leuckart F. E. C.

MUSIKALIEN-verlags-katalog, F. E. C. Leuckart. . . . Vollständig. Leipzig [1914]. pp.[iv].622. [10,000.]

Special Subjects

Liszt, Ferencz.

THEMATISCHES verzeichnis der werke von F. Liszt. Leipzig 1855. pp.97. [600.]

— Neue . . . ausgabe. Thematisches verzeichniss der werke, bearbeitungen und transcriptionen von F. Liszt. [1877]. pp.iv.162. [1000.]

PETER RAABE, Franz Liszt. Zweites buch. Liszts schaffen. Stuttgart &c. 1931. pp.[vi].380. [2000.]

HERBERT WESTERBY, Liszt, composer, and his piano works. Descriptive guide and critical analysis. [1936]. pp.xxii.336. [500.]

DENIS DE BARTHA, Exposition Fr. Liszt. . . . Catalogue. Musée historique hongrois [Magyar történeti múzeum]: Budapest 1936. pp.51. [450.]

Lute.

WOLFGANG BOETTICHER, Le luth et sa musique. . . . Bibliographie des sources de la musique pour luth. Centre national de la recherche scientifique: [1943]. ff.[i].69. [700.]*

MacDowell, Edward Alexander.

O[SCAR] G[EORGE THEODORE] SONNECK, Catalogue of first editions of Edward MacDowell.

Library of Congress: Washington 1917. pp.89. [400.]*

—— Supplement . . . containing notes on Columbia copies of MacDowell first editions. Columbia university libraries: Music library: MacDowell collections: New York 1943. ff.[iii]. 14. [50.]*

Malipiero, Gian Francesco.

MARIO LABROCA and BIANCAMARIA BORRI, Malipiero musicista veneziano. Con il catalogo analitico completo delle opere. Civiltà veneziana: Saggi (no.2): Venezia 1957. pp.75. [250.]

Marionettes.

LIST of references on marionettes, puppet shows, Punch and Judy, etc. Library of Congress: [Washington] 1925. ff.10. [144.]*

— [supplement]. [1936]. ff.12. [141.]*

GRACE GREENLEAF RANSOME, Puppets and shadows. A bibliography. Useful reference series (no.44): Boston 1931. pp.[vii].66. [marionettes: 1250.]

ALWIN NIKOLAIS, *ed.* Index to puppetry. A classified list of magazine articles published be-

tween 1910 and 1930 [*sic*, 1938]. [Hartford 1938].
ff.[vi].60. [1000.]*

[ELIZABETH LEWIS], The Rosalynde Stearn
puppet collection. McGill university: Library:
Special collections (vol.iv): Montreal 1961. ff.[60].
[700.]*

*the title is misleading; the collection consists of books
on puppets.*

Meyerbeer, Giacomo.

ALBERT DE LASALLE, Meyerbeer, sa vie et le
catalogue de ses œuvres. 1864. pp.31. [70.]

Moscheles, Ignaz.

[I. MOSCHELES], Catalogue thématique des
œuvres de J. Moscheles. Leipzig [1825].

THEMATISCHES verzeichnis im druck erschienenen kompositionen vom I. Moscheles. Leipzig
[1862.]

Mozart, Johann Chrysostomus Wolfgang Amadeus.

W. A. MOZART, Thematisches verzeichniss
sämmtlicher kompositionen von W. A. Mozart,

so wie er solches vom 9ten Februar 1784 an, bis zum 15ten November 1791 eigenhändig niedergeschrieben hat. Nach dem original-manuscripte herausgegeben von [Johann] A[nton] André. Offenbach a. M. 1805. pp.[v].63. [145.]

engraved throughout; there is also a french title-page; reissued in 1828.

THEMATISCHES verzeichnis derjenigen original-handschriften von W. A. Mozart . . . welche hofrath [Johann Anton] André in Offenbach a. M. besitzt. Offenbach 1841. pp.79. [280.]

CIPRIANI POTTER, A thematique catalogue of Mozart's pianoforte works, with and without accompaniment. [1848].

EDWARD HOLMES, Analytical & thematic index of Mozart's pianoforte works. [1852]. pp.24. [100.]

part of J. A. Novello's Catalogue.

THEMATISCHES verzeichniss werthvoller meist noch ungedruckter original-handschriften W. A. Mozart's. Berlin &c. [1856]. pp.16. [38.]

LUDWIG VON KÖCHEL, Chronologisch-thematisches verzeichniss sämmtlicher tonwerke Wolfgang Amade Mozart's. Leipzig 1862. pp.xx.551. [920.]

—— Dritte auflage, bearbeitet von Alfred Einstein. Leipzig 1937. pp.xlix.984. [5000.]

corrections and additions by Alfred Einstein appear in The music review *(1940), i.313–342; (1941), ii. 68–77, 151–158, 235–242, 324–331; (1942), iii.53–61; (1943), iv.53–61; (1945), vi.238–242.*

—— Dritte auflage ... mit ... 'berichtigungen und zusätze' von Alfred Einstein. Ann Arbor 1947. pp.xlix.1052. [5000.]

—— Vierte auflage in der bearbeitung von A. Einstein. Leipzig 1958. pp.xlix.984. [5000.]

ERNST CHALLIER, Sonaten-tabelle. Eine nach tonarten alphabetisch geordnete aufstellung sämmtlicher clavier sonaten von Clementi, Haydn, Mozart in allen ausgaben. 3ᵗᵉ ... auflage. Giessen 1890. pp.14. [Mozart: 300.]

[PAUL HIRSCH], Katalog einer Mozart-bibliothek. Frankfurt a. M. 1906. pp.[viii].75. [750.]
100 copies privately printed; Hirsch's interleaved and annotated copy is in the British museum.

[EMMANUEL] HENRI [PARENT] DE CURZON, Essai de bibliographie mozartine. Revue critique des ouvrages relatifs à W. A. Mozart et à ses œuvres. 1906. pp.39. [453.]

T[EODOR] DE WYZEWA and G[EORGES] DE SAINT-

FOIX, W.-A. Mozart, sa vie musicale et son œuvre. 1912–1946. pp.[iii].xiv.523+[iii].456+425+399 +369. [700.]

OTTO KELLER, Wolfgang Amadeus Mozart. Bibliographie und ikonographie zusammengestellt und nach materien geordnet aus dem musik- und theaterarchiv G. Fr. Hagen und anderen quellen. Leipzig 1927. pp.xi.274. [4250.]

[R. PAYER VON THURN and ROLAND TENSCHERT], Ausstellung die Zauberflöte. Mozarteum: Salzburg [1928]. pp.3–76. [500.]

ALFRED ERDMANN WERNER BOEHME, Mozart in der schönen literatur (drama, roman, novelle, lyrik), eine motivgeschichtliche abhandlung mit . . . bibliographie. Greifswald 1932. pp.[ii].179– 299. [424.]

KATALOG des Mozart-museums. Internationale stiftung Mozarteum: Salzburg [*c.*1935]. pp.12. [254.]

MOZARTS werkverzeichnis, 1784–1791. [Edited by] Otto Erich Deutsch. Wien &c. 1938. pp.32+ ff.[i].29. [145.]
a facsimile of the original manuscript.

W. A. MOZART, Verzeichniss aller meiner werke. Herausgegeben von E[rich] H[ermann] Müller von Asow. Wien &c. [1943]. pp.[vii].104. [144.] *contains also Johann Georg Leopold Mozart's 'Verzeichniss alles desjenigen was dieser 12 jahrige knab seit seinem 7ten jahre componiert und in originali aufgezeiget werden'.*

KARL FRANZ MÜLLER, W. A. Mozart. Gesamtkatalog seiner werke. Wien 1951. pp.448. [5000.]

ZDENĚK ZOUHAR, Wolfgang Amadeus Mozart. . . . Výběrová bibliografie. Universitní knihovna: Výběrové seznamy (no.11): Brně 1955. pp.36. [400.]

REMO GIAZOTTO, Annali mozartini. Milano 1956. pp.168. [1750.]

[FRANÇOIS LESURE], Mozart en France. Bibliothèque nationale: 1956. pp.xiv.78. [300.] *an exhibition catalogue.*

[ELEONORE HECKMANN], Wolfgang Amadeus Mozart. Städtische volksbüchereien: Musikbücherei: Frankfurt a. M. [1956]. pp.40. [200.] *an exhibition catalogue.*

[ALEXANDER HYATT KING], Mozart in the British museum. 1956. pp.28. [150.] *an exhibition catalogue.*

Special Subjects

OBRAS de W. A. Mozart executadas no Teatro municipal de Rio de Janeiro 1909–1956. Museu dos teatros do Rio de Janeiro: [Rio de Janeiro 1956]. pp.3–47. [150.]

EXPOSIÇÃO comemorativa do 2º centenário do nascimento de W. A. Mozart. Biblioteca nacional: [Rio de Janeiro 1956]. pp.19. [80.]

[ÅKE VRETBLAD], Wolfgang Amadeus Mozart, 1756–1956. Kungl. bibliotek: Utställningskatalog (no.5): [Stockholm 1956]: pp.10. [39.]

LIDIA F[ERENCZY] WENDELIN, Mozart Magyarországon. Új bibliográfiai füzetek (no.2): Budapest 1958. pp.203. [1000.]

OTTO SCHNEIDER and ANTON ALGATZY, Mozart-handbuch. Chronik — werk — bibliographie. Wien [1962]. pp.xv.508. [3900.]

Musical instruments.

ABRIDGMENTS of specifications relating to music and musical instruments, A.D. 1694–1861. Commissioners of patents for inventions: 1864. pp.xi. 376. [500.]

— 1694–1866. Second edition. 1871. pp.xv.520. [600.]

— 1867–1876. 1881. pp.xi.248. [400.]

335

ABRIDGMENTS of specifications. Class 88. Music and musical instruments. Patent office.

    1855–1866. pp.xi.96. [300.]
    1867–1876. pp.xi.102. [300.]
    1877–1883. pp.x.78. [250.]
    1884–1888. pp.xii.138. [400.]
    1889–1892. pp.xii.104. [300.]
    1893–1896. pp.xii.132. [400.]
    1897–1900. pp.xii.136. [400.]
    1901–1904. pp.xiv.188. [600.]
    1905–1908. pp.xvi.228. [750.]
        [*continued as:*]
    i. Musical instruments, automatic.
    1909–1915. pp.viii.163. [500.]
    1916–1920. pp.vi.35. [100.]
    1921–1925. pp.vi.53. [150.]
    1926–1930. pp.v.23. [75.]
    ii. Music and musical instruments other than automatic.
    1909–1915. pp.ix.150. [500.]
    1916–1920. pp.ix.39. [125.]
    1921–1925. pp.xi.92. [300.]
    1926–1930. pp.xi.81. [250.]
no more published.

PATENTS for inventions. Fifty years subject index, 1861–1910. Class 88. Patent office: 1913.

Special Subjects

i. Musical instruments, automatic. pp.8. [1000.]
ii. Music and musical instruments other than automatic. pp.15. [2000.]

KATHLEEN SCHLESINGER, A bibliography of musical instruments and archæology. Intended as a guide to the study of the history of musical instruments. 1912. pp.x.100. [1750.]

LUIGI TORRI, La costruzione ed i costruttori degli istrumenti ad arco. Bibliografia liutistica. 2ª edizione. Padova [1920]. pp.[iii].viii.43. [800.]

ELECTRONIC musical instruments. Public libraries and museum: Bibliographical series (no.1): Tottenham 1952. pp.31. [250.]

Mysteries.

G[ALINA] P[ETROVNA] BOGATOVA, Вековые загадки. Беседы о научно-популярных книгах (no.4): Москва 1958. pp.16. [20.]

Novello & co.

THE COMPLETE catalogue of music published by Novello and company, limited. [1912]. pp.[718]. [35,000.]

Special Subjects

Opéra, Paris.

[ÉLISABETH LEBEAU *and others*], Charles Garnier et l'Opéra. Exposition. Bibliothèque de l'Opéra. 1961. pp.40. [145.]

Oratorios.

ALFRED WOTQUENNE, Catalogue de la bibliothèque du Conservatoire royal de musique de Bruxelles. . . . Annexe I. Libretti d'opéras et d'oratorios italiens du XVIIᵉ siècle. Bruxelles 1901. pp.[iii].191. [450.]
250 copies printed.

Organ, organ music.

CATALOGUE of organ music; also sacred music with english words. Novello's catalogus (nos.1–2): 1866. pp.160. [4000.]

MUSICA sacra. Vollständiges verzeichniss aller seit dem jahre 1750–1867 gedruckt erschienener compositionen für die orgel, lehrbücher für die orgel, schriften über die orgelbaukunst. 1867. pp.56. [2000.]

MUSICA sacra. Abtheilung III. Vollständiges verzeichniss aller seit dem jahre 1750–1871 gedruckt erschienener oratorien, messen, cantaten und an-

derer werke der kirchenmusik im clavier-auszuge
oder mit begleitung der orgel. 1872. pp.26. [1000.]

B[ERNHARD] KOTHE and TH. FORCHHAMMER,
Führer durch die orgel-literatur. Leipzig 1890.
pp.viii.182. [3500.]
— — [third edition]. Vollständig neu bearbeitet
... von Otto Burkert. 1909. pp.viii.388. [6000.]

JOHN WATSON WARMAN, The organ. ... Writings and other utterances on its structure, procural,
capabilities, etc. Thornton Heath 1898[–1904].
pp.288. [1000.]
A–Nouveau only; no more published.

JOHN F. RUSSELL, List of compositions for the
organ and harmonium in the Henry Watson
music library. Public libraries: Music lists (no.5):
Manchester 1913. pp.56. [1500.]

FRANZ SAUER, Handbuch der orgel-literatur. Ein
wegweiser für organisten. Wien 1924. pp.62.
[750.]

R. WALKER ROBSON, The repertoire of the
modern organist. 1925. pp.[iii].152. [500.]

A. BROM, Catalogus van de bibliotheek der
Nederlandsche organisten-vereeniging onderge-
bracht in de bibliotheek der Rijks-universiteit te

Utrecht. . . . Tweede druck. Utrecht 1929. pp. viii.160. [2000.]

HENRY COLEMAN, Hymn-tune voluntaries for the organ. An index of organ pieces by british composers specially suitable for use in worship. 1930. pp.46. [250.]

BRUNO WEIGL, Handbuch der orgelliteratur. Leipzig 1931. pp.viii.318. [6000.]

HERBERT WESTERBY, The complete organ recitalist, international repertoire-guide . . . to foreign, british and american works. [1933]. pp.xii.120. [3000.]

F. MÜNGER, Protestantische chorāle und choralgebundene orgelmusik. Alphabetisches choralverzeichnis mit literaturangabe von orgelsätzen. Der organist (beilage): Zürich 1938. pp.16. [250.]

MUSIC for the organ. Nottinghamshire county library: [Nottingham] 1954. pp.12. [200.]

M. A. VENTE, Proeve van een repertorium van de archivalia betrekking hebbende op het nederlandse orgel en zijn makers tot omstreeks 1630. Académie royale de Belgique: Classe des beaux-arts: Mémoires: Collection in-8° (vol.x, no.2): Bruxelles 1956. pp.230. [327.]

[G. A. C. DE GRAAF], Literatuur over het orgel. [Amsterdam 1957]. pp.71. [900.]
limited in the main to books found in dutch libraries.

Ouseley, sir Frederick Arthur Gore.

JOHN S. BUMPUS, The compositions of the rev. sir Frederick A. Gore Ouseley. 1892. pp.34. [250.]
privately printed.

Pageants.

[JOHN GOUGH NICHOLS], London pageants. I. Accounts of sixty royal processions. . . . II. A list of lord mayors' pageants. 1831. pp.125. [100.]

—— [second edition]. London pageants. I. Accounts of fifty-five royal processions. . . . II. A bibliographical list [&c.]. 1831. pp.122. [100.]

—— [third edition]. 1837. pp.122. [100.]

FREDRICK W[ILLIAM] FAIRHOLT, Lord mayor's pageants: being collections towards a history of these annual celebrations. . . . Part I. History of lord mayors' pageants. Percy society: [Early english poetry (vol.x):] 1843. pp.[iii].xl.178. [50.]

[C. KNIGHT WATSON], Catalogue of a collection of works on pageantry bequeathed to the Society of antiquaries . . . by the late Frederick William Fairholt. 1869. pp.40. [200.]

Special Subjects

CAROLINE HILL DAVIS, Pageants in Great Britain and the United States. A list of references. [Public library:] New York 1916. pp.43. [1000.]

LIST of references on pageants, with separate sections on elizabethan pageants, pageants based on Shakespeare's plays and on postuming for pageants. Library of Congress: Washington 1916. ff.45. [589.]*

Paisiello, Giovanni.

E[UGENIO] FAUSTINI-FASINI, Opere teatrali, oratori e cantate di Giovanni Paisiello (1764–1808). Saggio storico-cronologico. Bari 1940. pp.3–208. [156.]

ULDERICO ROLANDI, Contributi alla bibliografia di Giovanni Paisiello. Lecce 1940. pp.28. [100.]

Palestrina, Giovanni Pierluigi da.

R. CASIMIRI, Il 'codice 59' dell'Archivio musicale lateranense, autografo di Giov. Pierluigi da Palestrina. Roma 1919. pp.ix.139.27. [250.]

Parody.

KARL FRIEDERICH FLÖGEL, Geschichte der burlesken. Leipzig 1794. pp.xii.260. [500.]

Special Subjects

ISRAEL DAVIDSON, Parody in jewish literature. Columbia university oriental studies (vol.ii): New York 1907. pp.xxiii.292. [421.]
also issued as a Columbia thesis.

SEYMOUR TRAVERS, Catalogue of nineteenth century french theatrical parodies . . . between 1789 and 1914. New York 1941. pp.132. [1225.]

HENRIQUE DE CAMPOS FERREIRA LIMA, As parodias na literatura portuguesa. Ensaio bibliográfico. Lisboa 1930. pp.92. [250.]

Petrucci, Ottaviano.

CLAUDIO SARTORI, Bibliografia delle opere musicali stampate da Ottaviano Petrucci. Biblioteca di bibliografia italiana (vol.xviii): Firenze 1948. pp. 3–219. [49.]

Pianoforte.

JULIUS KNORR, Führer auf dem felde der clavier-unterrichts-literatur. Leipzig [1849]. pp.[iii].108. [1500.]
— — Fünfte . . . auflage. Methodischer leitfaden für clavierlehrer. 1861. pp.viii.64. [500.]

LOUIS KÖHLER, Führer durch den clavierunterricht. Ein repertorium der clavierliteratur etc.

343

Leipzig &c. 1858. pp.[iii].126. [2500.]

— — Fünfte . . . auflage. 1874. pp.xi.172. [3500.]

F[RANZ LUDWIG] SCHUBERT, Wegweiser in der
musikliteratur für pianofortespieler. Leipzig 1860.
pp.96. [1500.]

— — Zweite . . . auflage. 1861. pp.122. [2000.]

MUSICA theatralis, d.i. vollständiges verzeichniss
sämmtlicher, seit dem jahre 1750 bis zu ende des
jahres 1863 im deutschen und auswärtigen handel
gedruckt erschienener, opern-clavier-auszüge mit
text, und sonstiger, für die bühne bestimmter
musikwerke. Erfurt 1864. pp.56. [2000.]

MUSICA sacra. Abtheilung III. Vollständiges verzeichniss aller seit dem jahre 1750–1871 gedruckt
erschienenen oratorien, messen, cantaten und anderen werke der kirchenmusik im clavierauszuge
oder mit begleitung der orgel. 1872. pp.26. [1000.]

HERMANN WETTIG, Führer durch die klavier-
unterrichts-litteratur. Bernburg 1884. pp.viii.309.
[5000.]

ADOLF PROSNIZ, Handbuch der clavier[klavier]-
literatur von 1450 bis 1830. Historisch-kritische
übersicht. Wien 1887. pp.xxvi.158. [4000.]

— — Zweite . . . auflage. Leipzig &c. 1908.
pp.[ii].xxii.167. [5000.]

—— 1830–1904. Leipzig &c. 1907. pp.xliv.179. [7500.]

JOHN F. RUSSELL, List of compositions for the pianoforte in the Henry Watson music library. Public libraries: Music lists (no.1): Manchester 1912. pp.72. [1750.]

ADOLF RUTHARDT, Wegweiser durch die klavier-literatur. . . . Achte auflage. Leipzig, &c. 1914. pp. xvii.461. [6500.]

BRIEF list of references on the piano and mechanical piano player industry. Library of Congress: [Washington] 1921. ff.8. [66.]*

ROBERT TEICHMÜLLER and KURT HERRMANN, Internationale moderne klaviermusik. Leipzig &c. 1927. pp.viii.200. [2500.]

WILHELM ALTMANN, Handbuch für klaviertrio-spieler. Wegweiser durch die trios für klavier, violine und violoncell. Wolfenbüttel 1934. pp. 237. [1000.]

WILHELM ALTMANN, Handbuch für klavier-quintettspieler. Wegweiser durch die klavier-quintette. Wolfenbüttel 1936. pp.178. [343.]

ALEC ROWLEY, Four hands — one piano. A list of works for duet players. 1940. pp.39. [400.]

Special Subjects

ALBERT LOCKWOOD, Notes on the literature of the piano. Ann Arbor 1940. pp.iii–xx.235. [5000.]

WILHELM ALTMANN, Verzeichnis von werken für klavier vier- und sechshändig sowie für zwei und mehr klaviere. Leipzig 1943. pp.133. [5000.]

CARLOTTA HELLER, Graded list of some useful works for piano study. Peabody conservatory preparatory department: Baltimore 1942. pp.35.

[K. H. ANDERSON], The piano, its music and literature. Public libraries: Catalogue of the music library: Liverpool 1949. pp.viii.103. [3500.]

ERNEST HUTCHESON, The literature of the piano. [1950]. pp.viii.3–374.xxxv. [2500.]

MARY ANNAROSE GRIFFIN, Piano materials. Graded . . . as an aid to instructors. Cardinal Stritch college: Milwaukee 1953. ff.59. [2000.]

JAMES FRISKIN and IRWIN FREUNDLICH, Music for the piano. A handbook of concert and teaching material from 1580 to 1952. Field of music (vol.v): New York 1954. pp.xi.432. [4000.]

HANDLIST of piano scores. City libraries: Music section: Newcastle-upon-Tyne 1954. pp.[iii].53. [1000.]

PIANO music. Nottinghamshire county library: [Nottingham] 1954. pp.34. [600.]

PIANO construction. Public library of South Australia: Research service: [Adelaide] 1956. ff.2+2. [30.]*

FRIEDRICH WILHELM RIEDEL, Quellenkundliche beiträge zur geschichte der musik für tasten-instrumente in der zweiten hälfte des 17. jahr-hunderts (vornehmlich in Deutschland). Landes-institut für musikforschung: Schriften (vol.10): Kiel 1960. pp.224. [1000.]

Pijper, Willem.

W. C. M. KLOPPENBURG, Thematisch-bibliogra-fische catalogus van de werken van Willem Pijper (1894–1947). Assen 1960. pp.xxxii.199. [104.]

Pleyel, Ignaz.

CATALOGUE thématique des œuvres de J. Pleiel qui se vendent chez Artaria à Vienne. Vienne [*c*.1870.]

Poulenc, Francis.

THE COMPLETE works of Francis Poulenc. 1946. pp.16. [100.]

Special Subjects

Praeger & Meier.

KATALOG (vollständig –1896) des musikverlages (und nebenzweige) der verlagshandlung Praeger & Meier. Bremen 1897. pp.ix.118. [3036.]
various supplements were issued.

Proch, Heinrich.

THEMATISCHES verzeichnis sämmtlicher werke von H. Proch. Wien [1854].

Purcell, Henry.

[ALEXANDER HYATT KING], Henry Purcell, 1659(?)–1695, George Frideric Handel, 1685–1759. Catalogue of a commemorative exhibition. British museum: 1959. pp.47. [Purcell: 66.]

FRANKLIN B. ZIMMERMANN, Henry Purcell. . . . An analytical catalogue of his music. 1963. pp. xxiv.576. [871.]

Raff, Joachim.

ALBERT SCHÄFER, Chronologisch-systematisches verzeichnis der werke Joachim Raff's, mit einschluss der verloren gegangenen, unveröffentlichten und nachgelassenen kompositionen. Wiesbaden [c.1900]. pp.[vii].164. [500.]

Special Subjects

Rakhmaninov, Sergei Vasilevich.

[E. BORTNIKOVA], Автографы С. В. Рахманинова в фондах Государственного центрального музея музыкальной культуры... Каталог–справочник. [Moscow] 1955. pp.35. [166.]

Recorder.

LINDE HÖFFER VON WINTERFELD and HARALD KUNZ, Handbuch der blockflötenliteratur. Berlin &c. 1959. pp.139. [1750.]

Refardt, Edgar.

[HANS PETER SCHANZLIN], Edgar Refardt, bibliographie. Schweizerische musikforschende gesellschaft: [Basel] 1962. pp.30. [400.]

Reger, Max.

WILHELM ALTMANN, Reger-katalog. Vollständiges verzeichnis sämtlicher im druck erschienenen werke, bearbeitungen und ausgaben Max Reger's. Berlin 1917. pp.56. [750.]
— — 2. . . . auflage. 1926. pp.56. [750.]

FRITZ STEIN, Thematisches verzeichnis der im druck erschienenen werke von Max Reger. Max

Reger-Gesellschaft: Veröffentlichungen (no.1): Leipzig [1933–1941].

— — [another edition]. Wiesbaden [1954]. pp. viii.617. [1000.]

incomplete; no more published.

Reinecke, Carl.

FRANZ REINECKE, Verzeichniss der bis jetzt im druck erschienenen compositionen von Carl Reinecke. Leipzig 1889. pp.[iv].76. [1250.]

Rimsky-Korsakov, Nikolai Andreievich.

V. A. KISELEV, Автографы Н. А. Римского-Корсакова в фондах Государственного центрального музея музыкальной культуры имени М. И. Глинки. Каталог-справочник. Москва 1958. pp.68. [312.]

Rubinstein, Anton.

CATALOG der im druck erschienenen compositionen von Anton Rubinstein. Leipzig 1889. pp.48. [300.]

Saint-Saëns, Charles Camille.

CATALOGUE général et thématique des œuvres de C. Saint-Saëns. 1897. pp.[iv].119. [600.]

— Nouvelle édition. 1908. pp.[iv].146. [750.]

Sarti, Giuseppe.

PIERO ZAMA, Opere musicale di Giuseppe Sarti possedute dalla Biblioteca comunale. Faenza 1933. pp.18. [250.]

Scarlatti, Giuseppe Domenico.

ULDERICO ROLANDI, Per una bio-bibliografia di D. Scarlatti. Roma 1935. pp.11. [4.]

D. SCARLATTI. Indice tematico (in ordine di tonalità e di ritmo) delle sonate per clavicembalo contenute nella raccolta completa riveduta da Alessandro Longo e nelle altre pubblicazioni della casa editrice G. Ricordi &c. Milano 1937. pp.37. [500.]

Schönberg, Arnold.

JOSEF RUFER, Das werk Arnold Schönbergs.
— — The works of Arnold Schönberg. . . . Translated by Dika Newlin. 1962. pp.3–214. [150.]

Schubert, Franz Peter.

THEMATISCHES verzeichniss im druck erschie-

nener compositionen von Franz Schubert. Wien
[1851]. pp.[ii].49. [500.]
engraved throughout.

A. WHISTLING, Systematisch geordnetes verzeichnis der im druck erschienenen compositionen
von Robert Schumann. Leipzig 1851. pp.52.
[250.]

VERZEICHNISS sämmtlicher lieder u. gesänge von
Franz Schubert, Rob. Schumann, Fel. Mendelssohn und Robert Franz. Halle 1868. pp.[ii].34.
[1750.]

[MARTIN] G[USTAV] NOTTEBOHM, Thematisches
verzeichniss der im druck erschienenen werke von
Franz Schubert. Wien 1874. pp.vii.288. [2500.]
*a copy in the British museum contains manuscript
notes by the author and others.*

[KARL GLOSSY], Schubert-ausstellung. Wien
1897. pp.xv.229. [500.]

[EMMANUEL] HENRI [PARENT] DE CURZON, Les
lieder de Franz Schubert ... suivie du catalogue ...
des lieder et d'une note bibliographique. 1899.
pp.113. [603].

[EMMANUEL] HENRI [PARENT] DE CURZON, Franz
Schubert. Société des études historiques: Bibliothèque de bibliographies critiques [no.4]: [1899].
pp.7. [50.]

OTTO ERICH DEUTSCH, Die originalausgaben von
Schuberts Goethe-liedern. Wien 1926. pp.24. [50.]

KATALOG der Schubert-zentenar-ausstellung der
stadt Wien. Wien [1928]. pp.viii.158. [500.]

WILLI KAHL, Verzeichnis des schrifttums über
Franz Schubert, 1828–1928. Kölner beiträge zur
musikforschung (vol.i): Regensburg 1938. pp.264.
[3122.]

OTTO ERICH DEUTSCH and DONALD R[UFUS]
WAKELING, Schubert. Thematic catalogue of all his
works in chronological order. 1951. pp.xxiv.566.
[999.]

Schumann, Robert Alexander.

THEMATISCHES verzeichnis sämmtlicher im
druck erschienenen werke R. Schumann's. Leipzig
&c. [c.1855]. pp.[ii].22.112. [750.]
— Vierte . . . auflage. [1868]. pp.[ii].112.
[1000.]

VERZEICHNISS sämmtlicher lieder u. gesänge von Franz Schubert, Rob. Schumann, Fel. Mendelssohn und Robert Franz. Halle 1868. pp.[ii].34. [1750.]

ALFRED DÖRFFEL, Literarisches verzeichniss der im druck erschienenen tonwerke von Robert Schumann. Leipzig [c.1880]. pp.48. [1500.]

Schütz, Heinrich.

AUS ZWEI jahrhunderten deutscher musik. Ausstellung zur Deutschen Bach-Händel-Schützfeier.

Preussische staatsbibliothek: Berlin 1935. pp.52. [Schütz: 21.]

WERNER BITTINGER, *ed.* Schütz-werke-verzeichnis. . . . Kleine ausgabe. Neue Schütz-gesellschaft: Kassel &c. 1960. pp.iii–xxxi.191. [496.]*

Shadow theatre.

G[EORG] JACOB, Schattenspiel-bibliographie. Erlangen 1901. pp.12. [100.]
— — Erwähnungen des schattentheaters in der welt-litteratur. . . . 3. Vermehrte ausgabe der bibliographie über das schattentheater. Berlin 1906. pp.49. [500.]
150 copies printed.

GEORG JACOB, Die erwähnungen des schattentheaters und der zauberlaternen bis zum jahre
1700. Erweiterter bibliographischer nachweis.
Berlin 1912. pp.18. [100.]
150 copies printed.

GRACE GREENLEAF RANSOME, Puppets and
shadows. A bibliography. Useful reference series
(no.44): Boston 1931. pp.[vii].66. [shadow theatre:
150.]

Simrock, Nicolaus.

VERZEICHNISS des musikalien-verlags von N.
Simrock.·... In alphabetischer reihenfolge ... vollständig bis 1897. Berlin [1898]. pp.lxxxvii.324.
[10,000.]

Skryabin, Aleksander Nikolaevich.

M. MONTAGU-NATHAN, Handbook to the piano
works of A. Scriabin. [1916]. pp.16. [250.]

Spohr, Louis.

J. JANTZEN, Verzeichnis sämmtlicher im druck
erschienener werke des . . . Louis Spohr nach
reihenfolge der opus-zahlen. Cassel [c.1855]. pp.
[ii].16. [250.]

H[ANS] M[ICHAEL] SCHLETTERER, Ludwig Spohr's werke. Historisches und systematisches verzeichnis der werke von Ludwig Spohr. Leipzig [1881]. pp.xl. [226.]

Stewart, sir Robert.

JAMES C. CULWICK, The works of sir Robert Stewart. . . . Catalogue of his musical compositions, such as have been performed, printed, or are still in manuscript: together with a list of his principal literary works. Dublin 1902. pp.24. [250.]

Strauss, family of.

CHR[ISTIAN] FLAMME, Verzeichnis der sämtlichen, im druck erschienenen kompositionen von Johann Strauss (vater), Johann Strauss (sohn), Josef Strauss und Eduard Strauss. Leipzig 1898. pp.90. [1250.]

ALEXANDER WEINMANN, Verzeichnis sämtlicher werke von Johann Strauss vater und sohn. Beiträge zur geschichte des alt-wiener musikverlages (1st ser., vol.2): Wien [1956]. pp.172. [1500.]

Strauss, Richard Georg.

RICHARD SPECHT, Vollständiges verzeichnis der

im druck erschienenen werke von Richard Strauss. Universal-edition (no.2756): Wien &c. [1910]. pp.42. [1000.]

E[RICH] H[ERMANN] MUELLER VON ASOW, Richard Strauss. Thematisches verzeichnis. Wien &c.
    i. Opus 1–59. 1959. pp.[iv].511. [3000.]
    ii. Opus 60–86. 1962. pp.[ii].512.1116. [1500.]
in progress.

Stravinsky, Igor Fedorovich.

IGOR STRAWINSKY. A complete catalogue of his published works. 1957. pp.39. [275.]

Symphonies.

CATALOGO delle sinfonie, che si trovano in manuscritto nella officina musica di Giovanno [*sic*] Gottlob Immanuel Breitkopf in Lipsia. [Leipzic] 1762. pp.28. [500.]

MUSIQUE symphonique. Conseil international de la musique: Répertoires internationaux de musique contemporaine (no.i): Frankfurt &c. 1957. pp.64. [900.]

Taubert, Wilhelm.

VERZEICHNISS sämmtlicher lieder und gesänge von Fr. Curschmann, Fr. Gumbert, Fr. Kücken,

Special Subjects

W. Taubert. Zürich 1876. pp.[ii].54. [2250.]

Taylor, William Franklin.

DETAILED list of progressive studies for the pianoforte and selected pianoforte studies by Franklin Taylor. [1902]. pp.16. [750.]

Valen, Fartein.

BJARNE KORTSEN, Thematic list of compositions by Fartein Valen. Oslo 1962. ff.141.*

Verdi, Fortunino Giuseppe Francesco.

CARLO VANBIANCHI, Nel 1º. centenario di Giuseppe Verdi, 1813–1913. Saggio di bibliografia verdiana. Milano &c. [1913]. pp.vii.118. [897.]

ULDERICO ROLANDI, Libretti e librettisti verdiani dal punto di vista storico-bibliografico. Roma 1941. pp.54. [40.]

Viola, violin, violoncello.

ALBERT TOTTMANN, Führer durch den violinunterricht. Ein kritisches, progressiv [*afterwards:* systematisches und nach den schwierigkeits-

graden] geordnetes verzeichnis. . . . Zweite . . .
auflage. [Edition Schuberth (no.1492):] Leipzig
1886. pp.xv.396. [3000.]

—— Führer durch die violin-literatur. 4. . . .
auflage, von Wilhelm Altmann. [1934–]1935.
pp.xv.472. [6000.]

reissued in 1935.

EDWARD HERON-ALLEN, De fidiculis bibliographia: being an attempt towards a bibliography
of the violin and all other instruments played with
a bow. 1890–1894. pp.xlvii.ff.220+[vii].ff.221–
416.lxxviii.[vii]. [1500.]

ERNST HEIM, Neuer führer durch die violin-
litteratur. . . . II^{te} . . . auflage. Hannover [1901].
pp.viii.358. [3500.]

CARL SCHROEDER, Guide through violin literature (and viola literature), being a re-print of
the appendix to Handbook of violin playing. . . .
Third edition [that is, reprinted from the third
edition of the Handbook]. Augener's edition
(no.9212 a): [1903]. pp.82. [2500.]

ALFRED EINSTEIN, Zur deutschen literatur für
viola da gamba im 16. und 17. jahrhundert. Internationale musikgesellschaft: Publikationen: Bei-
hefte (2nd ser.i): Leipzig 1905. pp.[v].120. [60.]

Special Subjects

G. SCHIRMER COMPANY, The violin teacher's guide. A graded & classified list of violin music. New York &c. 1910. pp.113. [4300.]

BRUNO WEIGL, Handbuch der violoncell-literatur. Wien &c. 1911.

—— III. . . . auflage. 1929. pp.357. [4000.]

MAX GRÜNBERG, Führer durch die literatur der streichinstrumente (violine, viola, violoncello). Kritisches . . . repertorium von instruktiven solo- und ensemble-werken, mit besonderer berücksichtigung ihrer nützlichkeit für den unterricht. Handbücher der musiklehre (vol.x): Leipzig 1913. pp.xii.218. [4000.]

M. VADDING and MAX MERSEBURGER, Das violoncello und seine literatur. Leipzig 1920. pp.172. [6500.]

the bibliography, by M. Merseburger, has a separate titlepage and title, Musikliteratur für violoncello.

ÉDOUARD NOGUÉ, La littérature du violoncelle. Choix de morceaux classés et annotés . . . avec la collaboration d'un groupe de violoncellistes. 1925. pp.152. [1750.]

[GUSTAV GROSCHWITZ], Violoncello-musik und kammermusikwerke. Vollständiges verzeichnis mit ausführlichen angaben. Leipzig [*c.*1930]. pp. viii.218. [2000.]

WILHELM ALTMANN and WADIM BORISSOWSKY, Literaturverzeichnis für bratsche und viola d'amore. Eine vollständigkeit anstrebende, auch ungedruckte werke berücksichtigende bibliographie. Wolfenbüttel 1937. pp.148. [4000.]

ALEXANDER FEINLAND, The combination violin and violoncello without accompaniment. Paramaribo 1944. pp.121. [300.]

FRANZ ZEYRINGER, Literatur für viola. Verzeichnis der werke für . . . viola. Hartberg [1963]. pp. 151. [3750.]

Vivaldi, Antonio.

MARIO RINALDI, Catalogo numerico tematico delle composizioni di Antonio Vivaldi. Roma [1945]. pp.3–311. [647.]

ANTONIO VIVALDI. Indice tematico. Istituto italiano Antonio Vivaldi: [*s.l.*] 1955. pp.[v].35. [200.]

Voice.

VOICE training: a bibliographical list. Library of Congress: Washington 1929. ff.3. [30.]*

Special Subjects

Volkmann, Robert.

HANS VOLKMANN, Thematisches verzeichnis der werke von Robert Volkmann. Dresden 1937. pp.xv.79. [300.]

includes also a bibliography of Volkmann.

Wagner, Wilhelm Richard.

EMERICH KASTNER, Wagner-catalog. Chronologisches verzeichniss der von und über Richard Wagner erschienenen schriften, musikwerke, etc. Offenbach a. M. 1878. pp.xi.132. [2000.]

NIKOLAUS OESTERLEIN, Katalog einer Richard Wagner-bibliothek. Nach den vorliegenden originalien zu einem authentischen nachschlagebuch durch die gesammte, insbesondere deutsche Wagner-litteratur bearbeitet. Leipzig 1882–1895. pp.xxx.322 + xl.356 + xxxi.518 + xvi.172. [10,180.]

vols.iii–iv have a second titlepage reading Beschreibendes verzeichniss des Richard Wagner-museums in Wien.

EMERICH KASTNER, Wagneriana. Beiträge zur Richard Wagner-bibliographie. . . . 1. theil. Briefe Richard Wagner's (1830–1883). Wien 1885. pp. viii.53. [413.]

Special Subjects

F. PARKINSON, Bibliography of Wagner's leit-motives and preludes. [1893]. pp.48. [400.]

HENRI SILÈGE, Bibliographie wagnérienne française ... donnant la nomenclature de tous les livres français intéressant le wagnérisme parus ... depuis 1851. 1902. pp.35. [150.]

[K. THOMASBERGER], Bibliophiles und kuriöses aus der Richard Wagner-literatur. [Vienna 1928]. pp.[ii].52. [100.]*

[PETER E. WRIGHT], Catalogue of the Burrell collection of Wagner documents, letters, and other biographical material. 1929. pp.xi.99. [1000.]

L. WINDSPERGER, Das buch der motive und themen aus sämtlichen opern und musikdramen Richard Wagners. Mainz [1931].

KATALOG. Zweite auflage. Richard Wagner-museum: Luzern 1935. pp.[ii].28. [189.]

INTERNATIONALE Wagner-bibliographie. Bayreuth.

    1945–1955. Herausgegeben von Herbert Barth. [1956]. pp.vi.56. [250.]
    1956–1960. Herausgegeben von Henrik Barth. [1961]. pp.345. [250.]

RYSZARD WAGNER a Polska ... Wystawa. Biblio-

Special Subjects

teka państwowej wyższej szkoły muzycznej: Katowice 1963. pp.40. [200.]

Walsh, John.

WILLIAM C[HARLES] SMITH, A bibliography of the musical works published by John Walsh during the years 1695–1720. Bibliographical society: 1948. pp.[iv].xxxiv.216. [636.]

Weber, Karl Maria Friedrich Ernst von.

FRIEDR[ICH] WILH[ELM] JÄHNS, Carl Maria von Weber in seinen werken. Chronologisch-thematisches verzeichniss seiner sämmtlichen compositionen, nebst angabe der unvollständigen, verloren gegangenen, zweifelhaften und untergeschobenen. Berlin 1871. pp.[vii].480. [5000.]

HANS DÜNNEBEIL, C. M. von Weber. Verzeichnis seiner kompositionen. Berlin 1942. pp.36. [1000.]

HANS DÜNNEBEIL, Schrifttum über Carl Maria von Weber. Vierte . . . auflage. Berlin &c. 1957. pp.95. [1000.]

Wolf, Hugo Philipp Jakob.

HUGO WOLF. Verzeichnis seiner werke. Leipzig [c.1930]. pp.[ii].61. [350.]

Special Subjects

FRANZ GRASBERGER, Hugo Wolf, persönlichkeit und werk. Eine ausstellung zum 100. geburtstag. Biblos-schriften (vol.25): Wien 1960. pp.128. [400.]

Wölfl, Joseph.

RICHARD BAUM, Joseph Wölfl (1773–1812). Leben, klavierwerke, klavierkammermusik und klavierkonzerte. Kassel 1928. pp.90. [100.]

Zieritz, Grete von.

GRETE VON ZIERITZ werkverzeichnis. Internationales musiker-brief-archiv: Grete-von-Zieritz-Fond: Berlin 1963. pp.11. [107.]*

Zither.

HENRY VRIES, General-katalog sämtlicher zither-musikalien. Leipzig [1902]. pp.389. [18,000.]